The BIG Book of ANIMALS

Editor: Daniela Majerna
Editorial Assistant: Tiziana Campana
Scientific Consultant: Marina Mansi
Art Editor: Viviana Cerrato

Illustrations: Cinzia Antinori, Amalia Arosio, Alessandra Micheletti
and in collaboration with Lorenzo Orlandi

ISBN 0-7097-1636-2

The BIG Book of ANIMALS

English edition translated from the Italian and edited
by Maureen Spurgeon

Brown Watson
ENGLAND

CONTENTS

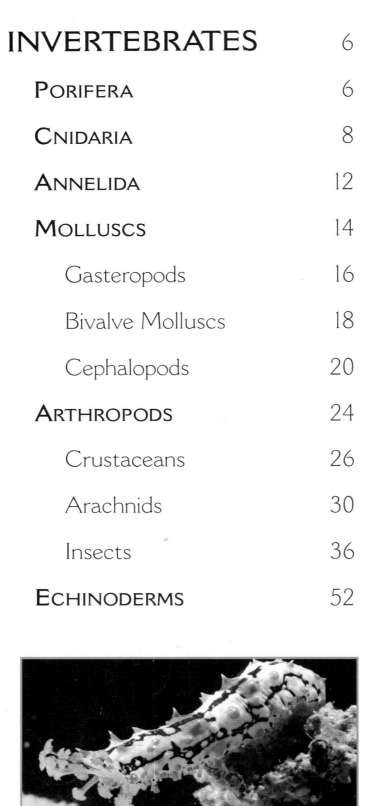

MAMMALS

PORIFERA

EVOLUTION

Animal life on Earth began with invertebrates – creatures without backbones. The oldest phylum (or 'family') of invertebrates dates back over three thousand million years ago. This is Protozoa, one-celled animals, some with simple structures, such as the amoeba, some more complex, like radiolaria. Two thousand million years later, Porifera, commonly known as sponges, probably developed from the one-celled animals of the Protozoa phylum.

NUTRITION

Sponges filter water as this enters through their pores, getting particles of food in this way. Waste products are expelled through larger holes called *oscula*. Sponges feed on bacteria, protozoa and tiny particles of animal and plant substances. This filtering system is extremely delicate. An excess of food particles can be extremely dangerous.

The *spongia officinalis*, the common bath sponge (centre) is widespread throughout the Mediterranean: it has lost its chalky spines, leaving just the spongy fibres of its skeleton. This can absorb a remarkable amount of water, equal to 20-35 times the dry weight of the sponge. Soft and strong, this type of sponge has been used since ancient times, for body hygiene, for medical uses and as a mask to protect against disease.

Right, the *Axinella polypoides*, a sponge with branches like a little yellow or orange plant, very common on rocky sea beds along the Mediterranean and Atlantic coastlines. The four species of axinella in the Mediterranean are spread in different ways, according to the current and the movement of the water.

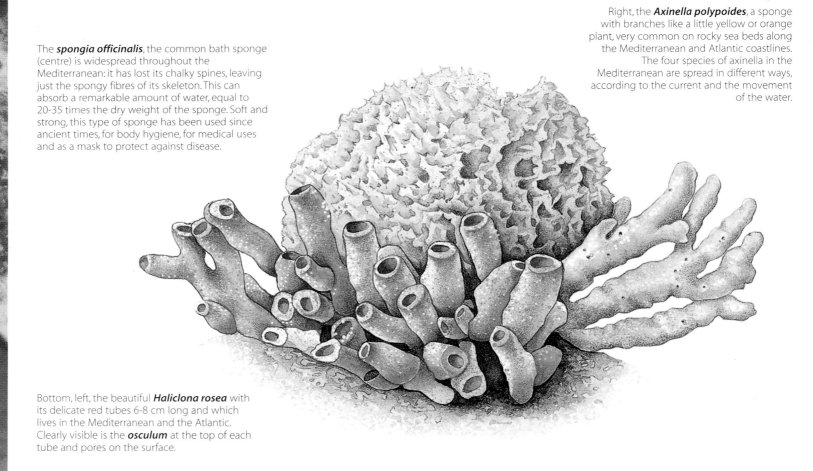

Bottom, left, the beautiful *Haliclona rosea* with its delicate red tubes 6-8 cm long and which lives in the Mediterranean and the Atlantic. Clearly visible is the *osculum* at the top of each tube and pores on the surface.

COMMON CHARACTERISTICS

All Porifera have a simple structure; a soft, irregular-shaped body, either like a bag or with branches, and supported either by silica or lime spines (or *spicules*) or by the *spongin*, a hard, horny-type fibre mesh. Water enters through numerous pores on the surface of the animal and goes out through a larger opening, called the *osculum*.

HABITAT AND DISTRIBUTION

There are over 3000 species of sponge which live on the sea beds, both in warm and in cold waters. Only some horny-coated species live in fresh water. Some sea sponges live in water which is only slightly deep, others live at depths from between 100 and over 1000 m.

Filtering to Live

Over a three thousand million years ago there were only **single-celled animals**, Protozoa. As animal life began to develop, some species of Protozoa probably **mated** to produce other creatures of two or more cells, which gradually became more complex. Porifera or **sponges** represent the first large group of multi-celled animals. Sponges have an extraordinary ability to **regenerate**. Not only can they renew lost or damaged cells, they can also be reproduced manually, by squeezing sponge cells through gauze or silk, or chemically, by taking out calcium and magnesium from the water in which they live. In both cases, once a group of cells settle on a surface, they begin to develop into a complete, living sponge.

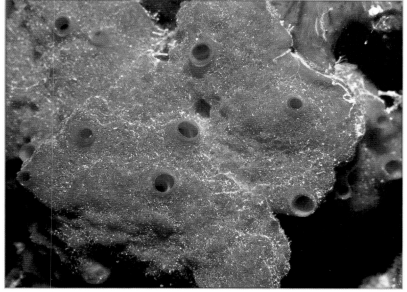

Photograph: Sponges have large openings called oscula, through which water flows.

As well as being able to reproduce by manual and chemical means, sponges can reproduce both sexually, through fertilization of the female egg by the male spermatozoa and asexually, by 'gemmating'. On the surface of a sponge, '**gemmae**' are formed, like little buds. Each **gemma** can multiply into a large number, which then detach from the body of the sponge, each one to begin life as an individual animal. The most primitive type of sponge is quite small, with a body in the form of a tube-like bag. But most sponges have irregular shapes, some bushy, others like little trees which can grow up to 2 m in diameter.

The body of a sponge has two layers of cells, criss-crossed with pores which come together in an internal cavity. This cavity is lined with special cells called **choanocytes**, which have structures like tiny whips which push the water which has entered in through the pores towards the **oscula**.

Sponges are fixed and unable to move. They feed by filtering useful substances carried along by the current of water.

According to the body structure, sponges are divided into three main classes:

Calcispongiae, the earliest type of sponge, is **calcareous** and sponges in this class have lime spicules. They live only in the deepest sea waters and they are small, reaching only 10 cm.

The **Hyalospongiae** have **silica spicules** with a body roughly shaped like a cylinder or a funnel, a tubular bag. They are present in all seas, in waters over 100 m deep. One of the most famous in this class is Venus's Flower Basket, with its delicate, white flower-like skeleton.

Sponges in the **Demospongiae** class have a horny, **spongin** body. This class is the largest and the most complex. They can be found both in seas, in the deepest waters of the oceans, and in fresh waters – such as the **Spongilla lacustris** which lives in lakes and has a characteristic green colour, due to the presence of the algae which live on its body. The **spongia officinalis** (common bath sponge) belongs to this class.

PHYLUM	CLASS	SPECIES
PORIFERA OR SPONGES	Calcispongiae	scypha
	Hyalospongiae	Venus's Flower Basket
	Demospongiae	bath sponge

CNIDARIA

EVOLUTION

The Cnidaria (or Coelenterata) phylum developed at the same time as sponges, first appearing in the seas and oceans more than 500 million years ago. Like sponges, Cnidaria are multi-celled creatures with a simple structure, but in many different forms, such as the beautiful **sea anemone**, the **transparent jellyfish** and tree-like **corals**.

NUTRITION

The central cavity of the Cnidaria body begins with an opening on the outside, through which the creature both gets its food and gets rid of waste. This opening is surrounded with numerous tentacles which attract prey, then paralyse it and take it down into the cavity to be digested.

The beautiful red coral, also called the noble coral, is found mainly in the Mediterranean Sea at depths of between 20 and 200 m, forming groups up to 20-25 cm high. Other similar species which live in Japan reach heights of up to 1 m and a weight of over 40 kg!

Red coral has been used for centuries in making ornaments and jewellery. Some has been found in a prehistoric tomb dating from the fourth century BC. It was used in Ancient China and Japan, and in Europe, red coral was widely used as a semi-precious stone and in jewellery, especially after the fifteenth century. People in Tibet used coral in place of money during the thirteenth century. At one time, coral was also valued for the power it was thought to have to cure many illnesses.

The coral which we know is in fact an external skeleton of calcium carbonate, hard and brittle and formed by tiny, hollow, tube-like structures called polyps. These form groups of branches, so that corals look like little trees, especially when they move their tentacles like the petals of flowers.

COMMON CHARACTERISTICS

All creatures in the Cnidaria phylum have a hollow, cylinder-shape body called a polyp. This is generally fixed at the bottom with an opening at the top surrounded by tentacles reaching upward. In some species, such as a jellyfish, a polyp develops into a medusa, where parts of the body are spread evenly around a central point, like the spokes of a wheel.

HABITAT AND DISTRIBUTION

Some Cnidaria can live fixed in water. Others can move about in the sea, especially in the warm waters of tropical seas. The Hydroida class have species both in the form of polyp and medusa. This class is mainly sea-dwelling. The Scyphozoa in medusa form is widespread in all seas. Creatures in the class Anthozoa are in polyp form. They can live alone or in large colonies.

Stinging traps

Cnidaria are multi-celled animals, very simple and with symmetrical shapes (equal on both sides). This type of body means that they can reach out for food and towards enemies with any part of their body and can attack or defend from either side, even when they cannot move.

The body of a Cnidaria animal has a single internal cavity which begins on the outside through a single opening, a mouth. The walls of the body are also used for breathing, digesting food and for getting rid of waste. The mouth is surrounded by tentacles armed with **stinging cells** (**cnidoblasts**). When prey comes in contact with a tentacle, it is stung by a tubular filament containing a poisonous liquid. Hundreds of these filaments fix themselves like this to the victim and paralyse it. Then, it is taken down into the mouth by the tentacles.

This means that the Cnidaria phylum are **fearsome predators**, often wonderfully hidden among underwater plants and feeding on small crustaceans and tiny fish. The two basic types of Cnidaria, the polyp and the medusa, can change during their development. For instance, the larva can be fixed, in the form of a **polyp**, and the adult mobile, like a **medusa**. Or the adult may be fixed like a polyp,

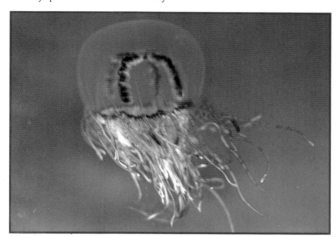

Photographs above: top, jellyfish, bottom, Sea Anemone.
Facing page: top, Sea Pen, bottom, Tube Anemone.

such as the coral.

The walls of the body are composed of two layers of cell tissues. The outer is called the ectoderma, the internal layer is called the endoderma. Between these two tissues there is a **jelly-like layer**, rich in water. The outer fibres make up the muscles lengthways. The fibres inside form the circular muscles. In the **darting movements** which characterise the jellyfish, these two muscular systems work together, relaxing and contracting.

Other cells develop into nerves; these line the internal surface of the body like a network and are extremely sensitive.

The three main classes into which Cnidaria are divided are – Hydroida, Scyphozoa and Anthozoa.

There are over 2700 species of **Hydroida**, all quite small, and in the form of both polyp and medusa. All can reproduce sexually or by 'gemmation' (see Sponges). They can live alone, like the Hydra, or in large colonies, such as the Milleporia corals.

The **Scyphozoa** are always alone, such as the colourful jellyfish with huge 'bells' or canopies. There are around 250 species of scyphozoa. The largest is the **Cyanea arctica** with a bell measuring over 2 m in diameter.

Anthozoa, with over 6500 species, is the largest class of Cnidaria. These are only in polyp form. They can be either solitary, such as the sea anemone, or, more often, living in groups, such as the stony corals and the madreporaria.

PHYLUM	CLASS	SUBCLASS	SPECIES
CNIDARIA	Hydroida		Hydra
	Scyphozoa		jellyfish
	Anthozoa	Alcyonaria	corals, gorgonians
		Zoanthinaria	madreporaria, sea anemone

PURPLE JELLYFISH

Diameter:	25-35 cm
Length of tentacles:	45-80 cm

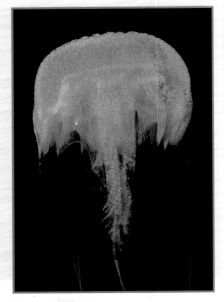

This jellyfish is very common in the Mediterranean and in the warmest parts of the Atlantic Ocean. It has eight tentacles which it can stretch and contract to a remarkable degree and a semi-circular bell. Its colour can range from pale purple to dark red. When disturbed or alarmed, this jellyfish reacts by acquiring a red-mauve luminous shine, easily visible at night-time. The life cycle of the Purple Jellyfish is very unusual. When its larva, called a **planula**, hatches from a fertilized egg, this does not go through the polyp stage. Instead, it develops directly into a baby jellyfish, called an **ephyra**. Because the purple jellyfish does not need to fix itself to a surface, like a polyp, it can live in the open sea. Often, enormous groups of Purple Jellyfish are swept towards a bank or a sea-shore by tidal currents, and then they are a serious danger for bathers who may be stung by their long, stinging filaments.

Some species of jellyfish can be very dangerous to humans, causing shock on contact.

TUBE ANEMONE

Diameter:	up to 60 cm, tentacles extended
Length of tube:	20-70 cm

The Tube Anemone belongs to the Anthozoa class and is one of the most beautiful of sea creatures. Its flowery appearance reminds us of the sea anemone, its distant relative.

The Tube Anemone, pictured below, lives in Japanese waters. It lives alone, protected by its tube-shaped skeleton which is rooted to the sea bed. Its tentacles, arranged in two concentric circles, are armed with poisonous glands. When disturbed, the creature withdraws completely inside its tube. The Tube Anemone feeds on small crustaceans and tiny fish, which it paralyses with liquid poison and then captures in its tentacles. Some tropical fish, such as the Clown Fish, are immune to the poison of the Tube Anemone. Instead, it likes to keep the Tube Anemone company, darting in and out of its tentacles. Then, at the least sign of danger, the Clown Fish will hide inside a bunch of the stinging tentacles.

Did you know...

The **Hydra** lives in fresh water and resembles a fine, delicate seaweed. Its tentacles are about six times the length of its body.

The **Xenia** is a most beautiful coral, rather like a little tree flowering with feathery tentacles.

The **Bunodactis Verrucosa** is a special type of sea anemone, because its base is covered in lumps. When it senses danger, it will withdraw its tentacles into its mouth, until it becomes a hard ball.

Because of its beauty, the **Tube Anemone** is often collected for large aquariums.

The **Sea Pen** has an external skeleton that is very soft and flexible, and which looks like a beautiful set of goose feather quills.

The **Sea Fan** is becoming very rare. It lives in large groups and its branches reach up to 70 cm in height. It is much sought after by divers because of its beauty.

The **Caryophylla Clava**, is a stony type of coral and it is quite common in the Mediterranean. It lives alone.

At the base of its tentacles, the **Bell Jellyfish** has cells which are sensitive to light.

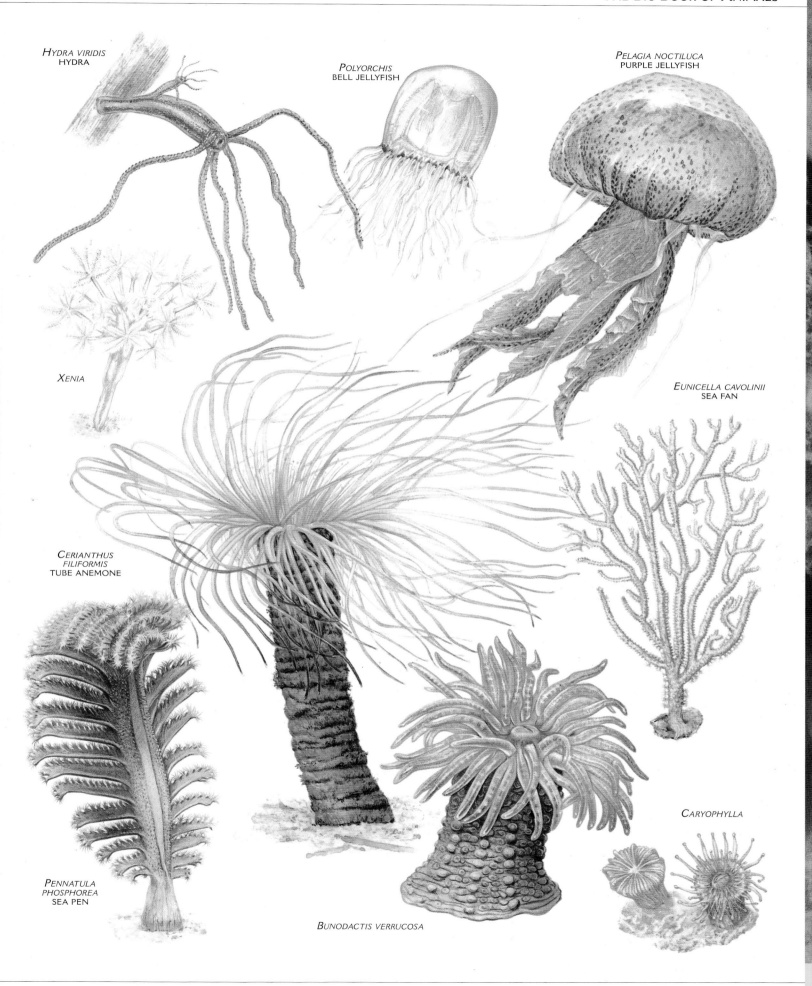

HYDRA VIRIDIS
HYDRA

POLYORCHIS
BELL JELLYFISH

PELAGIA NOCTILUCA
PURPLE JELLYFISH

XENIA

EUNICELLA CAVOLINII
SEA FAN

CERIANTHUS FILIFORMIS
TUBE ANEMONE

CARYOPHYLLA

PENNATULA PHOSPHOREA
SEA PEN

BUNODACTIS VERRUCOSA

ANNELIDA

EVOLUTION

The name **Annelida** comes from the Latin word *annulus*, meaning ring – because the body is covered with rings from the head to the tail. The segmented body structure of the Annelida phylum signalled the development of the *Arthropods*, such as insects.

HABITAT AND DISTRIBUTION

We know of around 9000 species of Annelida. The earliest form can be found living in the sea, such as the sea worm; the most developed have adapted to fresh waters, such as the leech, or in muddy depths in the earth, such as the well-known earthworm.

In the *Lumbricus Terrestris*, the common earthworm, we can see this marking very well. Each ring has four pairs of short, hairy bristles which enable the animal to make its way along the ground. These bristles are also sensitive to vibrations in the earth, and so enable the earthworm to escape when a mole, its most dangerous enemy, comes near. Only the earthworm's head has no bristles.

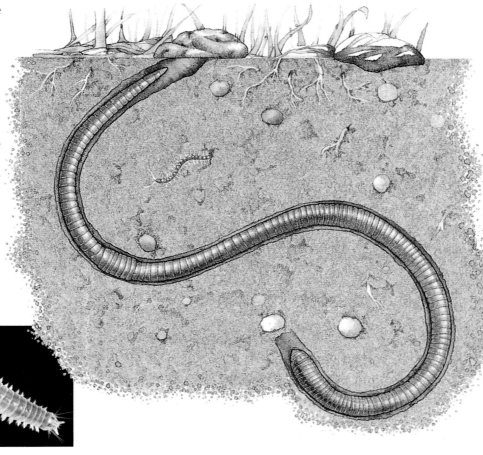

The earthworm seems to have neither a head nor tail, because it can move both forward and back. It opens its mouth in a fraction of a second. All members of the Annelida phylum have a digestive tube which begins at the mouth and opens up at the tail. Earthworms are very useful to farmers, because they feed on both vegetable waste and the soil, which they crumble up, 'digest' and then expel through the tail. In this way, earthworms break down the soil and keep it fertile.

When an earthworm is ready to mate, there appears a thickening in the middle of the body. This is called the clitellum and it is here that eggs develop into young worms, inside cocoons.

COMMON CHARACTERISTICS

The body is segmented. Each segment is called a **metamere**, and is similar to the one next to it. Each **metamere** is practically independent because it has all the organs necessary to survive.

Annelida creatures also have an internal body cavity called a **coelom**, which is full of liquid.

MOVEMENT

A good muscle structure in each metamere means that creatures in the Annelida phylum can wriggle and move in all directions, aided by the **coelom**, which can make a single metamere swell or shrink in many different ways. Some species can expand sideways with **parapodia**, rather like flat feet covered with hair. They use these to lever themselves along the ground.

'The Lord of the Rings'

The bodies of most Annelida are segmented and normally long and rounded. But sometimes, as with some **Polychaetes** (sea worms), it can be broad and flat and the segmentation is not so easily seen. The body is covered by a protective layer, or **cuticle** which is strong and very flexible. In the aquatic form, the body can also have bristles. Beneath the **cuticle** there is a circular, muscular layer, and, inside this, lengthways muscles which are different according to the various species.

This **muscular strength** enables Annelida to move very easily. Animals in the most highly developed classes of Annelida have a **digestive system** with a mouth, intestine and a hole for the waste to pass through.

These also have a circulation system whereby their blood circulates inside through a network of veins. Reproduction is generally sexual, but some species can reproduce asexually. The **earthworm** is a good example of this. If it loses a piece of its tail or its head, it just grows another!

There are about 9000 species in the Annelida phylum, divided into three classes – **polychaeta**, (marine or sea worms), **oligochaeta** (earthworms) and **hirudinea** or leeches.

There are over 5000 species in the **polychaeta** class and most live in the sea. At the deepest depths, we find the **free-living polychaetes** which move by means of their **strong tails** and **bristles** on the body.

The **sedentary polychaetes** live in tunnels dug out of mud and sand, or they dig tunnels in firm sand. These **polychaetes** cannot move. They get their food by rippling the water with the bristles on their tentacles around their mouths.

The **oligochaeta** comprise around 3000 species which live on the ground or in muddy fresh water. Their bodies are characterized by the presence of the **clitellum**, a swollen group of segments. Here the **cocoons** are formed to contain the eggs that will develop into baby worms. **Oligochaetes** move by contracting and extending the muscular segments. As well as the earthworm, the **Megascolides Australis** – a gigantic Australian worm which can reach 3 metres in length – belongs to the same class.

Photographs: top right, a marine worm of the Polychaeta class, above, a spendid Spriographis. Facing page: top right, the Hermodice carunculata (Bearded Fireworm), bottom left, Neried (sea worm).

Hirudinea is the most highly developed class of Annelida, with over 300 species. Some are the predators of the invertebrates, others are **ectoparasites**, such as the leech which attaches itself to the skins of animals and humans and sucks out the blood.

Echiurida constitutes a small group of sea creatures which live mostly along sandy and rocky coastlines. They have a proboscis (a long tube to suck with) at the tip of the front end. They are different to other Annelida because they have the typical metamere segments only in the embryo stage of development.

PHYLUM	CLASS	SUB-CLASS	SPECIES
ANELIDA	Polychaeta	free-moving	
		sedentary	
	Oligochaeta		earthworm
	Hirudinea		leech
ECHIURIDA			spoonworm

MOLLUSCS

EVOLUTION

The origin of molluscs began more than 500 million years ago, probably from the same creatures then living on the sea beds and from which the phylum Annelida also developed. This is confirmed by the fact that the larvae of Molluscs and Annelida are very similar. Some of the oldest fossils ever found have been tiny calcium carbonate mollusc shells.

NUTRITION

Molluscs feed on a variety of food depending on their surroundings. Some feed on algae (seaweed) and Cnidaria, others feed on plankton (tiny plants and sea creatures), algae and small invertebrates. There are some herbivore (plant-eating) species, such as the common snail, others carnivorous (meat-eating) such as squid and octopus.

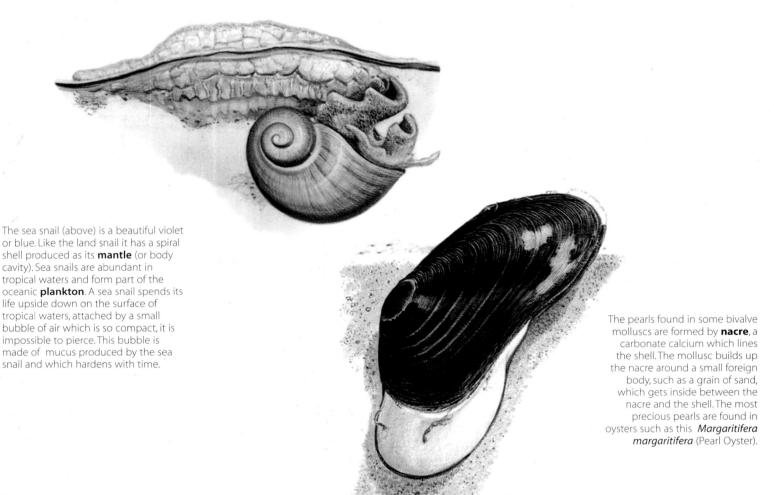

The sea snail (above) is a beautiful violet or blue. Like the land snail it has a spiral shell produced as its **mantle** (or body cavity). Sea snails are abundant in tropical waters and form part of the oceanic **plankton**. A sea snail spends its life upside down on the surface of tropical waters, attached by a small bubble of air which is so compact, it is impossible to pierce. This bubble is made of mucus produced by the sea snail and which hardens with time.

The pearls found in some bivalve molluscs are formed by **nacre**, a carbonate calcium which lines the shell. The mollusc builds up the nacre around a small foreign body, such as a grain of sand, which gets inside between the nacre and the shell. The most precious pearls are found in oysters such as this *Margaritifera margaritifera* (Pearl Oyster).

COMMON CHARACTERISTICS

All molluscs have a soft, compact body without an internal skeleton and which is sub-divided into a head and a trunk. They do not have jointed segments like the Annelida phylum. The particular characteristic of many species is the calcium carbonate shell.

HABITAT AND DISTRIBUTION

There is a large variety of molluscs living in all types of damp conditions. Some live on surfaces below ground or water, others in the mud and the sand, others are swimmers. Some species are able to live in the depths of the sea bed, others can live at an altitude of over 5000 m.

An incredible variety of shapes

All molluscs have soft bodies which are compact and wet because of the liquids made by their glands. There are two main parts – the head, with the sense organs (organs for sight, smell, taste and touch) the nervous system and the mouth, and the main body, with muscular-type feet and an internal bag. On the back of this bag is the mantle, which is wrapped around a cavity where the breathing organs are – **lamella gills** in aquatic molluscs, **lungs** in land molluscs. In the mantle, the mollusc secretes a calcium carbonate substance which forms the **shell** and which is connected to the feet by muscular bands.

Molluscs have a complete digestive system. At the top end of the digestive tube is a rasp-like tongue with lots of little teeth. This is called the **radula**. It is used to gather food in and to break it down.

Molluscs also have a proper heart at the back of the body, which enables the blood to circulate.

The nervous system is made up of a brain and four nerve cords which spread to all parts of the bottom of the body.

In molluscs the muscles are particularly developed. Reproduction of molluscs is sexual, the result of a male mating with a female. Many characteristics are the processes of development from the egg. In many molluscs the development to an adult proceeds through a larva called **veliger**.

There are at least 125,000 living species of molluscs, sub-divided into many classes. The most important classes are the Gastropods, the Bivalves and the Cephalopods.

The class of **Gastropods** have the most species of molluscs. They are recognized by the **spiral shell**. There are aquatic gastropods, living in fresh waters as well as land gastropods.

Bivalves have a **shell divided into two parts, or two valves** which are joined together by an elastic type of ligament, like a hinge. They do not have a true head or **radula**. Bivalves are mainly sea molluscs.

Cephalopods are almost all **without shells**. They are one of the most developed classes in the mollusc phylum, with a highly developed nervous system and sense organs. The octopus and the squid, have the most complex eyes amongst molluscs. Both live in sea water which has a high salt level.

Photographs: above, the dazzling colours of the Flabellina Lilla octopus, below, a Conus textile or Cone Shell, a marine snail.

PHYLUM	CLASS	SUB-CLASS	SPECIES
MOLLUSCS	Gastropods	Prosobranchs	acquatic, with shell
		Opisthobranchs	sea-dwelling without shell
		Pulmonates	land, such as snail and slug
	Bivalves or Lamellabranchs		with shell in two halves
	Cephalopods		with tentacles; nautilus, squid, cuttlefish, octopus

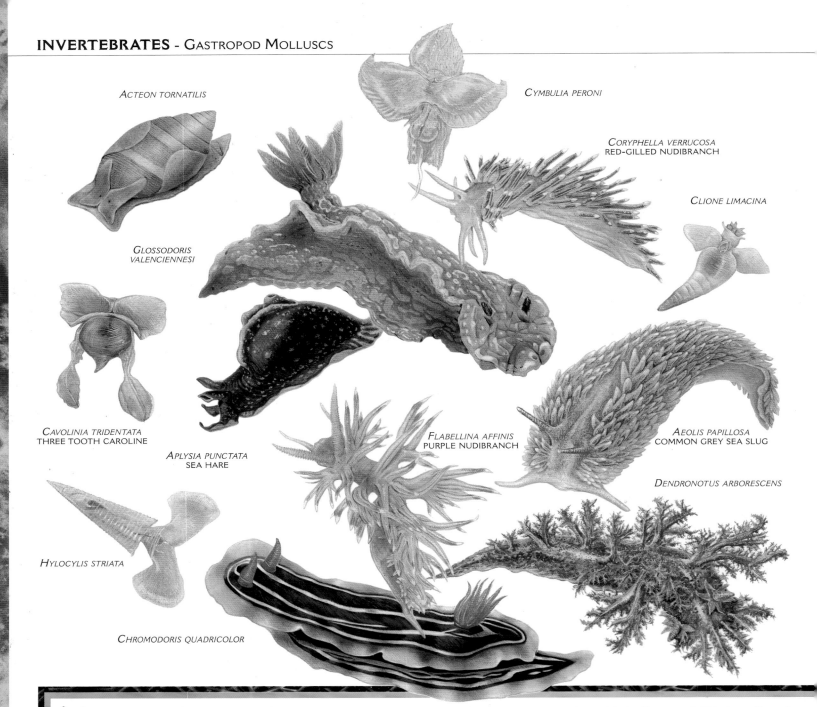

ACTEON TORNATILIS

CYMBULIA PERONI

CORYPHELLA VERRUCOSA
RED-GILLED NUDIBRANCH

CLIONE LIMACINA

GLOSSODORIS
VALENCIENNESI

CAVOLINIA TRIDENTATA
THREE TOOTH CAROLINE

APLYSIA PUNCTATA
SEA HARE

FLABELLINA AFFINIS
PURPLE NUDIBRANCH

AEOLIS PAPILLOSA
COMMON GREY SEA SLUG

DENDRONOTUS ARBORESCENS

HYLOCYLIS STRIATA

CHROMODORIS QUADRICOLOR

Did you know...

Acteon Tornatilis usually lives on the sandy beds of European seas. It feeds mostly on a type of seaweed called 'sea lettuce'. This mollusc has a shell rather like a shield, reaching up to its head and which the creature uses as a tool for digging short tunnels beneath the sand.

Widespread in all seas is the **Coryphelia Verusca**, or Red-Gilled Nudibranch, one of the most beautiful sea creatures because of its dazzling colours. Instead of a shell, it has numerous long spines around its body.

The **Hypselodoris Valenciennesi** and the **Chromodoris Quadricolor** are two gastropods with flat bodies. Each species has a tuft of secondary gills on its back which looks like a beautiful flower.

Sea butterflies are small plankton gastropods. They are among the most abundant of sea creatures. The **Cavolina Tridentata** (Three Tooth Caroline) is widespread almost everywhere, the **Cymbulia Peroni** and **Hylocylis Striata** are found mostly in the Mediterranean; the **Clione Limacina** is found in the cold waters of the Arctic.

The **Flabellina Affinis** (Purple Nudibranch) looks rather like a little bush. Feeding on jellyfish, this mollusc has stinging cells in its back spines which it uses to defend itself. Like the **Dendronotus Arborescens**, it lives along the European Atlantic coast and has a body with lots of branches. The Dendronotus Arborescens is also a stinging mollusc. It uses its gaudy colours as a signal to the would-be predator to go and find other prey.

The **Helix Hortensis** (White Lipped Snail) is known for its beautiful colours and the shape of its shell. It is nocturnal, coming out only when it is dark to go in

HELIX HORTENSIS
WHITE LIPPED SNAIL

DELIMA ITALA

ACHATINA FULICA
GIANT AFRICAN
LAND SNAIL

SUCCINEA PUTRIS
AMBER SNAIL

ARION RUFUS
RED SLUG

LIMAX MAXIMUS
GREAT GREY SLUG

POLYMITA PICTA

PLANORBARIUS CORNEUS
GREAT RAMSHORN SNAIL

LYMNAEA STAGNALIS
GREAT POND SNAIL

HELIX POMATIA
ROMAN SNAIL

LIGUUS DRYAS

search of leaves and nettles.

The **Delima Itala** is a small slug (15-20 mm) which likes hot climates.

The **Succinea Putris** (Amber Snail) is a European species which lives in very hot places, among the vegetation on the banks of rivers and marshes.

The **Limax Maximus** (Great Grey Slug) can be up to 15 cm long. It is found in woods and gardens after a storm. Although it seems to be without a shell, it does have a tiny, little one under the mantle.

The **Planorbarius Corneus** (Great Ramshorn Snail) is a gastropod with lungs. It is widespread throughout Europe and other temperate regions and lives in fresh water. The **Lymnaea Stagnalis** (Great Pond Snail) is also common in European ponds. Both eat water weeds and rotting plants; some species feed on tadpoles and newts.

The **Liguus Dryas** lives in hot regions.

The **Polymita Picta** is a multi-coloured snail which lives in the seas of the Caribbean.

The **Helix Pomatia** (Roman Snail) lives in vineyards and in zones which are not too damp, in undergrowth and bushes; in some countries, they are bred for food. About 80 fertilized eggs are laid in a hole which is specially dug. They have a calcium carbonate shell and, after 25-27 days, baby snails are born.

The **Achatina Fulica** (Giant African Land Snail) is a huge land Gastropod which originated in East Africa. It has a remarkable ability to adapt itself according to its surroundings. Every 2-3 months, up to 500 eggs are laid, each as large as a pea. But it needs temperatures above 24°C and very damp conditions.

TEREDO NAVALIS
SHIPWORM CLAM

TRIDACNA GIGAS
GIANT CLAM

CYRTOPLEURA COSTATA
ANGELWING CLAM

CARDIUM ACULEATUM
SEA NUT

EUCIROA TERAMACHI
SCALLOP

*PITAR
LUPANARIUS*

ENSIS ENSIS
RAZOR CLAM

LUTRARIA ELLIPTICA

GLOSSUS HUMANUS
HEART COCKLE

CALLANAITIS DISJECTA

*PENCILLUS
GIGANTEUS*

*CUSPIDARIA
CUSPIDATA*

Did you know...

The **Teredo Navalis** or Sea Worm Clam does considerable damage to the keels of ships by making holes in the wood.

The **Cyrtopleura costata** (Angelwing Clam) is a large bivalve which digs into clay and rock in the warm waters of the Atlantic.

The **Cardium Aculeatum** or Sea Nut, is a bivalve with ribs like rays, sometimes spiny. It lives in European seas. It has muscular feet which enables it to stay upside down.

The **Cuspidaria Cuspidata** is a small bivalve carnivore. It does not have any true gills. The **Euciroa Teramachi** belongs to the same order.

The spiny-looking **Pitar Lupanarius** and the **Callanaitus Disjecta** belong to the same family as the common clam. They live deep in muddy depths.

The **Lutraria Elliptica** is widespread from Norway to the Mediterranean and on to Senegal.

The **Pencillus Giganteus** is a small bivalve in a long tube-like shell, rather like an ornamental mace. The embryos of small snails attach themselves to this.

Glossus Humanus (Heart Cockle) has a thick, bulging shell in the form of a heart. Large numbers are found in the Mediterranean and in the northern Atlantic.

GIANT CLAM

Length: up to 1.5 metres or more.

Weight: up to 200 kg. or more.

The Giant Clam is a huge bivalve mollusc which lives on the coral reefs of the Indian and Pacific oceans. It has feet, gills and a downward mouth opening – but the whole mantle is turned 180° degrees, so that the back of the animal faces towards the opening of the shell and all the tummy part is turned towards the inside of the hinges. This strange structure has developed because the weight of the Giant Clam means it cannot move far. So, it needs to twist and turn to catch its prey. It is sometimes thought to be a danger to human beings. In fact, it is harmless and feeds on tiny creatures.

The edges of its mantle houses miniscule one-celled algae which receive food from the Giant Clam; and through the photosynthesis of the algae, the Giant Clam has a supply of oxygen. When the algae multiply too much, the Giant Clam is at risk of suffocation. So, it has to eat the algae to restore the balance. Its enormous hunger is not because of greed. Instead, it is a system of defence against aggressors.

When the Giant Clam senses danger, it slams its heavy valves shut, trapping whatever is in between.

RAZOR CLAM

Measurements: length of shell about 12-15 cm

This bivalve gets its name from the shape of its shell, like an old-fashioned razor.

It is very common in European waters. The **Razor Clam** spends much of its time deep in sand, feeding itself only at high tides. Then, out of the sand comes its short funnel called a siphon. Through this the Razor Clam sucks in water and with it oxygen and particles of food. These food particles become trapped in the mucus of the gills, which are covered with vibrating hair-like structures called cilia, then transferred to the mouth.

In the deepest seas, the Razor Clam retires beneath the sand. Then, every so often there is a tiny spurt of water which it has spat out. The Razor Clam moves by lifting itself off the sea bed with its feet and which it also uses to jump a few centimetres. It can also move by propulsion. First, it fills its body with water. Then it squeezes the water through its siphon, so that the force of the water pushes it forward.

NAUTILUS

This strange-looking cephalopod lives in tropical seas between depths of 50 and 650 m in the Indo-Pacific regions. Throughout its life, it is carried along by the currents.

The female has 90 tentacles and the male 60 which are poisonous. The shell of the Nautilus is a typical spiral shape, divided inside into spaces of air. Its soft little siphon contains an artery and passes through the dividing walls of each space. The siphon enables the Nautilus to vary the quantity of liquid and gas inside, so that it can control how it floats and descend down or rise up. The Nautilus can also move horizontally, by the same sort of propulsion as the Razor Clam; it sucks in water then uses its siphon to squeeze the water out through a cavity in the mantle.

It feeds on molluscs, and small fish which it catches with its tentacles and grasps in its beak-like mouth.

Respiration: 4 gills

Brood: 200-500 eggs, plankton-like larvae and slow development

Diameter of shell: about 30 cm

CUTTLEFISH

The cuttlefish is one of the most interesting molluscs, and one of the most highly developed. It has a remarkable sense of touch and of direction and is very intelligent. Common in the Atlantic and the Mediterranean, the cuttlefish has

two gills, two large eyes and ten poisonous tentacles.

Due to the structure of the shell, the cuttlefish can change colour very quickly, according to its surroundings. Despite this, the cuttlefish is the prey of rays, sharks and other fish, as well as human beings. To defend itself against attack, it squirts 'ink', a dark mauve substance which it expels through the funnel of a gland in the intestines. Its shell is internal and is wrongly called 'bone'. The cuttlefish has an system of siphons which enable it to move by means of propulsion, taking in water and expelling it in a jet.

Respiration: 2 gills

Brood: 200-300 eggs: 12 mm long on hatching

Total length: over 60 cm

Did you know...

The **Spirula Spirula** (Ram's Horn Squid) lives in the depths of tropical seas. It has a luminous organ which glows at the back end of its body.

The Californian **Abraliopsis Morisii** captures its prey by catching

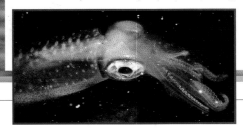

them on hooks at the ends of its longest two tentacles.

The **Chiroteuthis Imperator** is easily recognized by the very long tentacles hanging from its body.

The **Nautilus** has good eyesight — but this is no use in the dark depths of the sea where it lives! To find its way around, it uses its sense of smell, taste and touch.

The **Sandalops Melancholicus** has tentacles which are either short, or absent altogether.

The **Lycoteuthis Diadema** gets its name from about 22 different luminous creatures which cling to its body like a crown of precious stones.

Other **cephalopods** pictured on the opposite page have a shell which is reduced to a layer similar to a pen, and a slim, torpedo-shaped body.

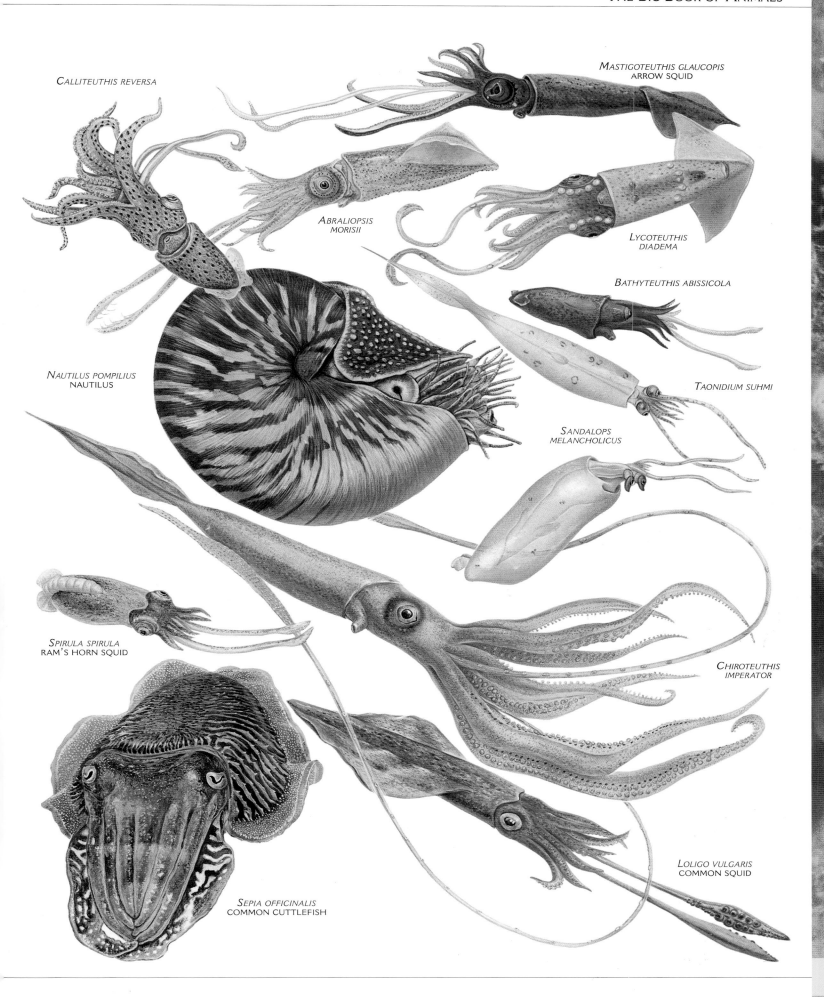

CALLITEUTHIS REVERSA

MASTIGOTEUTHIS GLAUCOPIS
ARROW SQUID

ABRALIOPSIS
MORISII

LYCOTEUTHIS
DIADEMA

BATHYTEUTHIS ABISSICOLA

NAUTILUS POMPILIUS
NAUTILUS

TAONIDIUM SUHMI

SANDALOPS
MELANCHOLICUS

SPIRULA SPIRULA
RAM'S HORN SQUID

CHIROTEUTHIS
IMPERATOR

SEPIA OFFICINALIS
COMMON CUTTLEFISH

LOLIGO VULGARIS
COMMON SQUID

21

PAPER NAUTILUS

Brood: 500 eggs

Length of adult:
female 30-40 cm; male 1.5-3 cm

Diameter of shell:
up to 25 cm

The Paper Nautilus lives in the Mediterranean and other warm seas. It is similar to an octopus with a bag-shaped body, eight poisonous tentacles, a mouth with a hard ridge and very prominent eyes.

But, unlike the octopus, the female Paper Nautilus makes herself a sort of shell, in the shape of a boat. She does this by using her first pair of tentacles as a framework, and then making a spiral, papery sort of shell.

This 'shell' has two functions. First, it helps the female to control her floating. Second, and more importantly, it is an egg-case, where she carries her eggs to develop.

The male Paper Nautilus is at least twenty times smaller than the female and has no shell. The one purpose of the male's existence is to fertilize the female.

OCTOPUS

Brood: 150,000 eggs

Size on hatching: 3 cm

Diameter of shell: up to 25 cm

The octopus is a cephalopod with eight quick, flexible tentacles each covered with two rows of poisonous cells. There are 150 known species of octopus, some reaching huge dimensions, such as the **Piovra** of Hong Kong, which, with open tentacles, can reach diameters of 10 m. The Common Octopus lives among the rocks in fairly shallow waters of the Mediterranean and in the area from the Canary Isles to the North Sea. It spends a great deal of its life alone in cavities among the rocks or in a shelter which it makes with stones on the sea bed. It moves slowly, clinging with its tentacles. Its presence is only noticed when it shoots out water from its siphon, in the same way as a cuttlefish. When it feels threatened, the octopus will squirt a jet of black ink, and then blend in with its surroundings by changing colour. The octopus is a fearsome predator: with its tentacles it will attack at the rear of its prey, generally crabs, shrimps and bivalve molluscs.

Did you know...

The **Opisthoteuthis Extensa** is an eight-footed cephalopod with poisonous tentacles, flat body and a tiny shell.

The **Eledonella Pygmaea** is also an eight-footed cephalopod but only a few centimetres long, with a jelly-like, transparent body. It is found at depths of 5400 m, or more.

The female of the **Common Octopus** watches over her tiny little eggs which she lays in a long, jelly-like row inside grottos and clefts in the sea. She gives them fresh water through her mouth, cleaning and stroking them, and never leaving her babies for at least one month.

An octopus which lives in the depths of the Caribbean seas and with a glossy appearance is the **Amphitretus Pelagicus**.

The **Vampyroteuthis Infernalis** (Vampire Squid) has a terrifying appearance. About 30 cm long, it lives at depths of between 1500 and 2500 m in tropical seas. Its thickset body is covered with a black membrane, which, with its tentacles forms an umbrella, and it has two dazzling eyes, red like glowing embers.

Among the Australian species of octopus is the **Hapalochlaena maculosa** (in the photograph). The saliva glands in the mouth produce a powerful poison which can kill its prey, even without direct contact.

The **Octopus cyanea** goes hunting by day in the coral reef, protected by its extraordinary ability to blend into its surroundings.

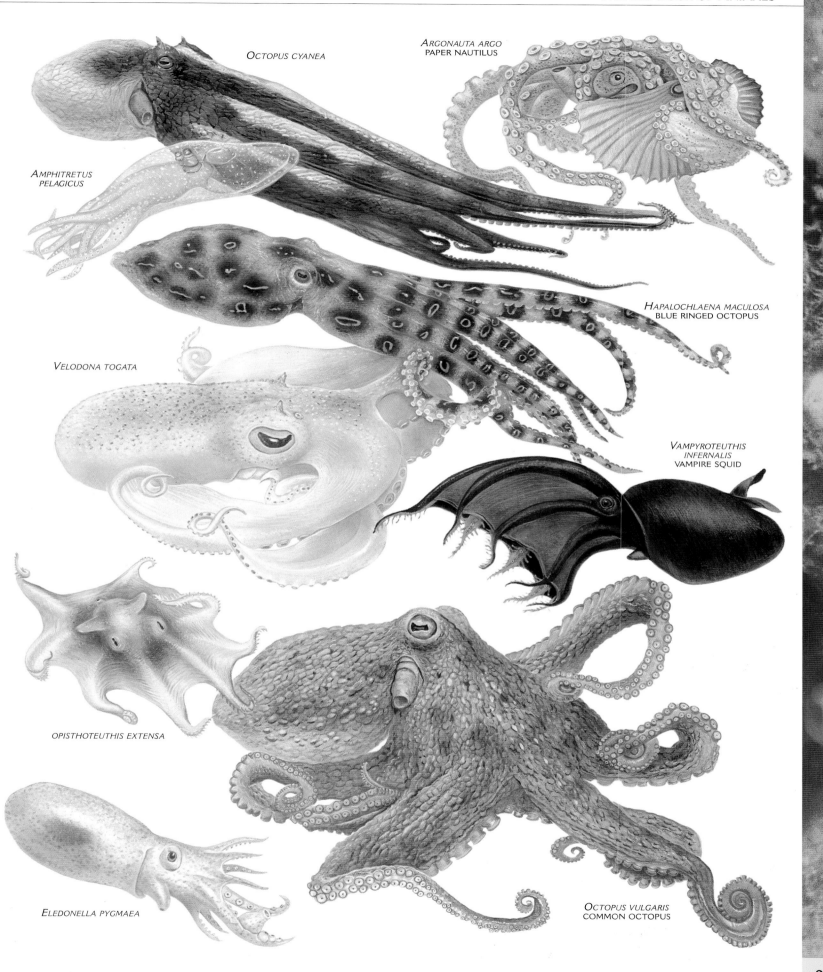

OCTOPUS CYANEA

ARGONAUTA ARGO
PAPER NAUTILUS

AMPHITRETUS
PELAGICUS

HAPALOCHLAENA MACULOSA
BLUE RINGED OCTOPUS

VELODONA TOGATA

VAMPYROTEUTHIS
INFERNALIS
VAMPIRE SQUID

OPISTHOTEUTHIS EXTENSA

ELEDONELLA PYGMAEA

OCTOPUS VULGARIS
COMMON OCTOPUS

ARTHROPODS

EVOLUTION

Of all the invertebrates, arthropods have been the most successful in development. This phylum originated over 500 million years ago from a branch of Annelida and they have the same segmented bodies.

DEVELOPMENT

All arthropods are covered with a rigid covering called a cuticle. This protects them like armour plating. Little by little, as an arthropod grows, it has to shed its old skin, so that it can grow one which is larger.

The metameric (segmented) body and numerous joints are very noticeable in all arthropods. All chilopods like the centipede have one pair of legs for each segment. Diplopods such as the millipede have two pairs of legs for each segment.

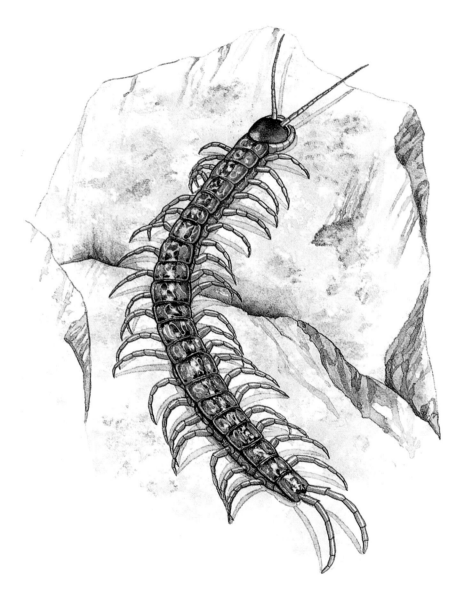

The centipede is a land arthropod. All are poisonous, but most are harmless to humans because they are so small. However, there are some tropical species which can grow to a length of over 280 mm.

Like all arthropods, the centipede has a body protected by a rigid cuticle and which acts as armour plating. It can die without sufficient dampness.

Many arthropods are predators. The centipede feeds on insects and small worms. Large species attack scorpions, lizards and even small birds.

COMMON CHARACTERISTICS

The body is divided into segments, generally in three parts – head, thorax and abdomen.
It has an external skeleton (the cuticle) and articulated (jointed) appendages which enable it to move freely.

HABITAT AND DISTRIBUTION

The Arthropod phylum is the largest and most widespread. There are Arthropods living everywhere – in the seas, in fresh water, on land, on surfaces below the level of the sea and at the highest heights, from the Equator to the North and South Poles.

PHYLUM	SUB-PHYLUM	CLASS	SPECIES
ARTHROPODS	Crustaceans	Branchiopoda	daphnia
		Ostracoda	small water species
		Cirripedes	barnacles
		Copepoda	plankton
		Malacostraca	krill, shrimps, lobster
	Chelicerates	Arachnids	spiders, scorpions
	Antennotrache	Chilopoda	centipedes
		Diplopoda	millipedes
		Insects	bees, beetles

A Successful Development

There are **more species** of Arthropods than any other phylum – about a million and a half species which are known and at least three million species all together, taking into account the ones which have not yet been classified.

Arthropods come in many forms – crabs and shrimps, spiders and scorpions, dragonflies and butterflies, coleoptera (beetles) and bees.

All have **jointed appendages**, legs with movable segments and which enable the animal to go in search of food without any trouble.

The body is **metamerical** (divided into segments) and generally in three parts, the head, thorax and abdomen. In addition, it has a rigid outer covering or skeleton, called the **cuticle.**

This is a substance containing nitrogen and produced within the surface **epithelium** tissue of the body made of chitin.

The cuticle protects the body but allows movement between one segment and the next, not only on the legs, but also various other parts of the animal's body. But because the cuticle itself is so rigid, it does stop the animal growing.

To overcome this problem, Arthropods renew the cuticle regularly in a process called '**sloughing**'. During sloughing, the animal remains weak and helpless.

The evolution (development) of Arthropods has proved very complex. For example – the development of senses in some species is remarkable compared to

their intelligence, memory and capacity for learning. Many arthropods have an 'open' circulation system which means that the blood is pumped into body cavities to supply internal tissues. From this point, the blood returns back to where it came from.

Breathing is by gills in aquatic species, by trachea or

Photograph: a Hermit Crab with a Sea Anemone.

lungs in land species.

Arthropods are egg-laying; larvae emerge from the eggs and these will develop through successive phases, or **metamorphoses** into adult creatures. The classification system of arthropods is summarized in the table (above). For more details on the types and various species, the following pages will give more information about the three main groups of arthropods – crustaceans, arachnids and insects.

CRUSTACEANS

COMMON CHARACTERISTICS

All crustaceans have a double pair of antennae, two-part (bifid) joints and one pair of jaws. The body is covered by a skin of varying thickness, called the cuticle. Many species of crustacean have a rigid shell. This can be in the form of a type of shield on the back called a carapace. In some crustaceans, the carapace is closed up and protects the whole body.

DISTRIBUTION AND HABITAT

Almost all crustaceans are aquatic. Most live in the sea, both in the open sea and near to the coast, in deep seas and on the sea beds, which is why they are often called 'sea insects'.

They are also very common in fresh waters, although a few, such as the Sow Bug, have adapted to life on the land.

The largest crustaceans and the most well-known are those which we see out at sea, in an aquarium, or served as food. Most of these belong to the Decapoda order, so-called because they have ten legs.

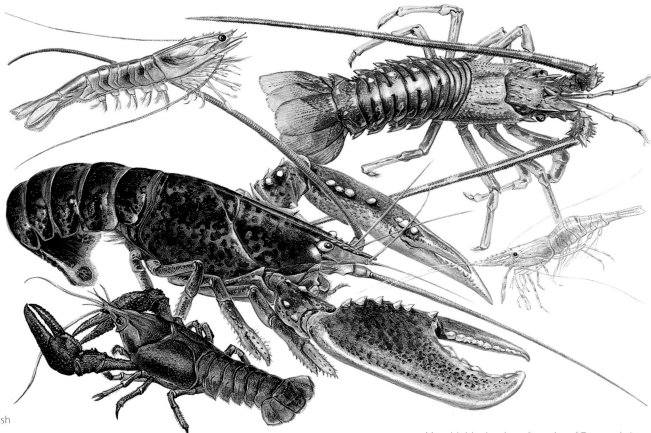

The name 'shrimps' actually covers many species of Decapoda which live in both fresh waters and the sea.

Most highly-developed species of Decapoda have a double pair of antennae, two-part legs and an 'armoured plating' (the carapace). Species such as the lobster and the river shrimp also have large, powerful nippers which are used like pincers to tear prey into scraps.

BREATHING

The smallest species of crustaceans breathe through a soft, fine film which covers the whole body. Crustaceans with a thick cuticle breathe through gills.

SENSE ORGANS

In all crustaceans, the sense organs are highly developed; they only lack the sense of hearing. On the body and legs there are numerous hairs and sensitive bristles for touching. There are also bristles on the antennae, used for taste and smell.

PHYLUM	SUB-PHYLUM	CLASS	ORDER	GENUS	SPECIES
ARTROPODS	Crustacean	Branchiopoda	Cladocera		daphnia
		Ostracoda			mussels
		Cirripedes			barnacles
		Copepoda			plankton
		Malacostraca	Amphipoda		Sand Flea
			Isopoda		Sow Bug
			Mysidacea	*Mysis Relicta*	Opossum Shrimp
			Leptostraca	*Nebalia*	
			Stomatopoda	*Squilla*	Mantis Shrimp
			Cumacea	*Diastylisgoodsin*	Hooded Shrimp
			Euphausia		krill
			Decapoda		shrimps, lobsters, crabs

Plated animals

It is estimated that at least 35,000 species of crustaceans live mostly in fresh water and the seas, and only a few on land. The body is made up of segments. The number of segments can vary. For example, the shrimp is divided into 19 segments, with a head, thorax (covered with a strong plating) and abdomen. Usually, the head and thorax are joined in one piece called the **cephalothorax**.

Each segment has a pair of **appendages** – apart from the first segment, where the eyes are. Crustaceans have two pairs of antennae, which are their tactile (touch) organs. The mouth has jaws, perfect for grinding food, and feet are often used for grinding as well. The joints used for moving sometimes have powerful pincers or **chelae**; these joints often have other special purposes, such as reproduction or carrying eggs.

Male and female sexes are separate in most species, although there are some **hermaphrodite** species

Photograph: above, a lobster has antennae which are longer than its body.
Facing page: top right, a common crab.

(where female and male reproductive organs are present in one individual). Crustaceans can be divided into two large groups – (1) **inferior crustaceans**, with nine classes. The four most important classes in this group are Branchiopoda, Ostracoda, Cirripedes and Copepoda. Then there are (2) the **superior crustaceans** where there are an estimated 18,000 species in just one class, the Malacostraca.

The **Inferior Crustaceans** vary a great deal in size and shape. Many are tiny and live in the ocean, where they make up the major part of **plankton**. In this they play an important part in the food chain of the sea; from one creature comes **huge quantities of larvae**. This constitutes an enormous food reserve for thousands of fish. These fish, in turn, follow shoals of plankton. Among crustaceans there is a huge range of dimension – some species of daphnia (water flea) are less than 3 mm long, whilst a giant Japanese Sea Crab can be more than 4 m in diameter with its claws open!

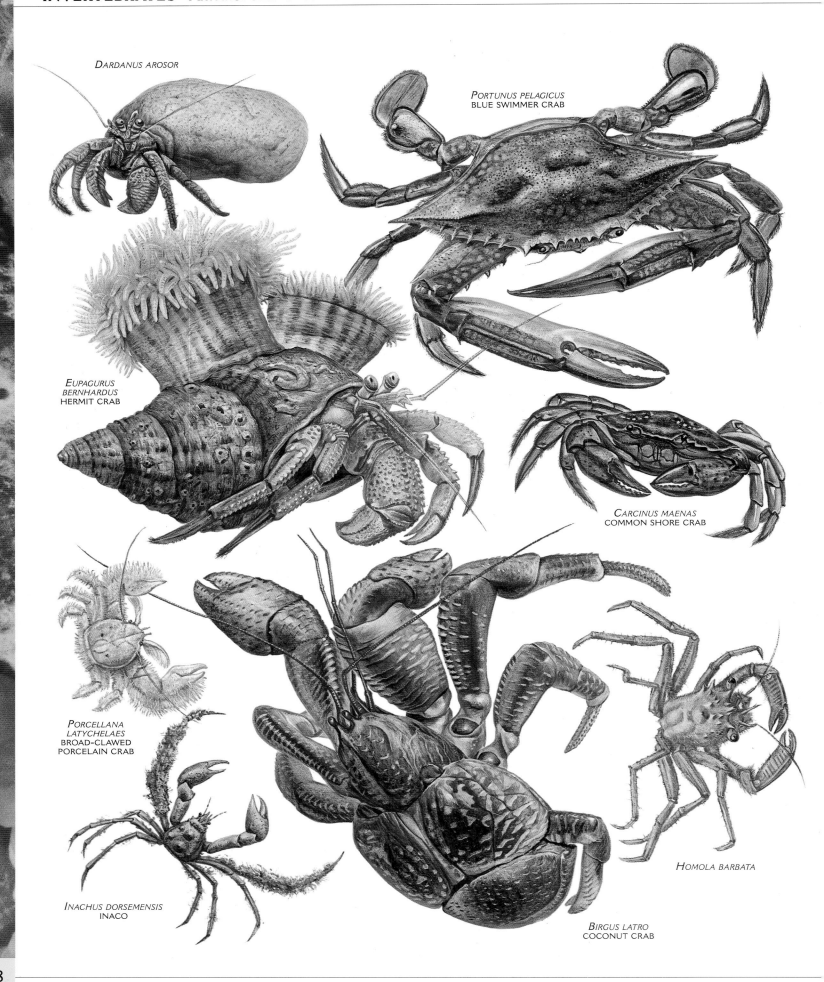

DARDANUS AROSOR

PORTUNUS PELAGICUS
BLUE SWIMMER CRAB

*EUPAGURUS
BERNHARDUS*
HERMIT CRAB

CARCINUS MAENAS
COMMON SHORE CRAB

*PORCELLANA
LATYCHELAES*
BROAD-CLAWED
PORCELAIN CRAB

HOMOLA BARBATA

INACHUS DORSEMENSIS
INACO

BIRGUS LATRO
COCONUT CRAB

COMMON SHORE CRAB

Habitat: the coast

Region found: Mediterranean

Length of carapace: 4-5 cm

Like all crabs, the Common Shore Crab belongs to the class Decapoda. It can be found along all European coastlines. At the least sign of danger, it runs and hides itself with its typical sideways movement.

The carapace (rigid plating) is black-green, rather like marble to look at, and its pincers are most clearly seen at the tip. At the front of its body, the Common Shore Crab

has three triangular teeth, set between its eyes which are on stalks. This crab is well used to ever-changing surroundings, which is why it is so easily found in harbours. It will eat anything, from small fish to shrimps and worms.

It is very aggressive and never lives with smaller crabs, or those which are weak due to the time of sloughing (shedding the carapace plating when this becomes too small). It can often be seen ready to do battle, raising its pincers which are always open; if necessary, it can defend itself by using only one leg if the other is broken off. Then it grows this again by successive sloughing.

COCONUT CRAB

Habitat: coast

Region found: East Pacific

Length: up to 46 mm

Weight of adult: 2-2.5 kg

Coconut Crabs can be found all along the Eastern Pacific coast.

This crab is a large crustacean which gets its name because it is supposed to be able to make coconuts fall to the ground, break them open and then eat them – but this is only a story.

The favourite foods of the Coconut Crab are the remains of fish or rotting molluscs which it finds along the beach. Only rarely does it feed on the flesh of a coconut and then it has to find one which is already open. Despite the strength of its pincers, it would not be able to lift a coconut, let alone open it. But, because of this story, this crab is also called the Robber Crab.

This crab reproduces in the sea and its larvae live in water until they develop into adults; once adult, the Coconut Crab swims towards the land. Because it breathes in oxygen from the air, it does not need to go into water again. The adult grows to about 1 m from head to tail.

Did you know...

The **Eupagurus bernhardus** or Hermit Crab (see photograph) has a soft, frail body, which is why it lives in empty shells for protection. After each sloughing, its body grows, and so the Hermit Crab goes in search of a larger shell. It lives in symbiosis (each creature helping the other) with the sea anemone. This sea creature feeds on the remains of the Hermit Crab's meals and in return protects the crab from enemies with its stinging appendages.

The **Dardanus arosor**, another type of hermit crab also shelters in empty mollusc shells and lives in symbiosis with the sea anemone.

The **crab Porcellana platychelaes** (Broad-Clawed Porcelain Crab), is a type of a hermit crab with a flat body – and so it goes in search of flat shells, not spiral.

The **Portunus pelagicus** (Blue Swimmer Crab) and the **Inachus dorsemensis** (Inaco) are fairly common in Mediterranean waters. The **Homola barbata** lives in very deep waters.

It is easy to distinguish the female of the **Common Shore Crab** from the male by examining the abdomen; in the female, this is large, because it has to carry eggs, whilst the stomach of the male is narrow and triangular.

ARACHNIDS

DEVELOPMENT, DISTRIBUTION AND HABITAT

The oldest forms of arachnids began a hundred million years ago with creatures similar to today's scorpions. Today, there are arachnids almost all over the world, mostly in very hot, damp regions. But some live in countries with temperate climates, and there are species of spiders which can be found within the Arctic Circle.

NUTRITION

Arachnids are meat-eaters and fearsome predators. For instance – scorpions feed on live prey, such as beetles, cockroaches and other arthropods, which it tears with its claws then sucks out the edible parts. The spider covers its prey with its gastric juices to 'melt' it before eating.

The *Salticus sanguinolentus* (Jumping Spider, see bottom left) has eight eyes arranged in three rows; those in the middle are larger than the others and work rather like the telephoto lens of a camera. This gives the spider an enlarged image of its prey, but with a limited range. So, this spider must move in quickly before hurling itself on its victim.

Almost all spiders can spin thread. The common and harmless house spider spins its thread into a web and lives in the thickest part.

The web of the *Micrathena* (Orb Web Spider) is much more intricate. With its plated, spiny abdomen, this is a spider typical of those living in hot countries.

COMMON CHARACTERISTICS

The body of an arachnid is divided into a front part and a back part (the cephalothorax and the abdomen). Arachnids do not have antennae; the first pair of appendages are formed either like a hook or as pincers which the arachnid uses to grab, grind up and then put the food in its mouth.

BEHAVIOUR

All arachnids are aggressive creatures, ready to attack and to conquer their prey.
The scorpion uses its poisonous sting to kill. Spiders are experts in making soft webs, transparent and sticky, to trap their prey. An adult Daddy Long-Legs has a pair of glands which secrete an evil-smelling liquid.

Land dwelling creatures

We know of around 36,000 species of arachnid, but many thousands more exist. Most live on the land although a few are aquatic.

All arachnids have the same type of body, in two distinct parts – a **cephalothorax** or a prosoma

Photograph: above, Crab Spider.
Facing page: top right, a Sac Spider.

(head and thorax fused together) protected on the back by a rigid cover called the **carapace**, and six pairs of jointed appendages – a pair of **chelicerae**, one of **pedipalps** and four pairs of jointed claws – and an abdomen or **opisthosoma**, which has no appendages. The pincer-like chelicerae, nearest the mouth, are also used to grip, for the injection of poison, as well as for spinning silk.

The **pedipalps** can have various forms and functions; sometimes they are used for chewing, sometimes as huge, powerful pincers, as organs of reproduction, for taste and for gripping. The fourth pair of claws are for moving, digging, swimming, for **winding silk** and catching prey.

Scorpions, spiders and some mites have **poisonous glands**. Spiders and some other arachnids have spinning glands. Breathing organs are tubular trachea or lungs. In many mites, breathing is through the skin. Males and females are often quite different, as is the case with spiders.

Reproduction is by laying eggs, rarely oviparous (where eggs are hatched in the body of the female before the young emerge).

Arachnids belong to the sub phylum of Chelicerates (animals with pincers) and are divided into many types.

Scorpions have two large pedipalps which end in pincers and a tail with a poisonous sting.

Psuedoscorpions (also called false scorpions) are very small (from 1–8 mm) and without a tail.

Solifugae (sun spiders) are large in size, covered with a thick fur and with two large claws shaped like pincers. **Uropygi** are nocturnal. They live in damp, tropical and sub-tropical regions. **Amblypygi** have small, flat bodies with very long, spiny pedipalps.

Spiders are the most numerous of all arachnids. There are over 26,000 known species.

The **Opiliones** (Daddy Long-Legs) have small bodies and very long legs. They live in temperate and tropical regions. Most mites are parasites, living off plant material or other animals. They are widespread on the ground and in both the sea and fresh water.

PHYLUM	SUB-PHYLUM	CLASS	ORDER	SPECIES
	Chelicerates	Arachnids	Scorpion	scorpions
			Pseudoscorpions	Book Scorpion
			Solifugae	Sun Spider
ARTHROPODS			Uropygi	Mastigoproctus giganteus
			Amblypygi	Tail-Less Whip Scorpion
			Spiders	Tarantula, Mygale, Black Widow
			Opiliones	Daddy Long-Legs
			Mites	Castor Bean tick

Did you know...

The gigantic **Mastigoproctus giganteus** belongs to the **Uropygi** order. It is about 7 cm long and lives in Mexico and in the southern United States. Despite its menacing appearance and its hunger for catching frogs and small toads, it is harmless to humans.

The **Prynichus reniformis** moves on three pairs of legs, walking sideways, whilst using its long, spiny **pedipalps** as a trap for catching insects and large cockroaches. The first pair of legs, long and soft, function as organs for touch.

The **Phalangim opilio** (Daddy Long-Legs) has only two eyes. It does not spin silk and the male is almost identical to the female. It risks losing at least one of its thread-like legs when it has to flee from danger. Unlike spiders, the lost leg does not grow again.

Among other species of **Opiliones** we find the **Ischyropsalis hellwig**, with its huge pincers.

The **Galeodes arabs** is a large nocturnal arachnid of the order of **Solifugae** living in Europe and Asia; with its highly-developed pincers it can catch and eat termites, lizards and small mammals.

There are thousands of species of **mites**, all very tiny and which live at all latitudes and altitudes (up to 5500m). They are very resistant parasites which feed on plants and animals, such as the Sheep Tick and Castor Bean Tick.

CASTOR BEAN TICK

Habitat: animal parasite

Length: about 15 mm

The Castor Bean Tick may not seem very interesting. But, this tiny mite can be a very dangerous enemy both for animals and humans.

Like many mites, the Castor Bean Tick can transmit many disease-carrying viruses, some of which can cause death. That is why it can be very dangerous to touch or even to go near certain types of ticks. One bite can have terrible consequences.

The tick feeds on the blood of whatever creature it lives on, sucking through a beak formed by the claws of its pedipalps. It draws out the liquid by pumping movements of the stomach.

The life cycle of the tick is simple. The innocent-looking larva climbs a blade of grass, then waits for an animal to come along on to which it can move. After various moultings, it reaches the adult phase. Then it mates on its host plant or animal and the female falls to the ground to lay her eggs and then die. The new-born ticks will continue the life cycle.

PSEUDOSCORPIONS: BOOK SCORPION

Habitat: fields, libraries

Length: just a few millimetres

There are more than 1500 species of pseudoscorpions which live in all hot and temperate regions throughout the world. They are related to scorpions, but they do not have a poisonous sting and the body is not so long.

All pseudoscorpions are small, no more than a few millimetres. They are lively little creatures which live in cracks, beneath sacks and under the bark of trees, in rotting material, in nests of small mammals and in the honeycomb of bees. One of the most widespread is the Book Scorpion. This is a harmless creature which lives in the pages of books or among powdery paper, in libraries or in old, damp documents. The favourite prey of the **pseudoscorpion** are insects, especially the small, wingless insect, the collembolan. Unlike the spider and the scorpion, the pseudoscorpion is not limited to sucking or eating the soft parts of their prey, they eat everything. Sometimes, they attach themselves to ants or to scorpions to be carried along.

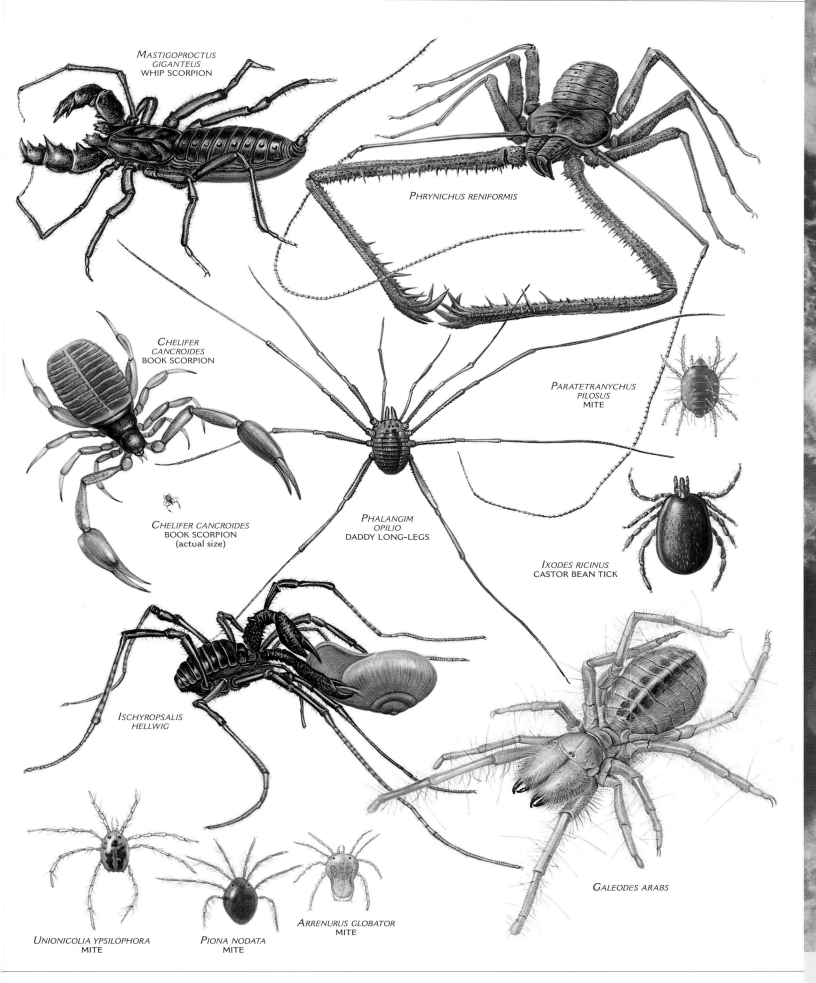

MASTIGOPROCTUS
GIGANTEUS
WHIP SCORPION

PHRYNICHUS RENIFORMIS

CHELIFER
CANCROIDES
BOOK SCORPION

PARATETRANYCHUS
PILOSUS
MITE

CHELIFER CANCROIDES
BOOK SCORPION
(actual size)

PHALANGIM
OPILIO
DADDY LONG-LEGS

IXODES RICINUS
CASTOR BEAN TICK

ISCHYROPSALIS
HELLWIG

UNIONICOLIA YPSILOPHORA
MITE

PIONA NODATA
MITE

ARRENURUS GLOBATOR
MITE

GALEODES ARABS

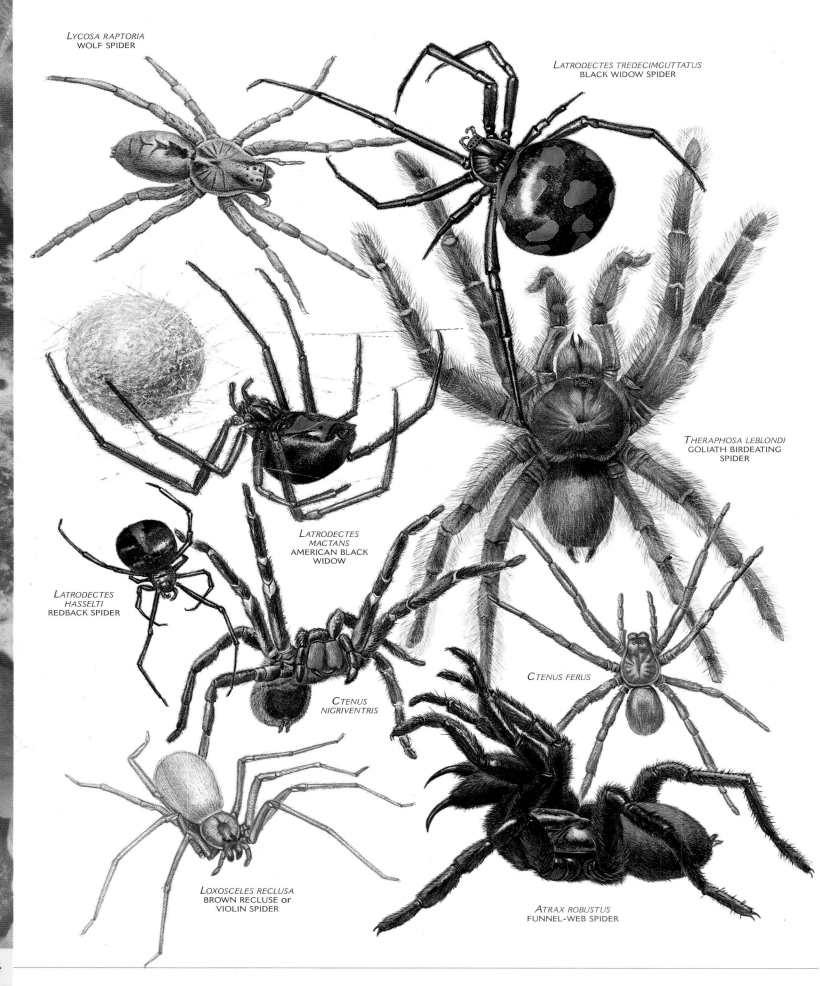

LYCOSA RAPTORIA
WOLF SPIDER

LATRODECTES TREDECIMGUTTATUS
BLACK WIDOW SPIDER

THERAPHOSA LEBLONDI
GOLIATH BIRDEATING
SPIDER

LATRODECTES MACTANS
AMERICAN BLACK
WIDOW

LATRODECTES HASSELTI
REDBACK SPIDER

CTENUS NIGRIVENTRIS

CTENUS FERUS

LOXOSCELES RECLUSA
BROWN RECLUSE or
VIOLIN SPIDER

ATRAX ROBUSTUS
FUNNEL-WEB SPIDER

BLACK WIDOW SPIDER

Habitat: low plants, stone, corners or walls

Web: ragged, irregular

Length: about 15 mm

Poison: deadly

Most spiders in the class **Latrodectes** are generally small, but poisonous – such as The Black Widow spider. There are six species of Black Widow. The most common lives in the area of the Mediterranean Sea and all very hot zones.

Although it is only 10-15 mm long, this spider is always hungry and is much-feared. It has a poisonous bite which can produce pain, sickness and temporary breathing problems. The bite, however, is rarely fatal to humans.

The female spider looks more frightening than the male, both in size and appearance, with her abdomen usually adorned with blood red spots. She hides among stones and bushes and spins a web made with threads of silk from the top of her body, abdomen turned upwards.

The Black Widow will not hesitate to attack animals larger than itself and grasshoppers are among its favourite prey. The female builds a clear-coloured sphere-shaped cocoon, where she lays her eggs. The spider gets the name of Black Widow due to the female's habit of eating the much smaller male after mating.

Did you know...

*The **spider** usually has 8 eyes, but those which live in caves have none. The average length of the body is 2 cm, but some tropical species, such as the bird-eating Mygale, measure 9 cm and with the legs can even be more than 20 cm!*

*The **tarantula** belongs to the class Lycosa. According to popular belief, its bite can cause a sort of frenzy which can lead to death. In fact, its bite is not very dangerous.*

*The male of the **Black Widow** wraps its sperm in a soft net which it takes to the female to fertilize her eggs.*

*Closely related to the European Black Widow is the famous **American Black Widow**, Latrodectes mactans.*

*The **Theraphosa leblondi** (Goliath Birdeating Spider) is from South America. At the approach of an enemy, it tears into the skin with its rear claws to confuse its victim, causing strong skin irritation.*

*Living in temperate regions are two spiders of the genus **Ctenus**, both very poisonous.*

*Another spider much-feared because of its poisonous bite is the **Atrax** (Funnel-Web Spider) widespread in tropical regions.*

LYCOSA

Habitat: ground

Web: underground covering

Length of body: about 25 mm

Length of legs: 25 mm

Poison: almost harmless

There are many species of **lycosa**, spiders of small or medium size, which are distinguished by their home.

Whilst other spiders make a web, the lycosa species finds a hole in the ground which it lines with a soft web of silk, to make it a comfortable underground sleeve, and which it can then close with a little silk cover. The cover opens or closes the entrance of the hole, making it into a trap. Each hole is inhabited by a solitary female; the male just keeps watch and goes in search of a mate only during the mating period, then flees before being eaten by his mate.

One species of lycosa is called the Ground Spider, or Wolf Spider because of its aggressive nature. The Wolf Spider runs fast across ground in search of prey, especially at night. It identifies its prey with the help of three rows of eyes – two medium-sized eyes in the top row, two large eyes in the middle row, and four small eyes in the bottom row.

INSECTS

EVOLUTION, DISTRIBUTION AND HABITAT

Even around 400 million years ago, insects were widespread on land, in fresh and salt water and after that, in the air. There are about 800,000 species of insect, more than any other class in the animal kingdom. Some insects, such as bees and silkworms, are useful to humans; others cause damage to agriculture and some are parasites.

DEVELOPMENT

The life cycle of an insect is made up of different stages of development, each one characterized by metamorphosis, or transformation. With each stage of metamorphosis, the insect, once it comes out of the egg, undergoes a transformation of the whole body – from the larva which develops into the chrysalis or pupa which develops into the adult insect.

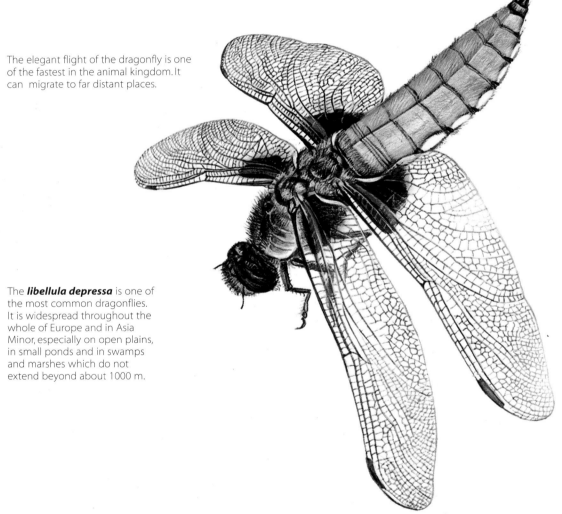

The elegant flight of the dragonfly is one of the fastest in the animal kingdom. It can migrate to far distant places.

This dragonfly prefers the sun and during hot days it stays hidden among the vegetation. It feeds on flies and butterflies and lays its eggs in flight, letting them fall on water plants. Dragonfly larvae are always hungry. They eat tadpoles and other small creatures. The adult dragonfly has a characteristic large, flat abdomen.

The **libellula depressa** is one of the most common dragonflies. It is widespread throughout the whole of Europe and in Asia Minor, especially on open plains, in small ponds and in swamps and marshes which do not extend beyond about 1000 m.

COMMON CHARATERISTICS

All insects have just one pair of antennae. These are their organs of touch and smell. Each has a particular form of mouth that can either lick, sting, suck or chew, three pairs of legs and a thorax and abdomen separated by a narrow 'waist'. Like all arthropods, an insect has an exoskeleton (a hard outer body covering).

BEHAVIOUR

Some insects such as ants, bees, wasps and termites, live in communities. In these communities, there are particular groups, each with a particular job to do – such as the feeding and the care of the young, collection of food and the construction of the home. In each group, the insects work together, carrying out their tasks in a very precise, regulated way.

So many different kinds

Nearly all the orders of insects which existed 230 million years ago still exist today, a length of time never achieved by any other animal. There are many reasons for this success; most important is the conquest of **flight** which has enabled insects to adapt to new surroundings, to gain access to new sources of food and to flee from predators.

Other reasons for this success are – small sizes, modest food needs and a hard body covering called the **exoskeleton** which protects like armour plating. This is solid yet light, made up of chitin and **sclerotin**.

On the head of the insect is a pair of antennae.

Some have two **compound eyes**, made up of many lenses, as well as **simple eyes** which can only make out light, dark and movement.

Most insects have a mouth with many parts, including an upper lip, a pair of jaws and a lower lip. The

Photographs: top, a hornet, bottom, a ground beetle. Facing page: a beetle of the Chrysomelidae family.

thorax is made up of three segments, with a pair of legs for each. Generally, the last two segments each have a pair of **wings**. The last segment of the abdomen has appendages which are used for reproduction.

There are some insects which can communicate by using sensitive cells on the legs or abdomen. By rubbing one part of the body against another they can make **sounds** which can be heard at a considerable distance. They detect different smells and explore their surroundings by using their antennae.

The **sight** and the perception of colour in insects is very much less than ours, and this also varies according to the species. Insects breathe by a network of tiny little tubes ('trachea') which distribute oxygen to the whole body. Almost all insects are born from the egg; only aphids and a few others give birth to live young.

In some insects, the **larvae** which emerge from the egg develop directly into an adult. This is known as incomplete metamorphosis. In others, the larvae pass through the phase of pupa and then into an adult insect. This is known as complete metamorphosis.

In insects, there is an enormous variety in the development of life cycles, which we often refer to as different **phases**.

PHYLUM	CLASS	SUB-CLASS	ORDER	SPECIES
ARTHROPODS	Insects	Pterygota	Odonata	dragonfly
			Orthoptera	cricket, locust
			Homoptera	aphids, cicadas
			Isoptera	termites
			Ephemeroptera	mayflies
			Heteroptera	bugs
			Thysanoptera	thrips
			Psocoptera	bookworms, silverfish
			Coleoptera	beetles, weevils
			Hymenoptera	bees, wasps, ants
			Raphidoptera	snakefly
			Neuroptera	lacewings
			Lepidoptera	butterflies, moths
			Diptera	flies, mosquitoes

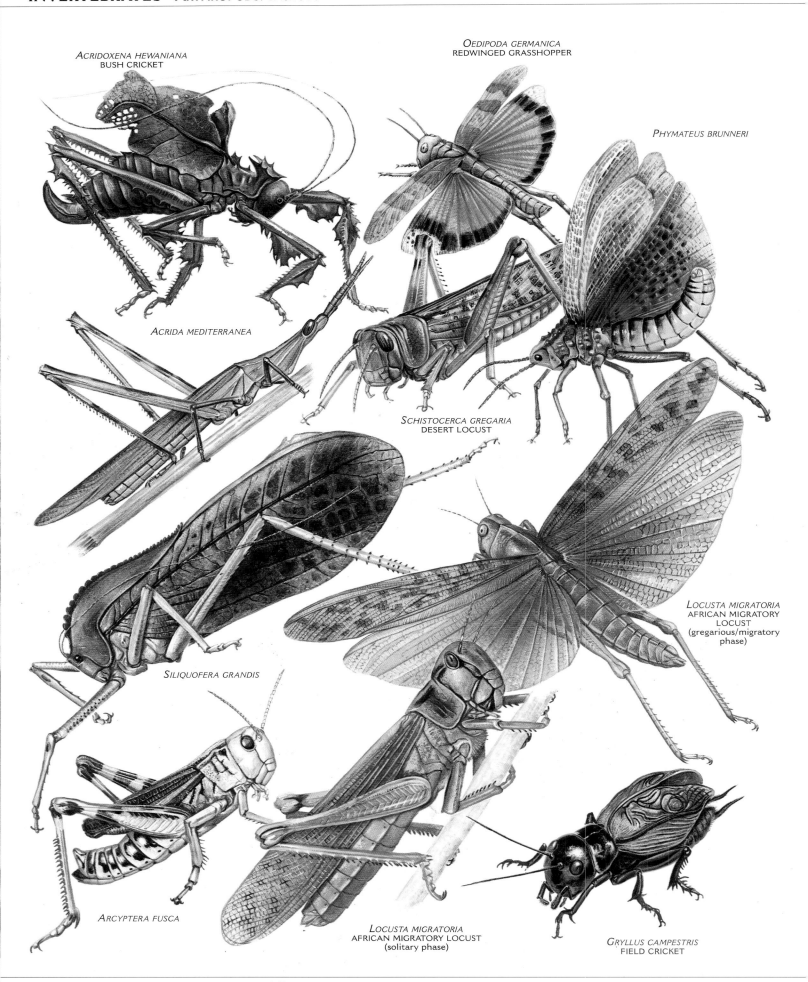

Acridoxena hewaniana
BUSH CRICKET

Oedipoda germanica
REDWINGED GRASSHOPPER

Phymateus brunneri

Acrida mediterranea

Schistocerca gregaria
DESERT LOCUST

Locusta migratoria
AFRICAN MIGRATORY
LOCUST
(gregarious/migratory
phase)

Siliquofera grandis

Arcyptera fusca

Locusta migratoria
AFRICAN MIGRATORY LOCUST
(solitary phase)

Gryllus campestris
FIELD CRICKET

Did you know...

The ability of the **Desert Locust** to destroy a whole crop of corn with astonishing speed has been known since Biblical times – a plague of locusts was one of the seven plagues to hit Ancient Egypt. The Desert Locust is gigantic, about 75 mm long.

The **Acrida mediterranea** is a grasshopper with a cone-shaped head and tapering legs. The female is up to 75 mm long. It does not 'sing' and lives in the warm, damp plains of southern Europe.

The **Redwinged Grasshopper** is a species with red rear wings. It prefers dry places.

The sound of the **Arcyptera Fusca** is high-pitched and consists of many short notes followed by a burst of three seconds. It lives in the mountain pastures of the Alps and the Pyrenees. The male insect flies, but the female does not.

The **Acridoxena Hewaniana**, (Bush Cricket) has wings looking like small, curled-up leaves. It is an excellent example of an insect which can mimic its surroundings.

In some parts of Africa, people eat **locusts**. As a food, they are a good source of protein.

A swarm of **locusts** can cover an area of over 1000 square kilometres and eat up to 20,000 tonnes of food per day.

FIELD CRICKET

Mouth: chewing

Movements: rarely jumps, prefers to fly and to run

Metamorphosis: incomplete

Length of adult: 3 cm

The Field Cricket belongs to the order of **Orthoptera** of insects and is found all over the world.

It is sometimes called the 'singing cricket' because of the loud, continuous sound it makes by lifting its front wings and rubbing one against the other. The sound is clearly heard, especially on warm, summer nights, but it is difficult to see the Field Cricket at close range.

It is very timid and at the slightest sign of anything strange, it will quickly flee into its underground lair. This can be up to half a metre deep, ending in a round chamber which is the actual nest. In front of the entrance to the lair, the cricket prepares a clean area where it sings to attract the female and to mark its territory. The female Field Cricket lays between 20 and 60 eggs during the autumn months. Young crickets are called 'nymphs' and they hatch in the spring. They shed their skins up to twelve times as they grow into adult crickets. Not all crickets sing. Some spend almost their whole lives underground. Others live in ant-hills, in symbiosis (helping and receiving help) with ants.

Although the cricket is related to the grasshopper and has hind legs ideal for jumping, it is not a great jumper and prefers to fly or to run rapidly over the ground. It eats leaves and small insects.

AFRICAN MIGRATORY LOCUST

Mouth: chewing

Movements: jumps, flies; migrates long distances

Speed: 10-25 km per hour

Metamorphosis: incomplete

Length of adult: 5 cm

The locust belongs to the **Orthoptera** order of insects. It is a species of grasshopper, and it can be found almost all over the world. From Biblical times, the African Migratory Locust has been known to cause serious damage to crops. But not all types of locusts are harmful. They are insects which usually live alone in what is called their 'solitary phase'. It is only when they congregate in thousands that they pose a danger. Then, under the influence of so many others, each locust changes its food, its size growing up to 70 mm long, and also its colour (yellow or mauve), becomes less bright. This is known as the 'gregarious phase'.

The locust eats mostly grasses; so, when thousands get together, no crops can stay undamaged. Also, eggs laid by a solitary female locust will spread about as they fall. But with many locusts all together, eggs will fall in a compact mass.

When the larvae hatch, they begin to group together in search of food - and once they reach the adult stage, they take to flight in swarms, swooping down on a field of crops and destroying it in a few hours.

PRAYING MANTIS

Mouth: chewing

Development: Metamorphosis: incomplete; larvae moult 6-12 times before reaching adult stage

Length of adult: 7-8 cm

Mantids belong to one of the higher order of insects. There are more than 200 species of mantids, all related to the grasshopper, to the leaf-insect and the stick-insect.

The Praying Mantis gets its name because of its pose as if in prayer, with 'hands together', when it is still, waiting to trap another insect. Then, with a sudden stretch of its front legs, the Praying Mantis catches its victim, holding it between two rows of sharp points then taking it to the mouth to be eaten.

The reproduction of the Praying Mantis is also very strange. Whilst male and female are in the act of mating, the female grasps the head of the male and begins to eat him, even before mating is finished.

As well as insects, a large Praying Mantis will even eat lizards, small frogs and birds. By doing this, the female will take in a sufficient amount of protein to hatch a lot of eggs – up to 200 in a sort of cocoon called an ootheca. The female makes the ootheca from a sort of foam and this soon hardens, becoming like parchment.

This opens in the spring-time, having survived even very low winter temperatures. Most species of mantid spend the winter in the egg phase. The first moulting of the larva happens with the splitting of the membrane in which it has been enclosed from birth. Even then, although it is still immature, the larva already has front legs with which it can catch its first tiny, little prey.

There are over 2,000 species of mantids. Most are found in tropical regions throughout the world, but some species are found further north, in Mediterranean countries.

Some mantids from Africa and South-east Asia are highly coloured, looking exactly like a flower or a leaf. European mantids can also blend in perfectly with the leaves among which they hide to attack their victims.

The Chinese Mantid originates in eastern Asia, but it is also the largest mantid found in North America, measuring up to 10 cm long.

Did you know...

The **Hymenopus coronatus** (Orchid Mantis) is a very beautiful species which comes from Java. Its vivid colouring simulates the shadow and the streaks of the flowers among which it lives. During moulting it can change colour, according to the flowers surrounding it.

The **Empusa pennata** (Horned Praying Mantis) is easily recognized by its long neck. It can be green or mauve and spends all winter in the larva phase. Generally, this is recognisable, because, only at this stage of development, the mantid keeps the abdomen folded up above the thorax.

Most **mantids** (see photograph) are generally bad fliers. Desert species have no wings, and so they do not fly. But they are excellent runners.

The **Idolum Diabolicum** (African Devil Mantis) is one of the largest in the world. It blends in so perfectly with flowers that it is very difficult to see. It hangs on a plant with its head down and the bumps which cover its front part become easily mistaken for the tiny insects intent on eating the 'flower'.

Among the most curious of mantids are the **Acanthus falcate** found in Brazil, the **Pseudocreobotra Wahlbergi** (African Flower Mantid) and the **Gonylus Gongyloides** (Wandering Violin) from South-east Asia.

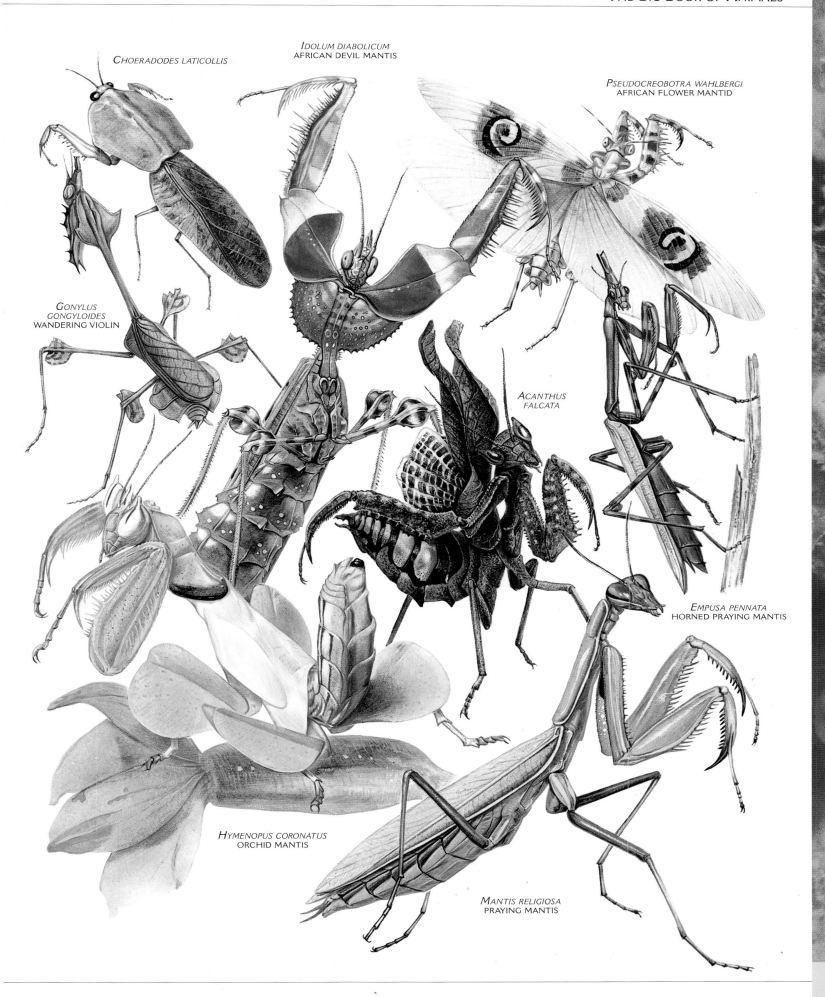

CHOERADODES LATICOLLIS

IDOLUM DIABOLICUM
AFRICAN DEVIL MANTIS

PSEUDOCREOBOTRA WAHLBERGI
AFRICAN FLOWER MANTID

GONYLUS
GONGYLOIDES
WANDERING VIOLIN

ACANTHUS
FALCATA

EMPUSA PENNATA
HORNED PRAYING MANTIS

HYMENOPUS CORONATUS
ORCHID MANTIS

MANTIS RELIGIOSA
PRAYING MANTIS

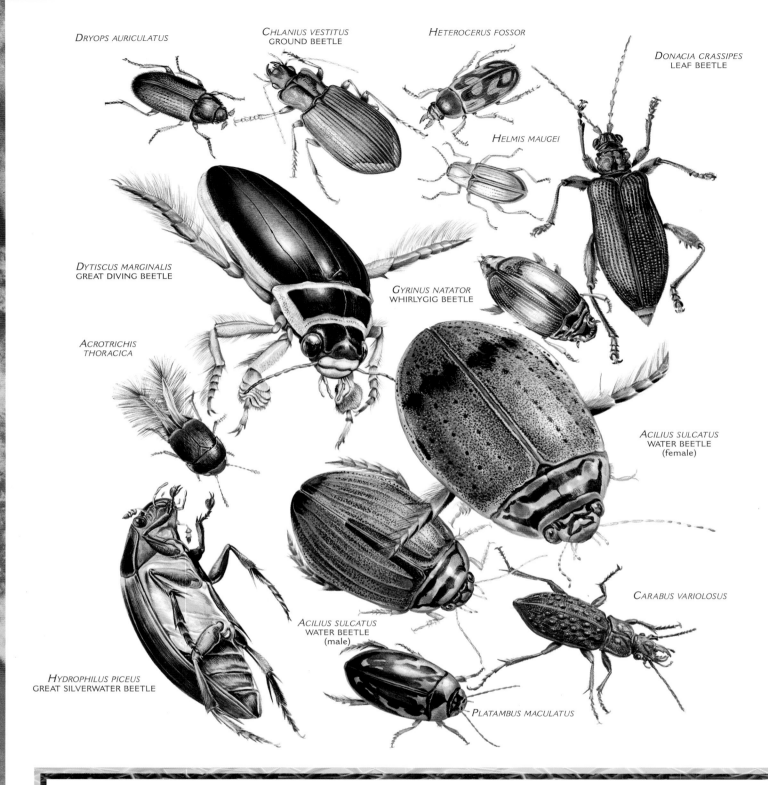

DRYOPS AURICULATUS

CHLANIUS VESTITUS
GROUND BEETLE

HETEROCERUS FOSSOR

DONACIA CRASSIPES
LEAF BEETLE

HELMIS MAUGEI

DYTISCUS MARGINALIS
GREAT DIVING BEETLE

GYRINUS NATATOR
WHIRLYGIG BEETLE

ACROTRICHIS
THORACICA

ACILIUS SULCATUS
WATER BEETLE
(female)

CARABUS VARIOLOSUS

ACILIUS SULCATUS
WATER BEETLE
(male)

HYDROPHILUS PICEUS
GREAT SILVERWATER BEETLE

PLATAMBUS MACULATUS

Díd you know...

There are many thousands of species of water beetles, all belonging to the insect order Coleoptera. The beetle, **Platambus maculates**, is a predator which lives mostly in flowing water.

The larvae of the **Dytiscus Marginalis** ('water tiger') pierces and sucks its prey until it is dry. The slow-moving adult is a water carnivore.

The **donacia** (leaf beetle) lays its eggs in the submerged stems of water plants. Their larvae never leave the bottom of ponds.

The female **Water Cockroach** fixes her cocoon containing her eggs beneath a leaf near the surface of the water.

The **Elater sanguineus** is one of the most brilliantly coloured coleoptera. It is a very rare species which feeds on dead and decomposing wood, especially the wood of the conifer.

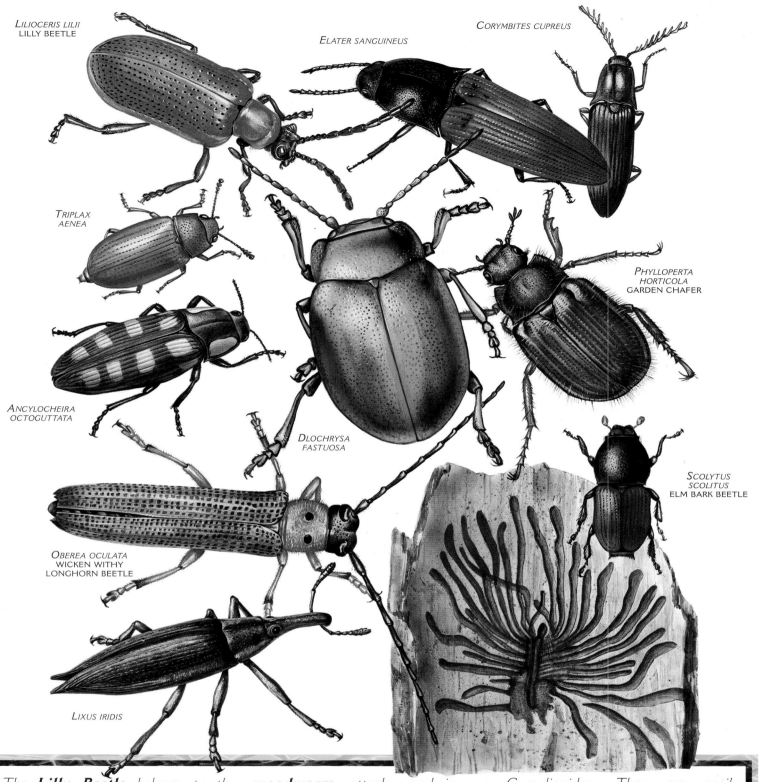

LILIOCERIS LILII
LILLY BEETLE

ELATER SANGUINEUS

CORYMBITES CUPREUS

TRIPLAX
AENEA

PHYLLOPERTA
HORTICOLA
GARDEN CHAFER

ANCYLOCHEIRA
OCTOGUTTATA

DLOCHRYSA
FASTUOSA

SCOLYTUS
SCOLITUS
ELM BARK BEETLE

OBEREA OCULATA
WICKEN WITHY
LONGHORN BEETLE

LIXUS IRIDIS

The **Lilly Beetle** belongs to the **Chrysomelidea** family, coleoptera characterized by bright colours and metal-like effects.

The **Elm Bark Beetle** digs long galleries beneath the bark of elm trees, seriously weakening the structure. Many species of coleoptera, commonly called **woodworm**, attack wood in our homes and in buildings.

To the Ancient Egyptians, the **Scarab Beetle** was a holy symbol of the Sun.

Coleoptera belonging to the genus **Lixus**, are wood-boring weevils. All are members of the family of Curculionidae. They are easily recognized by the rigid proboscis (nose tube) on which angular antennae are attached.

The **Phyllopertha orticola** belongs to the important family of Scarabaeidae of which there are at least 30,000 species, all feeding on plants.

OAK LEAF BUTTERFLY

Mouth: sucking	
Metamorphosis: complete	
Length of caterpillar: up to 8 cm	
Wing span: 8-9 cm	

The scientific name for this butterfly is **Kallima**, which in Greek means 'magnificent'. It is a name given to a group of tropical daytime butterflies which live mostly in Asia, but which can also be found in Africa and in Madagascar. The most notable feature of this butterfly is the way it can imitate perfectly the shape and the colour of narrow leaves when settling on trunks and branches of trees. In a resting position, the Oak Leaf Butterfly shows a central vein on the underside of its wings, which looks like a leaf. This 'disguise' protects the butterfly very well. Without ever showing itself too soon, it can fly away at the very last minute, when danger is almost upon it. Then it shows the coloured side of its wings, frightening away the unsuspecting predator and giving itself time to escape.

The Oak Leaf Butterfly prefers shady places and thick vegetation. It does not stay still for long and so it is difficult to pick out. It does not go in search of nectar from flowers, but feeds on the sap which oozes from the bark of the trees.

The larva (caterpillar) which feeds on nettles has two long 'horns' on its head, with rows of little spines on its back.

OWL BUTTERFLY

Mouth: sucking

Metamorphosis: complete

Length of caterpillar: up to 16 cm

Wing span: 12-14 cm

The butterflies of this genus are among the most beautiful in tropical America. They have brown wings, streaked on the upper side with a rich shade of shiny violet, like velvet. The underside is always brown with clear, black streaks.

The main feature of the Owl Butterfly are the two 'eyes' at the centre of the underside of the rear wings. In the past, some naturalists thought that these were 'false' eyes, similar to those of an owl. According to them, when predatory birds came near, the Owl Butterfly would bend its head down, and show its 'eyes' on the underside part, looking something like a bird of prey and scare enemies away.

In fact, the Owl Butterfly poses just like other butterflies; its head up, and resting its wings one on top of the other, with its strange 'eyes' no more than a beautiful decoration. It can look rather like a bat as it flies around at twilight and by night.

Did you know...

The order of **Lepidoptera** is one of the most numerous and most colourful groups of insects, with 165,000 known species. The word Lepidoptera means 'with scaly wings'. The tiny scales, however, fall off, even when they are not touched.

The mouth is in the form of a long proboscis, a tubular structure of two horny filaments which the insect uses for sucking. As the insect rests, the proboscis is sometimes curled up on top of the head. To suck the nectar from flowers, the butterfly extends its proboscis, thanks to a combined action of the muscles and pressure of the blood.

The **Lichen butterfly** belongs to a group of nocturnal butterflies. It has bright colours on the back of its body.

The **Death's Head Sphinx** butterfly gets its name because of the skull shape on the back of the thorax. It comes from Africa, but migrates every spring to Europe. Its back wings are yellow, with black streaks.

When the caterpillar of the **Cerura vinula** (Puss Moth) is disturbed, it withdraws its head and sticks out two long 'tails', looking like one, at the back.

The **cocoons** of Lepidoptera can last for years in dry conditions. The silk of which these are made is very strong and does not rot easily.

AUTOMERIS IO

THECLA LINUS

CALIGO EURILOCHUS OWL BUTTERFLY

CATOCALA NUPTA

KALLIMA INACHUS OAK LEAF BUTTERFLY (upper side)

THYSANIA AGRIPPINA

KALLIMA INACHUS OAK LEAF BUTTERFLY (underside)

ANOPHYLLA MAGNIFICA

ACHERONTIA ATROPOS DEATH'S HEAD SPHINX

CERURA VINULA

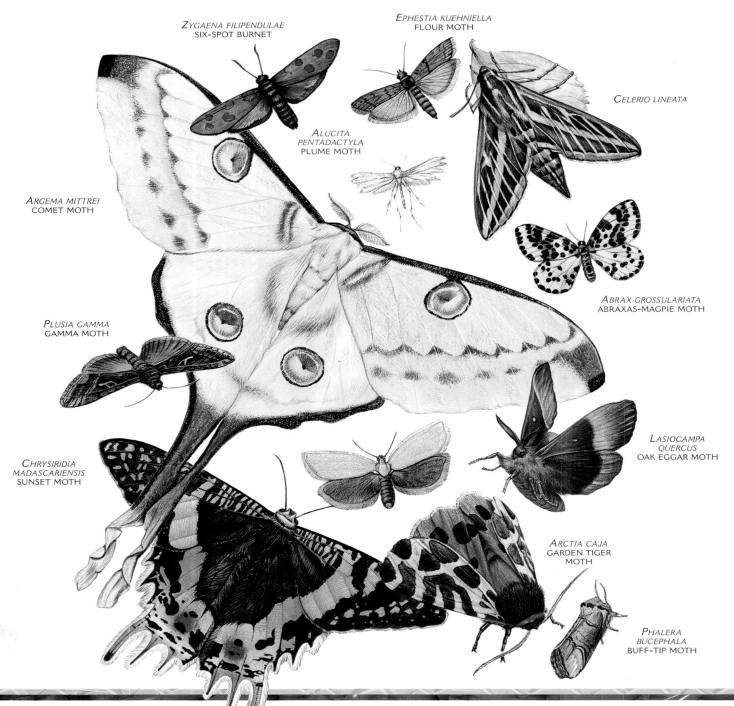

ZYGAENA FILIPENDULAE
SIX-SPOT BURNET

EPHESTIA KUEHNIELLA
FLOUR MOTH

CELERIO LINEATA

ALUCITA
PENTADACTYLA
PLUME MOTH

ARGEMA MITTREI
COMET MOTH

ABRAX GROSSULARIATA
ABRAXAS-MAGPIE MOTH

PLUSIA GAMMA
GAMMA MOTH

LASIOCAMPA
QUERCUS
OAK EGGAR MOTH

CHRYSIRIDIA
MADASCARIENSIS
SUNSET MOTH

ARCTIA CAJA
GARDEN TIGER
MOTH

PHALERA
BUCEPHALA
BUFF-TIP MOTH

Díd you know...

The **Garden Tiger Moth** may have markings similar to that of a tiger – but it avoids birds! However, it does make poisonous substances.

The rear wings of the **Comet Moth** end in two long 'tails'. In the male these can reach up to 20 cm. The female accumulates all the food she needs when in the caterpillar phase. As an adult, she neither eats nor drinks.

The Madagascar Giant Urania is one of the most colourful butterflies. Its colours take a long time to fade, even when exposed to strong light.

The bushy wings of the tiny **Alucita Pentadactyla** (Plume Moth) is split into five 'feathers'. It is so light, that it can easily be blown about by the wind.

When the **Zigaena Filipendulae** (Six-Spot Burnet Moth) is resting it almost seems to lose consciousness. Like this, it can be caught easily – however, the moment it is trapped, it releases a poisonous, yellowish liquid.

The **Owlet Moth** lives in all the temperate regions of the northern hemisphere. It belongs to the **Noctuidae** which is the largest group of Lepidoptera.

JOLANS
PROMETHEUS

APATURA IRIS
PURPLE EMPEROR

MORPHO DIDIUS
BLUE MORPHO

AGLAIS URTICAE
SMALL TORTOISESHELL
BUTTERFLY

BHUTANITIS LIDDERDALEI

PAPILIO ANDROCLES

AGRIAS CLAUDIA

MESOSEMIA CROEUS

PAPILIO ULYSSES
BLUE MOUNTAIN
BUTTERFLY

ERIHOEA DEHANI

PAPILIO CHILDRENAE

Moths and **butterflies** both belong to the Lepidoptera family. But, although some moths can be seen during the day, most moths are active by night. They also tend to be duller in colouring than butterflies, with smaller wings, fatter bodies, and distinctive bushy-like antennae.

The larvae of the **Tortrix viridiana** (European Pea-Green Moth) are a serious pest. They will attack any tree, particularly the oak, often stripping its leaves completely.

The **White Lined Sphinx** belongs to the **Sphingidae** (hawk moth) family. In tropical countries the wing span of a hawk moth can reach up to 20 cm.

The **Currant Moth** is one of the most typical of **geometrid moth**. The caterpillars of all moths in the geometrid family move with a strange 'looping' movement.

Brush-footed butterflies get their name because their forelegs are short and look like tiny brushes. Instead of proper front legs, this butterfly has a special organ which it uses to distinguish taste.

In the Amazon rainforest there are many examples of **nymphalaedea** butterflies. Their rare beauty in species such as the deep metallic blue **Morpho didius** makes them a sight to see.

COMMON MOSQUITO

Mouth: sucking

Metamorphosis: complete

Length: 8-13 cm

Life of Adult: 3-5 days

The common mosquito can be found almost anywhere in the world. It is harmless but very irritating. Normally, it sucks the blood only of birds and humans. Its abdomen is rather wide and covered in scales. The female's antennae are short; in the male, the antennae are long and feathery, so that the insect can collect the nectar on which it feeds. The male's antennae are also used to sense the high-pitched humming sounds made by the female and to recognize the presence of other mosquitoes. Both male and female have a long, hollow proboscis through which they suck their food. The common mosquito lays its eggs in all types of stagnant water.

To breathe, the larva positions itself vertically below the skin of the water, so that the bottom part of its body, where the respiratory organs are, is above the surface. The larvae feed on animal and vegetable matter, but the males of many species of mosquito 'fast' for the whole of their brief lives and survive by using up the reserves of food taken in during the larva stage. The female lives much longer than the male.

GARDEN MOSQUITO

Mouth: sucking

Metamorphosis: complete

Wingspan: 10 cm in the largest examples

The Garden Mosquito can be found almost all over the world. It is mostly noctural and looks very much like a giant mosquito, although it does not bite or sting.

The Garden Mosquito lives almost wholly in fields. It is quite lazy and, right from the start of its brief life, prefers to spend its time among the grass, always flying just above the surface of the ground in a clumsy, heavy sort of flight.

The adult feeds on nectar and other vegetable juices. But the long, soft larvae are very harmful because they feed only on the roots of vegetables, especially carrots. They are very resistant to pesticides and farmers see them as a pest and a danger.

Like all mosquitoes, the Garden Mosquito needs water. The female lays her eggs on muddy or moist surfaces, and as rain falls, so the larvae hatch. When the land is uncultivated, the larvae satisfy themselves with the roots of grasses.

Did you know...

Unlike all other flying insects, those which belong to the **Diptera** class have only one pair of true wings. The hind wings are in the form of 'halteres' — tiny, little fin-like organs which enable the insect to keep its balance during flight. In many of the larger insects in this class, the halteres are covered with scales.

The male and female of **Bibio Hortulanus** (Mark's Fly) are quite different to each other; the female has a more narrow head and smaller eyes. They live particularly near trees, and close to farms and gardens where they attack the roots of plants.

The adult male of the **Anopheles Mosquito** (see larvae in photograph) is easily recognized by its feelers, which look like little golf clubs. It is the female which carries malaria, and she, too, has long feelers. In a resting position, the adult keeps the abdomen leaning towards the surface on which it has landed, whereas the mosquito larvae lie horizontally on the surface of the water.

The female of the **Black Fly** sucks the blood of many mammals, injecting them with a poisonous substance with her saliva.

The female **Sand Fly** carries the germs which can cause serious illnesses in humans, for example, a tropical disease called Pappataci Fever.

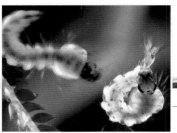

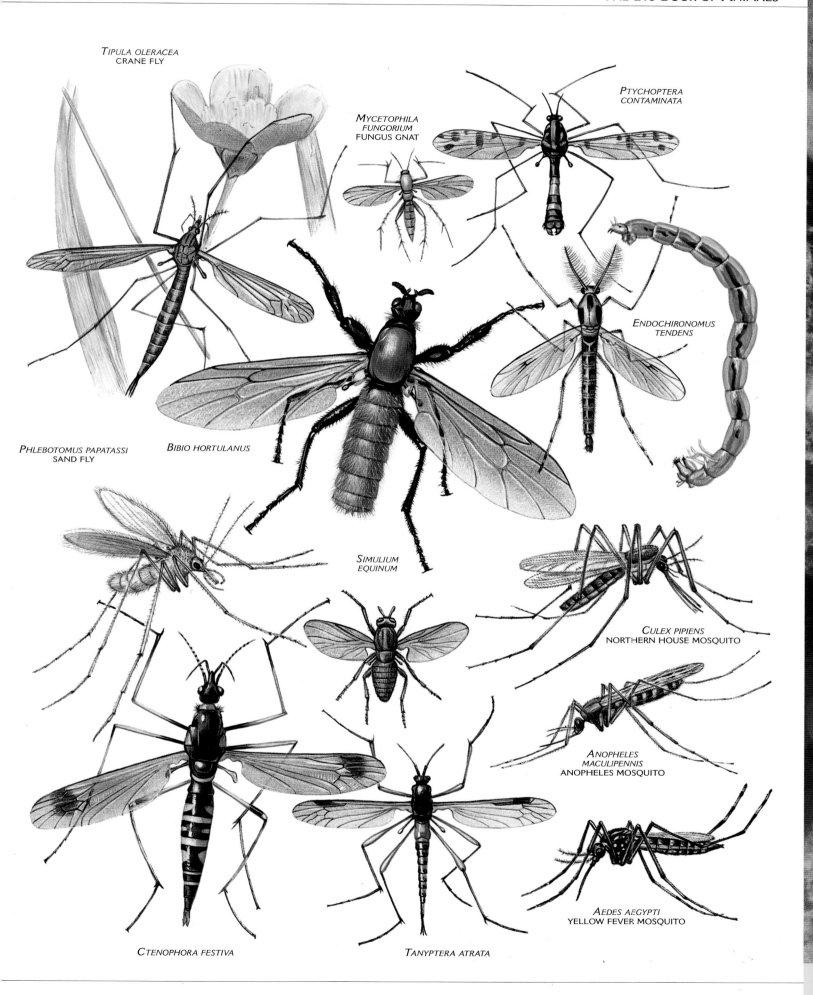

TIPULA OLERACEA
CRANE FLY

MYCETOPHILA
FUNGORIUM
FUNGUS GNAT

PTYCHOPTERA
CONTAMINATA

ENDOCHIRONOMUS
TENDENS

PHLEBOTOMUS PAPATASSI
SAND FLY

BIBIO HORTULANUS

SIMULIUM
EQUINUM

CULEX PIPIENS
NORTHERN HOUSE MOSQUITO

ANOPHELES
MACULIPENNIS
ANOPHELES MOSQUITO

AEDES AEGYPTI
YELLOW FEVER MOSQUITO

CTENOPHORA FESTIVA

TANYPTERA ATRATA

TSETSE FLY

Mouth: sucking

Metamorphosis: complete

Length of adult: 10-13 mm

The Tsetse Fly may look harmless, but it is the carrier of terrible disease which can strike many species of animals, including all domestic animals, as well as humans. It lives mainly in Africa in the southern region of the Sahara Desert.

It feeds by breaking the skin of its victim with its beak-like mouth then sucking the blood. Unlike the horsefly and the mosquito, where only the female feeds on blood, in the Tsetse Fly, both sexes are 'blood-suckers'.

So far, twenty similar species have been discovered, some living in the open spaces of desert and jungle regions, others among thick vegetation.

When it comes to reproduction, instead of laying a certain quantity of eggs, the female Tsetse Fly produces only one which she carries inside her body. Here, the larva develops, nourished by a food which the female produces by special glands, having sucked enough blood for the development of the egg. As the larva develops, it breathes through two ducts which develop from a swelling on the female's body.

FRUIT FLY

Mouth: sucking

Metamorphosis: complete

Length: 4.5-5 mm

There are many species of Fruit Fly, all seen as serious pests to fruit farmers. The Mediterranean Fruit Fly is common in the USA and most of Europe. It has grey-red wings, spotted with black at the bottom. The thorax is black with spots and covered with a fine silver down. After mating, the female will use a type of sting to break open the ripened skin of citrus fruits such as oranges and grapefruit, then lay her eggs inside. Some are killed by the oils in the skin of certain types of citrus fruits, but with up to 500 eggs laid, some are bound to survive. Once hatched, the larvae feed on the flesh of the fruit. In the case of the Apple Fruit Fly, the larva will eat the flesh to the core, so the fruit goes rotten and then falls. The Fruit Fly was identified in Malaysia at the beginning of the 18th century. After that, it invaded all hot and temperate countries in the world. In the USA, a 'war' is constantly being waged against all types of fruit flies, especially in Florida and in Hawaii. Crops are sprayed with pesticides during the mating season of the Fruit Fly, and there are strict quarantine laws to regulate all fruit imported from other countries. But, the Fruit Fly continues to survive.

Did you know...

The female of the **Tabanus Atratus** (Black Horse Fly) can suck up to 55 mg of blood with just one bite, attacking its victim near the eyes. But the male Black Horse Fly feeds only on nectar and dew.

One of the names for the Devil is Beelzebub, which means 'Lord of the Flies' – and the ugly appearance of the **fly** does make many of us think of this insect as a 'devilish' creature, especially when we know the fly to be a tireless pursuer which is able to feed on rubbish. In addition, a flies can cause illness and disease, and it is virtually indestructible.

The **Killer Shore Fly** from North America has front legs similar to the Praying Mantis.

The larvae of both the **Warble Fly** and the **Cattle Fly** develop beneath the skin of cattle. This causes painful lumps which have to be lanced.

Flies belonging to the **Diosophilidae** family and especially the **Vinegar Fly** were first studied by an American biologist in 1900. It was soon discovered that they can be easily bred and reproduce very quickly, which is why these insects have since become important in the study of the heredity of characteristics in human beings. In addition, the Vinegar Fly has only four pairs of chromosomes in the protein molecule nucleus of a cell, and this feature makes research into the DNA which carries hereditary information much easier.

BRAULA COECA
BEE LOUSE

OCYPTERA BRASSICARIA

ASILUS CRABRONIFORMIS
ROBBER FLY

OCHTERA MANTIS
KILLER SHORE FLY

CERATITIS CAPITATA
MEDITERRANEAN FRUIT FLY

LUCILIA CAESAR
GREEN BOTTLE

CHRYSOPS CAECUTIENS
HORSE FLY

GLOSSINA PALPALIS
TSETSE FLY

CONOPS QUADRIFASCIATUS
WASP FLY

HYPODERMA BOVIS
WARBLE FLY

CYRTUS GIBBUS

CELYPHUS

ECHINODERMS

EVOLUTION

The earliest fossils of Echinoderms are the remains of species fixed to levels of ground beneath the sea. These fossils date back 500 million years ago – although these sea creatures probably originated much earlier than that. The reason that Echinoderms have survived to the present day is largely due to their strong, protective covering.

MAIN CHARACTERISTICS

All Echinoderms, although in different shapes (star, spherical or elongated) have the same type of symmetrical shape (equal on all sides). This means that the body can be divided into five equal parts branching off from a central disc or axis, like the spokes of a wheel.

The **Marthasterias glacialis** (Spiny Starfish) is very large, with a strong body. Its five arms are covered with six or seven rows of sharp, cone-shaped prickles. It is dark green in colour and is usually found in deep waters.

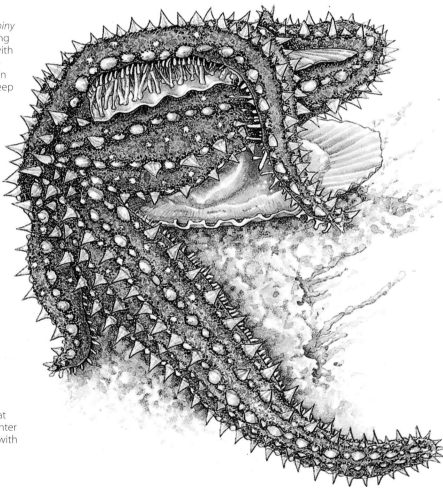

Like all starfish, it is a hungry predator and attacks its victims, oysters, mussels and other bivalves, grasping it with the strong pressure of its arms. It uses the suction of its tube-feet to force open the shell of the bivalve, then it takes the prey into part of its stomach where it is digested before the starfish actually swallows it. When it is very hungry, it will not hesitate to attack also the well-armoured sea urchin. Starfish will generally avoid the light, but the Spiny Starfish is attracted by it.

Other larger species which live at depths of over 100 m have brighter colours, from red to red-brown with white blotches.

MOVEMENT

Except for the feather stars and sea lilies which are fixed on the sea bed, Echinoderms can move about on tube-feet on the lower part of the body. As these tube-feet draw in water and pump it out, they contract and expand, enabling the animal to make slow movements.

HABITAT AND DISTRIBUTION

Echinoderms live mostly in the sea. Only those belonging to the Crinoidea family (feather stars and sea lilies) are fixed to underwater surfaces, many of these species in the deepest depths of the ocean. All other species live and move about close to the sea bed, in shallow and deep depths.

Rays in a Pattern

Even by looking closely at a starfish or a sea urchin it is not easy to distinguish the front part from the back. The sea urchin looks like a ball covered with prickles, the starfish has two flat surfaces with five points, apparently all the same. In fact, all Echinoderms are without a head and almost all have the mouth and the anus in line, on an upright axis through the centre of the body. The mouth is on the bottom surface whilst the anus, if there is one, is on the upper surface. The structure leads out from a central disc, spreading into **five equal parts**. This structure is very clear in the starfish, but it is more difficult to make out in the sea urchin. The walls of the body are divided into three layers – external, intermediate and internal. The external is the most delicate and covers the entire body. The intermediate layer is the connective tissue and forms the internal skeleton. In sea urchins, this skeleton is a compact shell covered with prickles; in the starfish and other species it is made of plates fused together. The internal layer covers the whole of the inner cavity which contains organs for digestion and for reproduction. It is inside this cavity that the five double rows of **tube-feet** begin, appearing on the body like rays. These tube-feet can move by a system of little canals which fill up with water and then empty, making the tube-feet contract and expand so that the animal can crawl along the sea bed. Breathing is done in the same way, taking in oxygen from the outside and expelling waste air.

The circulation system is made up of blood vessels called lacunas. These penetrate between the organs and the tissues, and the muscles in the lacunas contract to make the blood circulate.

Photograph: a colourful example of a Starfish

The nervous system also follows the same radial (ray-like) pattern.

The sex of echinoderms is almost always separate, but there are some species which are hermaphrodite; as a rule, the egg and sperm come together in the water. Swimming larvae develop from the egg, and these have a bilateral (two-sided) symmetry. Only after a complex metamorphosis (transformation) do the adults develop the five-point symmetry. Echinoderms are divided into six classes:

Crinoidea, comprising about eighty known species. These have one foot which fixes the animal to the sea bed. The body is cup-shaped with five or more coloured, feathery arms. After the early stages, some species detach themselves from the feet and move around freely.

Echinoidea, the family of sea urchins, with more than 850 species.

Holothurioidea, commonly known as sea cucumbers, of which there are 500 species, all with the typical long shape. The body has calcite little plates and moving tube-feet.

Asteroidea, the starfishes with over 2000 species.

Ophiuroidea (basket stars and brittle stars), with a little less than 2000 known species. These are rather like starfish, but with softer arms, long and flexible.

Concentricycloidea (sea daisies).

PHYLUM	CLASS	SPECIES
ECHINODERMS	Crinoidea	feather stars, sea lilies
	Echinoidea	sea urchins
	Holothurioidea	sea cucumbers
	Asteroidea	starfish
	Ophiuroidea	brittle stars
	Concentricycloidea	sea daisies

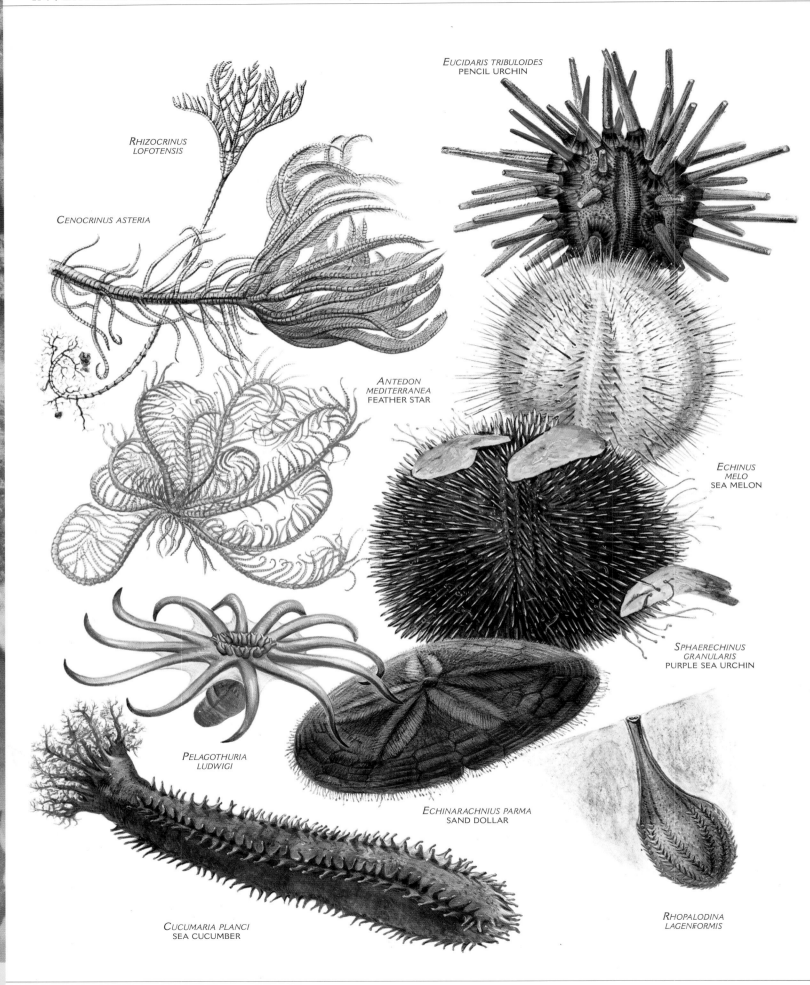

RHIZOCRINUS LOFOTENSIS

CENOCRINUS ASTERIA

EUCIDARIS TRIBULOIDES PENCIL URCHIN

ANTEDON MEDITERRANEA FEATHER STAR

ECHINUS MELO SEA MELON

SPHAERECHINUS GRANULARIS PURPLE SEA URCHIN

PELAGOTHURIA LUDWIGI

ECHINARACHNIUS PARMA SAND DOLLAR

CUCUMARIA PLANCI SEA CUCUMBER

RHOPALODINA LAGENFORMIS

PURPLE SEA URCHIN

Shape: spherical

Diameter: from 6-7 cm to 15 cm

Appendages: numerous short prickles

This sea urchin is one of the largest. It often reaches a size of 6 or 7 cm in diameter, but sometimes the largest reach a diameter of up to 15 cm.

Its surface is thickly covered with short, violet-coloured prickles, fading to white at the ends.

It is very common in the Mediterranean and in the Atlantic, and from the English Channel to the Gulf of Guinea, at depths of between 30 and 100 m.

It lies on its lower side, the same side as its mouth opening. The anus is on the opposite side, in the centre.

As in all sea urchins, the internal skeleton is made up of 10 double rows of calcite plates which form a rigid covering. Some of these plates have the larger nodules (swollen bases) for the roots of the prickles; other plates have the smaller nodules where the pedicellariae (small pincers) begin. The sea urchin uses these pedicellariae to defend itself.

From the actual body of the sea urchin emerge the five double rows of tube-feet which enable it to move. The sea urchin is egg-laying.

Did you know...

The **Rhizocrinus Lofotensis** is a 'dancer' of the sea, with a delicate hanging stem, about 7 cm long, and short grey or yellowish feathery arms. It is found in the northern Atlantic at depths of between 140 and 480 m. The **Cenocrinus Asteria** is another 'dancer'; it lives in the western Indian Ocean at depths of between 200-600 m; it is yellowish-brown, with a body 1.7 cm diameter and arms 10 cm long.

The feather star **Antedon Mediterranea** is very common in the Mediterranean. It lives among the algae on the sea bed, attached to the rocks and on the deep coral beds, at depths of up to 200 m.

Sea cucumbers in European seas are purple, grey or yellow, whilst those on or near coral reefs are brightly coloured. On the **Pelagothuria Ludwigi**, the front part of the trunk is encircled an umbrella-shaped membrane, with 13-16 tentacles which enable it to swim like a jellyfish.

The **Rhopalodina Lagenformis** keeps the lower part of its body sunken, whilst the upper part comes out of the sand to take in the water.

The **Sea Urchin** feeds on dead fish and carcasses of other sea creatures, seaweed and even wood. There are three main examples: the **Eucidaris Tribuloides** (Pencil Urchin), which lives in the Caribbean seas and the East Atlantic coast; the **Echinus Melo** (Sea Melon) in the Mediterranean Sea and the Atlantic Ocean, and the **Echinarachnius Parma** (Sand Dollar) which lives along the Atlantic coast of North America.

SEA CUCUMBER

The Sea Cucumber has a cylinder, worm-like shape, which makes it look rather like a vegetable cucumber. Unlike the starfish and the sea urchin, it does not rest on the ground on its 'face' but on one side of its body. This is because its mouth is at the

Shape: long

Length: 20-35 cm

Appendages: 20-39 tentacles around the mouth

end of its front and its anus at the end of its rear. It moves on the sea bed by moving tube-feet on the abdominal surface of the body; only a very few species swim by means of moving appendages. About twenty tentacles encircle the mouth. Some tentacles are branching. Others are simple, especially those which retract most quickly and which are used to catch small prey.

The Sea Cucumber can also take in the sand and the mud on the sea bed, from which it can absorb organic particles for nourishment. Its eggs are laid in the sea and incubated in the body of the female. Some species live in symbiosis with the small pearlfish, which shelter inside the body of the Sea Cucumber.

ASTROPECTEN AURANTIACUS

Diameter:	from 10 to 28 cm
Shape:	arms branching out from a central disc; plated edging and prickles
Habitat:	sandy surfaces from depths of 1 to 20 m.

This starfish belongs to the family of Asteroidea. The Echinoderma in this family have broad plates on the edges of the body, which is covered by prickles and bumps. It is easy to see this beautiful red-orange starfish, with its five arms edged with prickles, on the fine, sandy beaches of the Mediterranean and the Atlantic.

It lives very near the coast, and at low tide, it buries itself in the sand, showing only the centre of its upper side which is swollen in the form of a cone. This cone acts like a sense organ. When it is touched, the cone contracts and the starfish buries itself in the sand once again. Then at high tide, the starfish reappears on the surface of the water. It buries itself in the sand to shield parts of its body from the rays of the Sun, especially the bottom surface which has no coloured pigment and is therefore particularly sensitive.

This starfish is a carnivore and feeds on the molluscs which it catches with its arms and then takes to the mouth. The prey is then trapped by the long, moving prickles around the mouth cavity.

BRITTLE STAR

Diameter:	from 5 to 15 cm, arms extended
Shape:	arms clearly separated from the central disc; presence of spines
Habitat:	from depths of 0 to 475 m on rocky or slimy sea beds

This highly-coloured species is sometimes called the Serpent Star. Its arms are flexible, but so fragile that they can be broken off and re-grown easily.

The Brittle Star is found on the rocky coasts of Europe, in the Mediterranean and in the Atlantic, where it lives at the flattest part possible on the rough surfaces there. Sometimes it likes to be with other Brittle Stars, when a large group will gather together.

If the current is calm enough, the Brittle Star will extend its arms upwards to catch tiny food particles and fragments of debris floating in the water. The food reaches the mouth by quick movements of the tube-feet along the arms.

If the current is strong, the Brittle Star will squash itself against the sea bed, so as not to be carried away.

When a Brittle Star finds itself on its wrong side, it can turn itself back again within about 40 seconds. It can do this by making all the muscles in its body work together.

Did you know...

The **Linckia laevigata** (Blue Linkia) is a blue starfish which lives in the seas of Australia. It is remarkable because of its ability to re-grow; from a single arm, it can grow its whole body again. During this process, it presents the so-called 'comet shape' with one large and four small arms.

Unlike many other starfishes, the **Astropecten Aurantiacus** moves very quickly, between 30-60 cm in one minute.

The **Acanthaster planci** (Crown of Thorns Starfish) is a poisonous starfish. With its 11-21 short arms and its long prickles, it can attack and destroy the coral reefs.

The **Crossaster Papposus** (Spiny Sun Star) lives in the northern Atlantic. It has 8-14 arms, and a large disc with a diameter of 34 cm.

The **Fromia ghardaqana** (Hurghada Star) with its gaudy red colouring and white spots, is found in the Red Sea.

In the **Amphilycus androphorus**, the female is large-sized. The male is much smaller and stays with the female all his life.

The **Ophioderma longicauda** lives in the Mediterranean and in the Atlantic Ocean. The **Ophiura albida** lives in the Mediterranean in the Atlantic and in the eastern Baltic Sea.

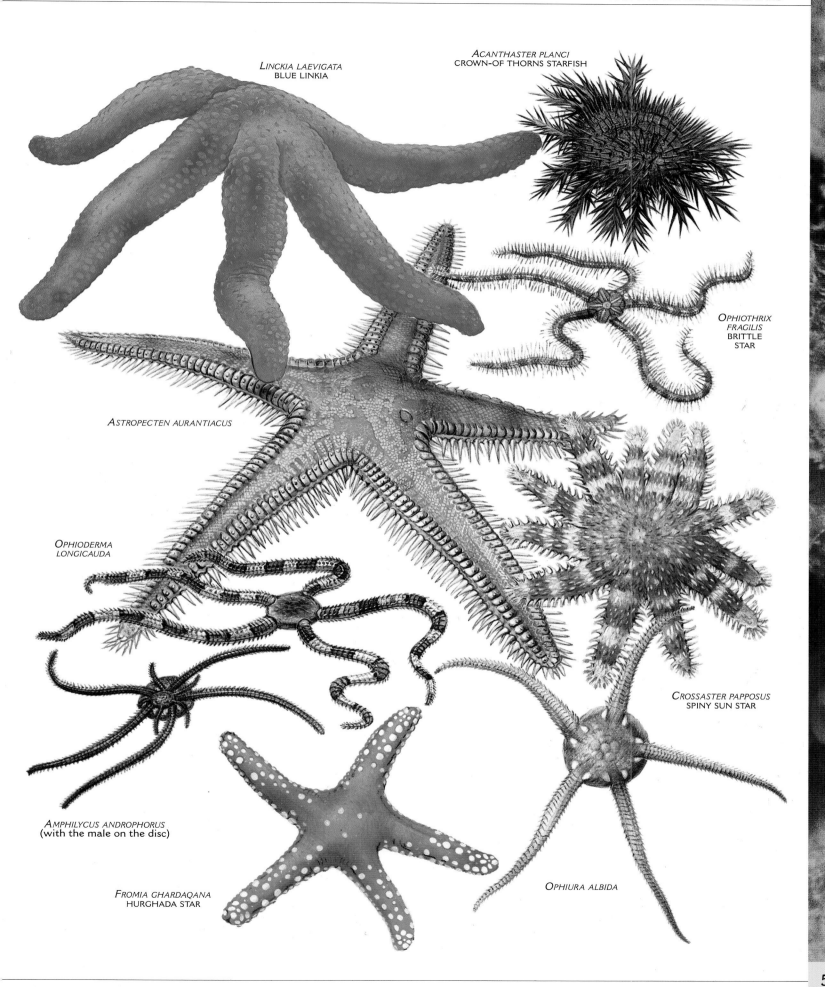

LINCKIA LAEVIGATA
BLUE LINKIA

ACANTHASTER PLANCI
CROWN-OF THORNS STARFISH

*OPHIOTHRIX
FRAGILIS*
BRITTLE
STAR

ASTROPECTEN AURANTIACUS

*OPHIODERMA
LONGICAUDA*

CROSSASTER PAPPOSUS
SPINY SUN STAR

AMPHILYCUS ANDROPHORUS
(with the male on the disc)

FROMIA GHARDAQANA
HURGHADA STAR

OPHIURA ALBIDA

CHORDATA

EVOLUTION

The phylum Chordata represents the link between the most primitive animal life through to the most highly developed, and on to human life. The earliest forms of Chordata were small animals, thin and sometimes transparent.

The Ascidian or Sea Squirt (right) is a very primitive Urochordate. It has a distinctive pouch-shaped body covered by a rigid 'tunic' of live tissue, with a siphon at the mouth through which water enters (and from which the animal extracts food particles and gets the oxygen for breathing), and another siphon through which the water is expelled.

MAIN CHARACTERISTICS

The body of a chordate is always symmetrical. This means that is is equal on both sides. In the embryo or larva state, it is supported by the **notochord**, which is like a flexible rod and runs through the length of the body.

The Amphioxus or Lancelet is a Cephalochordate. It is a tiny, semi-transparent sea creature which lives in the bottom of the sea. In the Lancelet, we can see evidence of the transition from invertebrates to vertebrates. It has a nerve notochord and tail muscles similar to those of a fish. But it has no brain, sense organs, jaws or a skeleton.

The Lamprey is one of the most primitive vertebrates. It has a long body but without jaws or limbs. Its system of feeding is very strange; the mouth is a sort of funnel covered with numerous horny teeth, set out in concentric circles at the centre of which is the tongue. The lamprey seizes its prey in its mouth, sticking on to it like a sucker and sucking out the blood. From pictures, it is possible to make out the gill slits through which the water which the Lamprey has ingested is expelled.

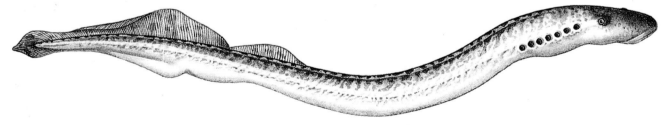

NERVOUS SYSTEM

Another characteristic which distinguishes Chordates from invertebrates is the presence of a central nervous system, which is always controlled from the top of the **notochord**. In the earliest Chordates, the nervous system was very simple. In the course of evolution, this has developed into various degrees of complexity.

HABITAT AND DISTRIBUTION

Among Chordates, only the vertebrates have been able to adapt to every type of surroundings, from water to the land and at all latitudes. The other two groups – the Urochordates and the Cephalochordates – have never succeeded in abandoning the waters of the seas and the oceans.

A strong and flexible support

All Chordates have a **notochord** – a solid, yet flexible rod of cells to support the body and the muscle structure. They also have organs necessary for the capture and filtering of tiny organisms, the 'gill slits'. Water is inhaled through the mouth and expelled through the **gill slits**, whilst the food particles present in the water are trapped.

The gill slits are also used for breathing.

The circulation system comprises a pulsating organ, the **heart**, and veins through which blood circulates. Over the centuries, this system has developed more and more, also becoming an important part of the process of respiration (breathing). In the majority of cases, reproduction is by the meeting of two animals of the opposite sex, although some Urochordates are hermaphrodite.

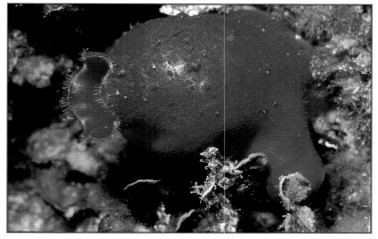

Photograph: above, a Sea Squirt, below, a colony of salps, creatures belonging to Thaliacea, another class of Urochordates.

Chordates are divided into three subphylums – **Urochordates** or **Tunicates**,

Cephalochordates and Vertebrates. Urochordates or Tunicates are sea creatures which can vary in size from a few millimetres to tens of centimetres. Some are fixed, like the Sea Squirt, others move freely. They are formed in one 'piece' and the body is similar to a pouch or bag. The spinal chord (or notochord) is present only in the tail and in some species only in the larva stage. Also, both the circulation system and the nervous system are reduced.

Cephalochordates are the closest to Vertebrates. The body is compressed sideways and covered with an epidermis (top layer of skin). The notochord runs through the whole body and remains in adults. Instead of limbs, **Cephalochordates** have fins for swimming, with various segmented organs repeated along the whole body. The mouth is at the front of the stomach and this has many filaments which trap food filtered through the water. The circulation system has only veins. Sexes are separate and fertilization takes place in water.

Vertebrates are the most complex of Chordates. The notochord is present only in the embryo; in the adult this is replaced by the **spinal column** which supports the whole skeleton. Two pairs of limbs are joined to the spinal column and these are used for movement. The skin protects the body and this has two layers, the dermis and the epidermis.

The **nervous system** consists of the brain, the spinal cord and various nerves. Blood is pumped around by the heart, circulating through a network of arteries, veins, and capillaries,. The respiratory (breathing) system consists of gills in aquatic vertebrates and lungs in land-dwelling vertebrates.

All vertebrates have separate sexes and can be oviparous (egg-laying), ovoviviparous (the egg is carried inside the female's body until it comes out) or viviparous (the embryo develops in the uterus of the female).

PHYLUM	SUB-PHYLUM	CLASS	SPECIES
CHORDATES	Urochordates		Sea Squirt
	Cephalochordates		Lancelet
	Vertebrates	cyclostomes	Lamprey
		fish	
		amphibians	
		reptiles	
		birds	
		mammals	

FISH

BEHAVIOUR

Most fish take little care or no care at all of their young. However, there are some species that build nests and keep guard over both the eggs and the young.

There are fish which 'walk' on the sea bed, fish that can fly, change colour or look like rocks and there are fish which can inject poison.

COMMON CHARATERISTICS

A fish has a tapering body which, in most cases is protected by scales, and dorsal (back), ventral (stomach), pectoral (breast) caudal (tail) and anal (end) fins. They breathe through gills and most species have a swim bladder which prevents them from sinking when they are not swimming.

The Coelacanth **(Latimeria Chalumnae)** shown below was discovered in the1930s. Before then, it was believed that this strange fish had been extinct for 70 million years. The coelacanth is a 'living fossil', one of the few survivors of a group of prehistoric fish, unaltered since the time it was widespread on Earth. It has a swim bladder, but this is full of fat and does not carry out any function in keeping the fish afloat. It has long pectoral fins which enables it to 'walk' on the sea bed, supported by 32 feelers.

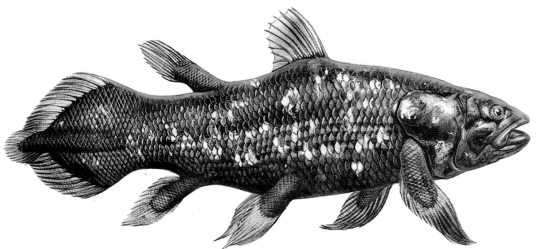

The Siamese Fighting Fish **(Betta Splendens)** in the photograph above, originated in Thailand. Little by little, as they were inbred by humans, they became more warlike, hence the name. It is not a sociable fish. A male lives with a female, defending its territory from other males. Unlike most fishes, it takes care of the young along with the female. She lays her eggs in a nest of bubbles of air, covered by saliva. The nest floats to the surface of the water.

FEEDING

Fish can be herbivore or carnivore. In both cases, there are some species with teeth strong enough for them to feed on large plants and sea creatures and some which can eat only the microscopic organisms in plankton which they filter through the water.

EVOLUTION, DISTRIBUTION AND HABITAT

The first vertebrates lived on earth about 400 million years ago. There are believed to be around 27,000 species, most living in seas and oceans all around the world, up to 9000 m deep. An estimated 5000 live in fresh water. Some can migrate from the seas to rivers and vice versa.

Gills, fins and a spinal column

Fish are divided into two main classes – cartilaginous fish and bony fish. Among the **Cartilaginous Fish** are the sharks, rays and chimaera. All sharks have a body which is perfectly hydrodynamic – ideal for moving through the water – but they do not have a **swim bladder**. Therefore, so as not to sink, the shark has to swim continuously. The ray has a very flat body which is made larger by the pectoral fins being fused together. Sometimes, the tail is sharp and has a very poisonous sting. Some rays give off strong electrical charges. The Chimaera, which lives in the deepest depths of the sea, is of medium size and has a very odd, somewhat monster-like form. Its appearance is somewhere between a cartilaginous and a bony fish. Like the Coelacanth, the Chimaera is an ancient species and a

Photograph: an example of a ray.

'living fossil'.

All the other known species of fish, of many different shapes and colours, belong to the class of **bony fish**, with a bony skeleton. Bony fish have separate sexes and often the male and the female are very different. The eggs can be pelagic (floating in water) and may contain a **drop of oil** which enables them to be carried along by the currents, drifting some way down from the surface and getting mixed with the plankton. The tuna lays this type of egg. Alternatively, the egg may have a heavier density than that of the water and so sinks to the bottom. This is what happens with the eggs of the coast-dwelling, and fresh water fish. When fertilization is 'external' the male bathes with his sperm the mass of eggs which has been laid; when fertilization is internal, the male fertilizes the female by way of a special organ called a **gonad**. In fish, the number of eggs laid can reach many millions; but then the larvae become easy prey for other animals and so few reach the adult stage.

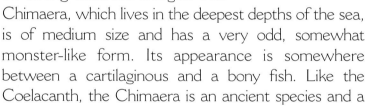

PHYLUM	SUB-PHYLUM	CLASS	ORDER	SPECIES
CHORDATA	Vertebrate	Cartilaginous Fish	Selachii	shark
			Batoidei	ray
			Chimaeriformes	Chimaera
		Bony Fish	Acipenseriformes	paddlefish
			Coelacantthicae	Coleacanth
			Clupeiformes	herring
			Mormyriformes	Nile Mormyrus
			Anguilliformes	eel
			Cypriniformes	carp, tench
			Bolonidae	garfish
			Gadiformes	cod
			Gasterosteiformes	Sea Horse
			Lampridiformes	Moonfish
			Zeiformes	Boarfish
			Perciformes	tuna
			Pleuronectiformes	sole, flatfish
			Tetraodontiformes	Puffer Fish
			Lophiiformes	Batfish

WHITE SHARK

Length:	6-7.5 m
Reproduction:	viviparous
Distribution:	worldwide

The White Shark belongs to the class of cartilaginous fish. It can be found in the open seas, especially in areas up to 1000 m deep, but also near to the coast. It lives all over the world, but is rare both in the tropics and in the Mediterranean. Its huge, solid body is silver grey or brown and the stomach white. It is recognized mainly by its cone-shaped, pointed nose, its tail shaped like a crescent moon and its terrifying mouth, with its grooved lips and rows of pointed teeth, all razor-sharp. The White Shark's largest teeth can reach a length of 8 cm. So, we can understand how easily it can tear its prey apart. The White Shark feeds on small sea creatures and occasionally larger prey such as dolphins, seals and other sharks. The stomachs of White Sharks often contain rubbish thrown overboard from ships, even tin cans. The shape of its body may lead us to think that it can swim very fast, but hunters using harpoons would seem to contradict this. Although the White Shark is so easily recognized, there are still many aspects of its life about which we do still do not know very much.

CARCHARODON CARCHARIAS **WHITE SHARK**

Did you know...

The largest shark — and the largest of all fish — is the **Whale Shark** with a length of 20 m and a weight of about 20,000 kg.
It swims slowly, keeping its mouth open. This alone can reach 2 m in length, but the Whale Shark eats only plankton and small fish.

The tail of the **Thresher Shark** is as long as the head and the body put together and it weighs up to 450 kg. But despite its appearance, it is quite harmless to humans. It is always hungry and can swallow in one gulp almost all the fish it can hold in its mouth at one time. It is unpopular with fishermen because it causes serious damage to their nets.

The young of the **Basking Shark** have a very long nose, like the proboscis of an insect. In the adult, this stays relatively thin.

The skin of the **Small Spotted Catshark** is covered with scales like dense teeth — no wonder this was once used like sandpaper! This fish lays its eggs in hard, rigid cases 10 cm long.

The mouth of the **Spotted Wobbegong** shark is surrounded by numerous curling skin appendages rather like the form of some invertebrates or algae. These helps them to disguise themselves as creatures on the deepest sea beds and to identify food.

The **Sand Shark** lives in the shallow water along all ocean coastlines except those which are too cold. Only two species of sand shark are considered to be dangerous.

Although it is always very hungry, the **Blue Shark** is not one of the most dangerous sharks. It also swallows non-edible material and often follows the whaling ships to eat the rubbish thrown overboard.

CETORHINUS MAXIMUS
BASKING SHARK

CHLAMYDOSELACHUS ANGUINEUS
FRILLED SHARK

SCYLIORHINUS CANICULA
SMALL SPOTTED CATSHARK

ALOPIAS VULPINUS
THRESHER SHARK

RHINCHODON TYPUS
WHALE SHARK

CARCHARODON CARCHARIAS
GREAT WHITE SHARK

CARCHARIAS FEROX
SAND SHARK

PRIONACE GLAUCA
BLUE SHARK

ORECTOLOBUS MACULATUS
SPOTTED WOBBEGONG

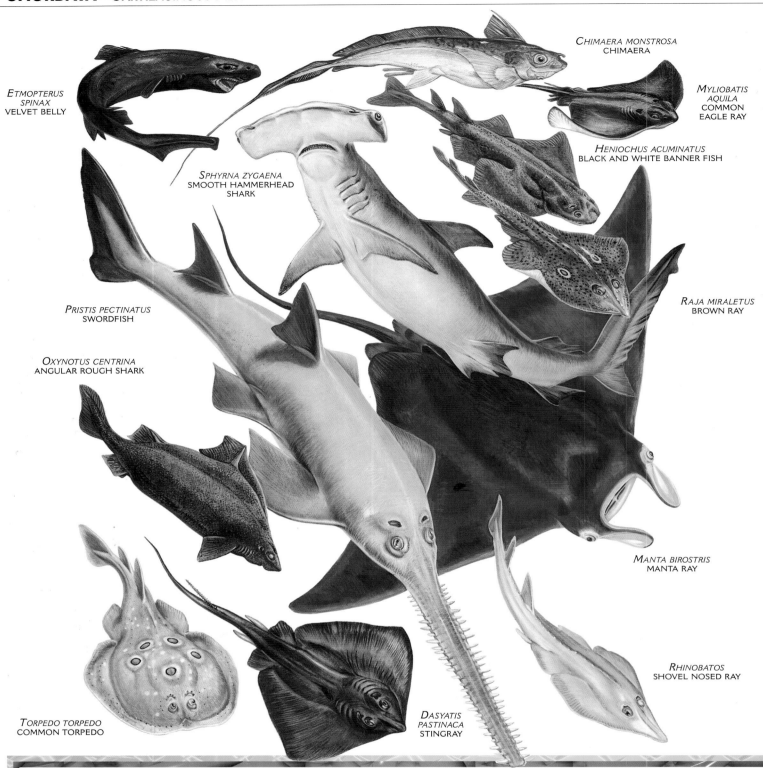

ETMOPTERUS
SPINAX
VELVET BELLY

CHIMAERA MONSTROSA
CHIMAERA

MYLIOBATIS
AQUILA
COMMON
EAGLE RAY

SPHYRNA ZYGAENA
SMOOTH HAMMERHEAD
SHARK

HENIOCHUS ACUMINATUS
BLACK AND WHITE BANNER FISH

PRISTIS PECTINATUS
SWORDFISH

OXYNOTUS CENTRINA
ANGULAR ROUGH SHARK

RAJA MIRALETUS
BROWN RAY

MANTA BIROSTRIS
MANTA RAY

TORPEDO TORPEDO
COMMON TORPEDO

DASYATIS
PASTINACA
STINGRAY

RHINOBATOS
SHOVEL NOSED RAY

Díd you know...

Because of its appearance and its position in the table of evolution, the **Black and White Bannerfish** is widely regarded as the link between sharks and rays.

The weapon of the **Swordfish** is a very long armed beak equal to a quarter or a third of its total length. As well as stunning other fish, the Swordfish also uses its beak to search in the mud of the sea bed for molluscs and other sea creatures to eat.

The **Common Eagle Ray** often appears as the 'monster' in sea legends. It has a tail like a dagger, 'armed' with spines and both tail and spines are poisonous. By moving its pectoral fins very rapidly, it can suddenly rise up from the deep and this is when it seems as if it is really flying.

The dorsal fins of the **Angular Rough Shark** each have a large spine; the front fins lean forward.

STINGRAY

Reproduction: viviparous

Number of young: 2-4

Length: up to 1.5 m

Weight: up to 20 kg

Where found: sea beds of the Mediterranean and the Eastern Atlantic

Feeds on: molluscs and crustaceans

The Stingray (in photograph) is one of the most common species of poisonous rays. It can be reddish in colour, or olive green or grey and it has a triangular snout and a long tail, one and a half times the length of the body, and this has at least one sharp spine. To defend itself, the Stingray uses its tail like a whip. This can pierce the bottom of a boat and cause serious injury to humans. In some regions of the Pacific, the caudal spines of the Stingray are used by inhabitants to make poisonous daggers.

The Stingray lives half-hidden in the sand, which it leaves only to go in search of food – molluscs, crustaceans and other invertebrates. Its enormous pectoral fins act as huge fans which, when waved about near muddy depths, uncovers the sea creatures which live hidden in the sediments of the sea bed.

The Stingray chews its prey with lots of strong teeth which are set out in rows. Some species of stingray have been known to swim up into the estuaries of rivers.

HAMMERHEAD SHARK

Reproduction: viviparous

Number of young: 30-40

Length of adult: up to 6 m

Width of head: up to 80 cm

Where found: worldwide

The Hammerhead Shark is one of the strangest members of the shark family. The reason for its curiously-shaped head, which can be up to 80 cm wide, is not known. Its side lobes, with the eyes at the end of two bulges in the skin and which are very large compared to the tiny pectoral fins, wave about to enable the Shark to maintain balance. Hammerhead Sharks can be up to 6 m long. They live in open, deep waters, in tropical and in temperate seas. In the Caribbean seas and along the coast of Florida, gatherings of hundreds of young Hammerhead Sharks can often be seen.

The Hammerhead Shark feeds mainly on cartilaginous fish, crustaceans and crabs which it finds on the sea beds. When it is hungry, there is nothing safe from its poisonous rays – the unmistakeable sting of the Stingray has been found in the flesh of some Hammerhead Sharks which have been caught.

The female gives birth to lots of living young many times in her lifetime.

The **Brown Ray** is egg-laying and fertilization is internal. The egg comes contained in a horny, rectangular shell with an appendage of variable length at any angle.

The **Manta Ray** is a real giant; it can measure over 8 m wide and weigh 3000 kg. Its square-shaped head has two small fins turning inward.

In the times of the Ancient Romans, doctors would use the **Common Torpedo** to cure some illnesses. The Torpedo is one of the few fish which can give an electric shock. This can be equal to approximately 200 volts. The organs which generate electricity are luminous and situated at the each side of the head, within the

folds of the body.

The **Chimaera** is sometimes known as the Ghost Shark and is a fascinating creature. It lives in the depths of the sea bed and has a tail similar to a thin whip. As the last representative of an extinct animal family, it is regarded as a 'living fossil'.

SALMON

The Common Salmon lives in fresh water and also the sea. It is a tireless traveller. This fish leaves the sea when, having reached sexual maturity and accumulated remarkable reserves of fat, it feels the moment of reproduction has arrived. Then it swims towards the mouth of the river, which leads it to the source. Here, the very cold waters are rich in food. Overcoming many obstacles, waterfalls, rapids and barriers, the salmon covers hundreds of kilometres. After losing one third of its weight, it reaches the place where it will reproduce.

Because of serious organic deterioration, some salmon die after laying their eggs, or become easy prey for fish, birds or mammals. It is calculated that only 5% of salmon have carried out a first migration successfully and returned to the sea. The young salmon, born in the highest reaches of the rivers, migrate towards the sea when they reach a length of 10-12 cm, at 1 - 2 years of age. When they reach the time to reproduce, they go back to exactly the same river in which they were born. It seems that salmon have a highly developed sense of recollection, even after 5 - 6 years, for the smell, the temperature and the chemical features of the water in which they were born.

Reproduction: egg-laying

Length: 1.20-1.50 m

Lives in: the sea and fresh water

PIKE

Reproduction: egg-laying

Length: up to 1.35 m

Weight: up to 23 kg

Lives in: fresh water

The Pike is a freshwater fish with a dreaded reputation; it is the most fearsome predator of European rivers, if not the whole northern hemisphere. The Pike does not like strong currents of water because these prevent it from staying still so that it can surprise and then attack its prey. Instead, it prefers the calm waters of lakes and non-raging rivers.

The clear colour of the skin with dark stripes enables it to stay hidden among the water plants. The strong tail and the backward-bending fins give the Pike enormous spurts of speed, so that it can dive down on a fish from a distance of 10 m before the prey is aware of the danger.

The adult Pike even attacks ducks, coots and other water fowl. Because of its appetite and its mouth with its sharp teeth, curving inside like hooks, the pike is called 'the freshwater shark'.

The female lays her eggs on submerged water plants.

Did you know...

Freshwater fish live at different levels of rivers according to the temperature of water and the amount of oxygen that they need.

When the time comes for them to spawn, all species of **Shad** swim from the sea to rivers ready to lay their eggs, like the salmon. The Shad belongs to the herring family.

The **Grayling** has a huge dorsal fin, rather like a sail. Because it needs lots of oxygen, this fish is sensitive to the features of water and also pollution.

The **Red Salmon** lives in the Pacific and returns to Asiatic and African rivers.

The **Schelly** belongs to the group of white fish which in European waters are almost extinct.

The **Gizzard Shad** is found in the rivers of Central and Northern America and in Atlantic waters. It belongs to an order of fish which is very popular as a food in the United States.

The **Alaska Blackfish** is found in North America and Siberia. It also lives in the stagnant waters of the Arctic tundra.

HIODON TERGISUS
MOONEYE

ALOSA FALLAX
THWAITE SHAD

THYMALLUS THYMALLUS
GRAYLING

COREGONUS LAVARETUS
SCHELLY

ONCORHYNCHUS NERKA
RED SALMON

ESOX LUCIUS
PIKE

DALLIA PECTORALIS
ALASKA BLACKFISH

SALMO SALAR
ATLANTIC SALMON

DOROSOMA CEPEDIANUM
GIZZARD SHAD

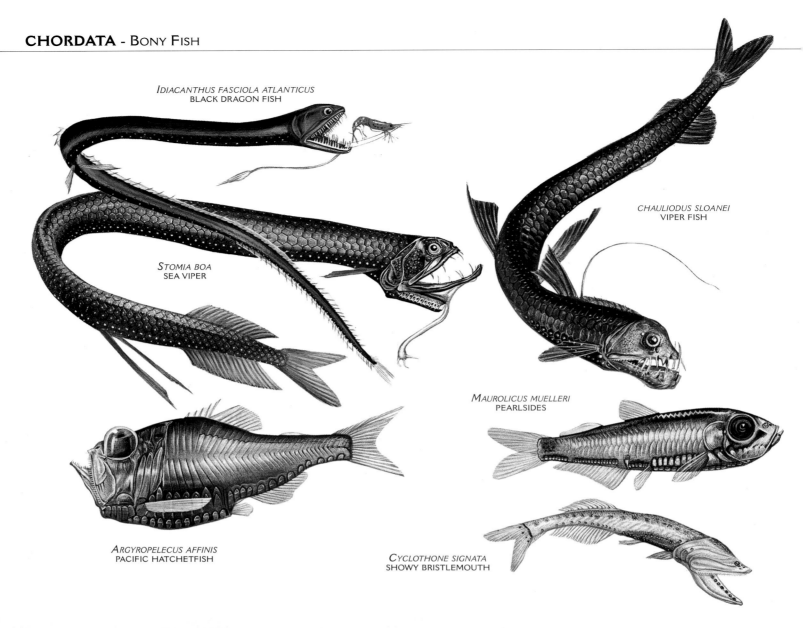

IDIACANTHUS FASCIOLA ATLANTICUS
BLACK DRAGON FISH

STOMIA BOA
SEA VIPER

CHAULIODUS SLOANEI
VIPER FISH

MAUROLICUS MUELLERI
PEARLSIDES

ARGYROPELECUS AFFINIS
PACIFIC HATCHETFISH

CYCLOTHONE SIGNATA
SHOWY BRISTLEMOUTH

FISH OF THE OCEAN DEPTHS

The Black Dragon Fish lives at depths of between 300 and 2000 m. This fish has a monster-like appearance, with its long body, coloured spots, hexagonal scales, and dorsal and anal fins near the tail. It also has huge jaws which it can open very wide, showing its sharp teeth, some long, others short and which are typical of carnivores. Its 'squashed' looking sides and the snout have numerous luminous organs called **photophores**, one under each eye.

The jaw has a filament, or thread, which is often very long. This, too, is luminous and attracts prey like a bait. Black Dragon Fish probably live in groups.

The **Sea Viper** is grey and has many luminous organs on its underside.

The **Viper Fish** has a very mobile head and the jaw can

open up wide enough to form an angle of 90 degrees.

The **Pearlsides** and the **Showy Bristlemouth** are mainly found in the Mediterranean, but also everywhere else except the Arctic. Both have a slightly bony skeleton, a silver body and **photophores**. Both are an important part in the food chain of sea creatures, because they are the food of other predators which live at the same depth. The **Pearlsides** has very large eyes and goes up near the surface of the water only at night-time.

The **Pacific Hatchet Fish** is widespread in the Mediterranean. It has large photophores which glow with a pinkish light.

The larvae of the **Black Dragon Fish** have long stalks. Their eyes are located at the end of these stalks.

SOME TROPICAL FRESHWATER FISH

Some of the largest tropical freshwater fish belong to the order of Clupeiformes.

The **Knifefish** has no dorsal fins and has just one very long fin, because the caudal, the ventral and anal fins are all joined up together.

The **Piracucu** is a terrible freshwater marauder which lives in the large rivers of Brazil and Guayana. It can measure up to 5 m long and weigh over 200 kgs. The male builds a nest where there is no vegetation, ready for the female to lay up to 11,000 eggs. The male always takes care of the young, and when it has to move, he carries them in his mouth for protection. The North American Indians catch them for meat, using the tongue for a nail-file.

The **Arawana** hatches its eggs in its mouth, in a sort of pouch between the bones of the lower jaw. It has a very flat, metallic-looking long body and beneath the lower jaw are the long whiskers, or sensory appendages, with which it identifies its prey, especially shrimps. It swims just below the surface of the water and shelters among the plants which grow on the bank.

The **Butterfly Fish**, which lives in the rivers Niger and the Congo, is also very flat. Its pectoral fins are similar to large wings, whilst the ventral fins have large thread-like rays which it uses as organs of touch.

The Butterfly Fish feeds on small fish, and, by staying quite still just below the skin of the water, it can also catch the insects bouncing down outside on the surface and making the most of those which fall into the water. The name 'Butterfly Fish' is misleading. Rather than being a true 'flying fish' it can only jump up in the air and cover a distance of about 2 m.

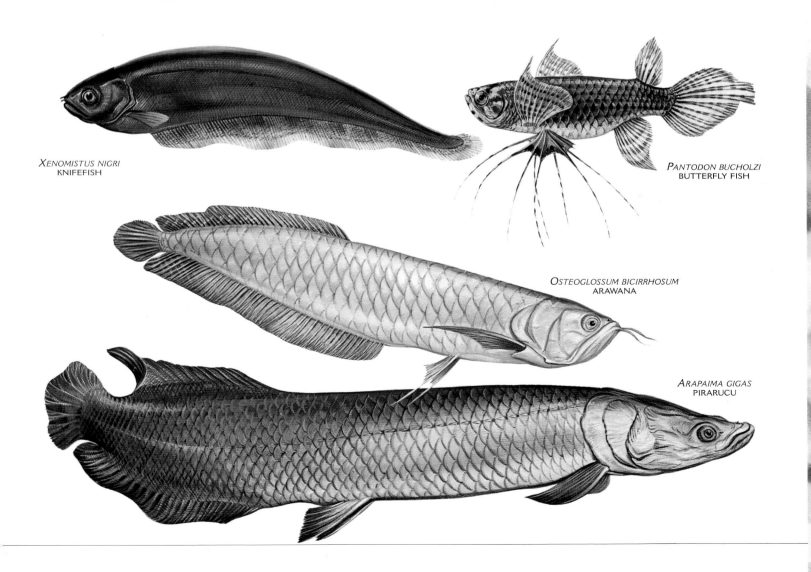

XENOMISTUS NIGRI
KNIFEFISH

PANTODON BUCHOLZI
BUTTERFLY FISH

OSTEOGLOSSUM BICIRRHOSUM
ARAWANA

ARAPAIMA GIGAS
PIRARUCU

EEL

Reproduction:	oviparous
Length:	up to 1.5 m
Habitat:	sea and fresh water

The freshwater eel is a night-time predator, long-lived and a remarkable migrator. The eel looks very much like a snake. It has no ventral fins. Instead it has a dorsal fin more or less the length of its body, which is supported by about 260 vertebrae. The male is about 50 cm long; the female can be up to 1.5 m. Outside the water, the eel can crawl through damp and wet grassy land for hours, sometimes days. Its thick, slimy skin may seem bare, but it is actually embedded with tiny scales.

The most notable feature of this 'sea snake' is its capacity for covering very long distances; the spread and the migration of eels has been one of the most long-standing mysteries which has puzzled naturalists for hundreds of years. Only in the twentieth century did some aspects of its life become clearer, when in particular zones of the Atlantic Ocean between the Sargasso Sea and the European coast, groups of eel larvae were identified at different stages of development and which gradually moved eastward. From this, it was discovered that the female eel lays her eggs only in the depths of the Sargasso Sea.

The long journey of the larvae begins at a depth of 400 m. It lasts around four years, mostly at more shallow depths, carried along by the Gulf Current. By the time it nears the European coast, the larva has been transformed into an eel with a short, cylindrical body, between 6 and 8 cm long, after which time it follows the course of rivers until it reaches a calm location.

The eel does not abandon fresh water for many years, until it reaches sexual maturity. Then, from the end of the summer until the beginning of autumn it begins to swim along the course of European rivers ready to swim into the sea, across the Atlantic Ocean and reach the Sargasso Sea. After spawning, the eels die. But the larvae, as if attracted by an irresistible call, undertake their first journey towards the places where their parents came from.

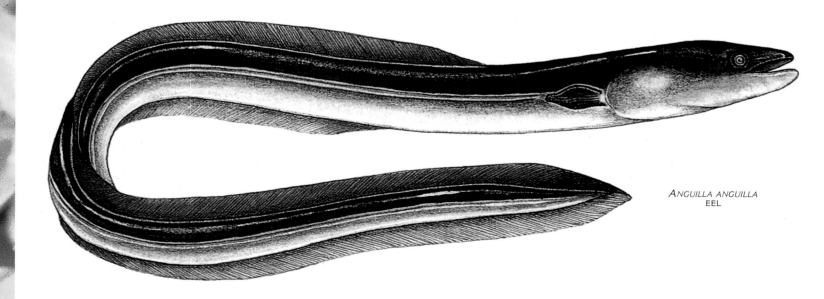

ANGUILLA ANGUILLA
EEL

MURAENA HELENA
MEDITERRANEAN MORAY EEL

MORAY EEL

The Moray Eel belongs to the same family as the common eel. It looks very much like the eel, except that it is much more muscular and compressed at the sides. It has a more aggressive appearance, with pointed teeth, strong jaws and small eyes, its long snout thrusting forward. Its head is small and it has no tongue or fins.

The skin of the Moray Eel is very thick, without scales but with glands which secrete mucus. In almost all species the skin is coloured and patterned; some moray eels – for example, the Mediterranean Moray Eel – have a marble-like yellow and black pattern; others have a pattern like the coat of a leopard. It has a very distinctive snout, with nostrils at the front which are like tiny little tubes, and rear nostrils in the form of simple, round holes situated above or near to the eyes. Also, the mouth of the Moray Eel can open up wide enough to reach its eyes. This fish is very strong in any kind of battle and can survive for a long time outside water.

The Moray Eel is found in all tropical and sub-tropical seas. It lives along rocky coasts and in coral reefs where it shelters in cracks and cavities in wait for prey. Normally, it spends the daylight hours in this way, going in search of food at night.

It feeds mainly on fish, molluscs and crustaceans which it seizes and then grinds up between rows of strong teeth. For humans disturbing the Moray Eel, a bite from those teeth can cause serious injury.

The Moray Eel is eaten in some countries, but the flesh of some species can be poisonous. In 92 BC, Ancient Romans built reservoirs to breed the Mediterranean Moray Eel for this purpose, considering it to be a great delicacy.

Reproduction: oviparous

Length: up to 1.3 m

Habitat: sea water

SEA HORSE

Reproduction: oviparous

Length when born: about 1 cm

Length of adult: 15-20 cm

Habitat: sea

The Sea Horse is one of the most eccentric and delightful of sea creatures. Its shape is well-known, with its head bent down towards its body and its tube-shaped mouth, making it look rather like the 'knight' piece in a game of chess. Its way of reproduction is interesting. After a refined courtship, which consists of little more than the male parading in front of the female, the male empties its ventral pouch of water so that the female can insert her ovipostor (egg-laying organ) and lay her eggs inside. The male then fertilizes the eggs and incubates them for some weeks.

When the eggs are ready to come out, the male pouch opens and the moment the little Sea Horses touch the water, they swim towards the surface to fill their swim bladders with air. Sea Horses can move upright because of their dorsal fin, which vibrates very quickly. This also draws in plankton and small prey. When the sea horse is still, it can 'anchor' itself to algae and coral with its prehensile (able to grasp) tail.

GARFISH

Reproduction: oviparous

Length when born: 13 mm

Length of adult: 90 cm

Habitat: sea

The common Garfish with its brilliant green-blue colouring, belongs to the group of fish which are able to jump out of the water when they are being chased or simply for fun.

An elegant and fast predator, the Garfish has a thin body, with jaws in the form of a long beak, thin and flat. The beak's small, sharp teeth enables the Garfish to skewer small prey such as herring, squid and crustaceans as it swims.

The Garfish reproduces along the coast in spring-time, the female laying round eggs which she 'anchors' to algae and submerged plants with a thin adhesive thread from her body. In winter, the Garfish goes out into the open sea. It lives in banks in the Mediterranean and the Atlantic Ocean. In the Black Sea and in other seas the Garfish is widely fished.

Did you know...

The **Stickleback** builds its nest by binding the fronds of plants together with its mucus; Sticklebacks mate for life and both take care of their young.

The **Blackspot Grenadier** belongs to the family of **Macrouridae** which are also called the rat-tails or rat fish.

The **Trout Perch**, otherwise known as the **Bull Trout**, is recognized by its upper 'lip', which is significantly larger than the lower jaw. Its scales are embedded with tiny little spines.

The **cod** is one of the most numerous fish in the world. Cod are excellent migrators and because they live in enormous shoals, they are widely fished.

Because of its rigid, flat body, the **John Dory** has had to develop a very careful plan of attack. By making barely noticeable movements only of the fins and the tail, it succeeds in nearing its prey slowly and without being seen.

The **Cypselurus Heterurus** belongs to the family of flying fish. A vigorous push from the tail gives it a short burst of speed outside the water

and then it can jump up to a metre above the surface of the water and float for up to 10 metres with its wide pectoral fins open like the wings of a bird.

The **Opah**, also called the **Moon Fish**, can reach a length of 2 m and a weight of 100 kg.

The pipefish **Syngnathus Typhle** has a long, thin body and can stay immobile vertically, hidden among water plants.

The **Tetra Black Ulrrey** is an eel that can withstand periods of drought by immersing itself in mud and breathing through its skin.

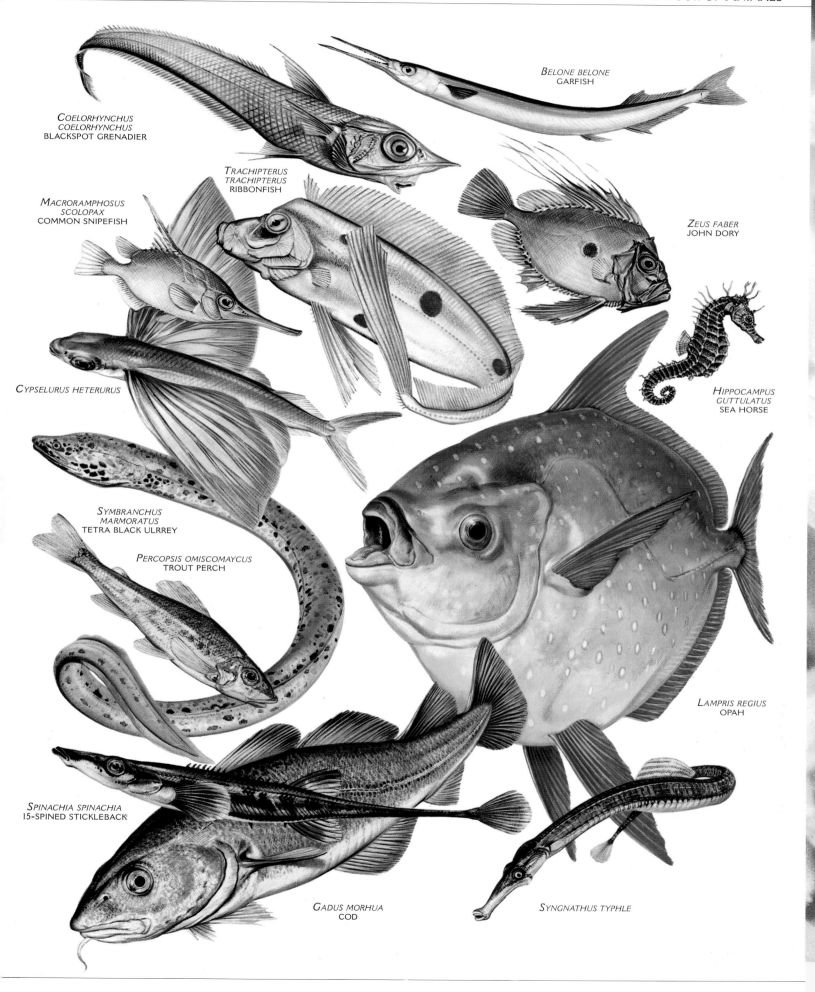

BELONE BELONE
GARFISH

COELORHYNCHUS
COELORHYNCHUS
BLACKSPOT GRENADIER

TRACHIPTERUS
TRACHIPTERUS
RIBBONFISH

ZEUS FABER
JOHN DORY

MACRORAMPHOSUS
SCOLOPAX
COMMON SNIPEFISH

HIPPOCAMPUS
GUTTULATUS
SEA HORSE

CYPSELURUS HETERURUS

SYMBRANCHUS
MARMORATUS
TETRA BLACK ULRREY

PERCOPSIS OMISCOMAYCUS
TROUT PERCH

LAMPRIS REGIUS
OPAH

SPINACHIA SPINACHIA
15-SPINED STICKLEBACK

GADUS MORHUA
COD

SYNGNATHUS TYPHLE

SPHYRAENA BARRACUDA
BARRACUDA

AMMODYTES
LANCEOLATUS
SAND LANCE

ATHERINA HEPSETUS
MEDITERRANEAN SAND SMELT

THUNNUS
THYNNUS
TUNA

MUGIL CEPHALUS
MULLET

CYCLOPTERUS LUMPUS
LUMPSUCKER

XIPHIAS GLADIUS
SWORDFISH

ANARHICHAS LUPUS
WOLF FISH

PTEROIS VOLITANS
LION FISH

DACTYLOPTERUS VOLITANS
FLYING GURNARD

TRIGLA LUCERNA
TUB GURNAND

TUB GURNAND

Reproduction: oviparous

Length: 40-70 cm

Habitat: sandy sea beds of the Mediterranean

The Tub Gurnard (also known as the 'Sea Robin') has very long pectoral fins each with three lower rays, rather like thin fingers, which sink into the sand like the runners on skis. By beating its fins energetically, the Tub Gurnard stays on the sea bed with the same ease as with which it swims. At the point of these 'fingers', which are its organs of touch, the fish has taste buds by which it can find a feed of crustaceans and molluscs in the sand.

Its enormous pyramid-shaped head is not the only reason for this fish being considered rather odd. By using a group of special muscles to make the walls of its swim bladder vibrate, it can make loud, rumbling noises of various kinds – moans, grunts, rumblings. Experts believe that this is a way of communicating with other fish of its own kind.

TUNA

Length: up to 3 m

Weight: up to 400 kg

Habitat: Mediterranean Sea and Pacific Ocean

The Blue Fin Tuna with its characteristic long, scythe-shaped fins, is one of the largest fish in the sea. The body temperature of all tuna fish is 10°C higher than that of the water and this helps to increase its power – a warm muscle contracts and relaxes more quickly than a cold muscle.

No other bony fish carries out a longer migration in the oceans at such high a speed: the tuna swims at 15 - 30 km/h, but, when it sees prey it can reach a speed of 70 km/h in just a few seconds.

As with all cold-blooded animals, all this movement uses up great quantities of oxygen. But the tuna has a small mouth, and to draw in lots of water, it must swim always holding this open wide.

The favourite prey of the tuna are herring, mackerel and sardine.

Did you know...

The **Wolf Fish** feeds on shrimps and echinoderms. It breaks the shells of crustaceans and molluscs before eating them, using its teeth which it re-grows each year.

There is no other fish which is more hungry or more 'nosey' than the **Barracuda**. It can grow up to 2 m long, and when it hunts, it proves that it has very sharp eyesight.

Unlike most other fish, the **Swordfish**, up to 6 m long, has an active circulation, and, like the tuna, has a body temperature higher than that of the water which surrounds it. So it can move very quickly and do spectacular jumps.

During winter, the **Mullet** stops feeding and stays almost quite still, in a state of torpor, near the sea bed. It carries out seasonal migrations in search of cooler water in summer and hotter water in autumn.

The **Sand Lance** is also called the sand eel – although it is not an eel at all. It inhabits the coastal waters of the Mediterranean, and, like the **Sand Eel**, it hides itself among the sand on the sea bed.

The **Mediterranean Sand Smelt** is sometimes called 'silverside' because of its colour. It lives in shoals in coastal waters and swims very near the surface with its snout barely submerged.

During the period of reproduction, the **Lumpsucker** acquires a bright red-orange colour.

The **Lion Fish** (in the photograph) with a length of 20 - 30 cm has a majestic ornamental skin and looks like a Chinese dragon. For this reason it is much loved by aquarium owners, even though it is poisonous; the stings of the dorsal fins are as poisonous as the teeth of a cobra.

AMPHIBIANS

COMMON CHARACTERISTICS

All amphibians have two pairs of limbs with claws. In the larva phase, breathing is by gills. By the time the amphibian is adult, its body has adapted from living in water to living on land, and so it is has lungs for breathing. The skin is bare and with glands which produce mucus to avoid dehydration.

EVOLUTION AND HABITAT

Over 350 million years ago, some of the animals living in water began to live on land, some partially, some completely. These animals were the first amphibians, a name meaning 'of double life'. All four-legged vertebrates (tetrapods) evolved from these creatures.

The Caecilian is very different to other amphibians. Because of its long-shaped body, it is impossible to disguise its head from its tail. The skin is covered with bony scales and it has a skull with jaws – very much like prehistoric amphibians. In fact, it is generally believed that the Caecilian is a direct descendent of the first amphibians.

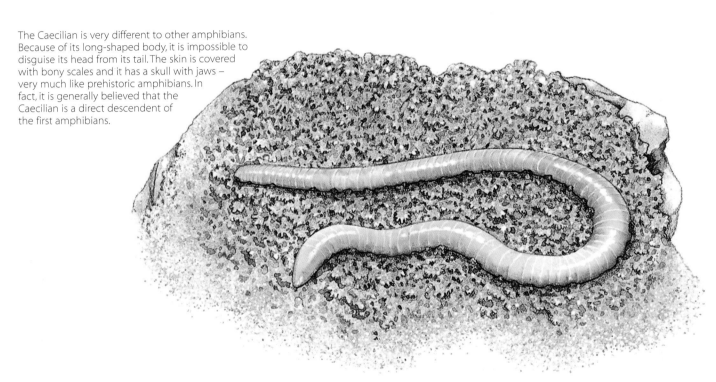

The Caecilian lives hidden in warm, damp earth near water. It rarely comes to the surface. After hatching from the egg, the larva becomes adult in the same way as other amphibians. When its metamorphosis is complete, the adult Caecilian comes out of the water of a pond and crawls on to the bank, where it digs a hole for shelter.

The length of the Caecilian can vary from a few centimetres to over one metre. It is a carnivore, feeding on earthworms and arthropods. The largest species also eat small earth-digging snakes. It lives only in America.

BEHAVIOUR

Amphibians are very intelligent. Each one lives within a precise territory, which it can recognize on its return, even after it has travelled a considerable distance. Amphibians can defend themselves against enemies, either by changing colour to blend in with their surroundings, or by poisons which they secrete in special glands in their skin, as happens with some toads.

FEEDING

As amphibians adapted to life on land, they developed a proper tongue, with its own muscles and glands. An amphibian uses its tongue to grasp, to moisten and to swallow its food. At the larva stage, it eats only plant matter. Adult amphibians also eat arthropods, molluscs, worms and also small vertebrates.

The double life of Amphibians

There are about 25,000 species of amphibians, with a great variety of shapes and sizes. Most are quite small, usually with four limbs which have claws. They are cold-blooded animals, which means that their body temperature depends on the temperature of their surroundings. Because amphibians cannot stand very low winter temperatures, they go into hibernation. In summer, if the temperature is too high, they remain inactive and immobile.

Their **bare skin** is rather thick, warm and damp, but offers little protection against dehydration. However, many amphibians do breathe through the skin. Due to the risk of dehydration, all amphibians live near lakes, rivers and fresh water or in very damp conditions. As well as the skin, which is shed and renewed at regular intervals, it has numerous **glands** in layers of skin below the surface. These glands secrete irritating and toxic substances, and also **chromatophores**. These are the pigment-bearing cells. By contracting and expanding, they determine the colouring of the body.

With most amphibians, the eggs are fertilized outside the body; the female lays the eggs in water, where the male fertilizes them. The eggs are round and non-transparent, often with gelatinous layers which absorb the water and swell up until each egg reaches a diameter five times larger than when it was laid. The larvae are born in water, breathing through gills. Later, they will undergo a **metamorphosis** and be transformed into adults. Some larvae grow rapidly and leave the water after one week. Others stay there for up to five years. In adults, which are capable of breathing on land, lungs are formed, limbs sprout, the skin thickens, the tail shrinks, muscles and the skeleton changes and the digestive tube shortens until it reaches the same measurement as the body. Some amphibians lay their eggs on land. Others give birth to perfectly-formed young, ready to breathe with their lungs.

Amphibians are divided into three orders.

Apoda are amphibians similar to earthworms. They live in the layer of humus and rich soil which covers the ground of tropical forests. Fertilization is internal and the eggs are laid in the ground; the larvae complete their metamorphosis in water. **Caudata**, such as the salamander and the newt, are characterized by a **tail** which the animal has all its life. **Anura**, such as the frog, the toad and the tree frog have a bulging body, hind legs which are more developed than the front legs, and bulging eyes. The adult has no tail. The embryo hatches from an egg, becomes a **tadpole** and undergoes a slow metamorphosis to the adult stage. By that time, it will have a strong skeleton, a bony skull, jaws with teeth and a spinal column composed of a varying number of elements (6 - 9 in Anura, up to 300 in some Caudata).

Photographs: top, a Fire Salamander with its gleaming black background and yellow patches, which can vary so much in number and size that no two individuals are the same. Bottom, a Tree Frog.

PHYLUM	SUBPHYLUM	CLASS	ORDER	SPECIES
CHORDATA	Vertebrates	Amphibians	Apoda	Caecilian
			Caudata	salamander, newt
			Anura	frog, toad

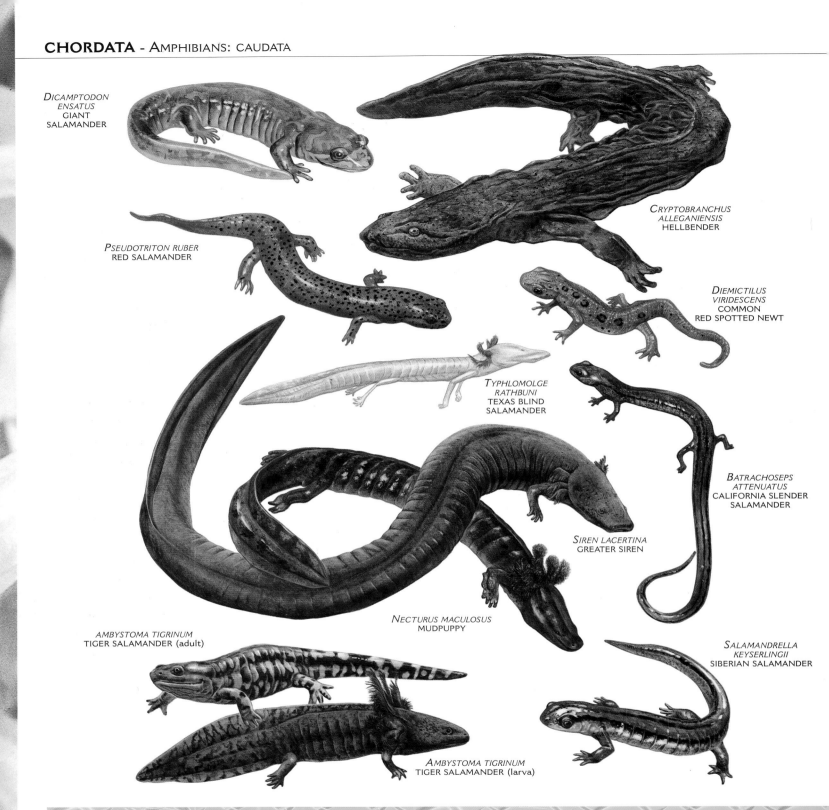

DICAMPTODON ENSATUS GIANT SALAMANDER

CRYPTOBRANCHUS ALLEGANIENSIS HELLBENDER

PSEUDOTRITON RUBER RED SALAMANDER

DIEMICTILUS VIRIDESCENS COMMON RED SPOTTED NEWT

TYPHLOMOLGE RATHBUNI TEXAS BLIND SALAMANDER

BATRACHOSEPS ATTENUATUS CALIFORNIA SLENDER SALAMANDER

SIREN LACERTINA GREATER SIREN

AMBYSTOMA TIGRINUM TIGER SALAMANDER (adult)

NECTURUS MACULOSUS MUDPUPPY

SALAMANDRELLA KEYSERLINGII SIBERIAN SALAMANDER

AMBYSTOMA TIGRINUM TIGER SALAMANDER (larva)

Díd you know...

The **Giant Salamander** is a land-dwelling species distinguished by its large head and small eyes. Despite its 30 cm length and its slightly comical appearance, it can climb trees easily. It feeds on invertebrates, small snakes, amphibians and small mammals.

The **Hellbender**, sometimes called the **Alligator Salamander** can grow up to 70 cm long. It only undergoes partial metamorphosis from larva to adult, and so the adult has withered gills. It lives in the rivers of the eastern United States. In summer, the female lays a gelatinous chain of hundreds of eggs, ready to be fertilized by the male.

Commonly found in North America is the **Tiger Salamander**. It has a strong body with a length which can vary from 19 to 33 cm. This salamander can withstand periods of drought by seeking refuge in the lairs of other animals. At the larvae stage, it is frequently known as an **axolotl**.

The **Red Salamander** breathes

CALIFORNIA SLENDER SALAMANDER

Habitat: underground

Respiration: through the skin

Length: up to 10 cm

The California Slender Salamander has a very tapering body and tiny limbs. Along with another 180 species, it belongs to a family of Caudata living mainly in North and Central America and is characterized by having no lungs. Instead, this animal breathes through its skin and by means of the mucus which covers the mouth cavity.

The California Slender Salamander has adapted to life on the land, where it spends the major part of the year. When it leaves its lair, it crawls along in the same way as a snake. If the ground is wet, it will dig a proper lair for itself; but if the ground is too compact, then it will find a hole which another animal has left empty.

It does not dig very deep and it can often be found beneath the trunk of a tree or under large stones, rolled up in a ball. It is very important that the surroundings are damp.

It feeds on small insects, their larvae and those of other invertebrates which it finds in the ground. It lays its eggs in water in the autumn.

Often a few females lay their eggs (up to 21) in the same place. Then, for most of the time, one or more females stay near the place where the eggs are. The tadpoles are born the following spring,

GREATER SIREN

Habitat: water

Breathing: gills and lungs

Number of eggs: up to 300 laid in bunches

Length of larvae: 5-10 mm

Length of adult: up to 1 m

The Greater Siren is one of only three species belonging to the Sirenidae family. From the time that metamorphosis is complete, it has an appearance which is halfway between a larva and an adult form. The eyes are not covered by eyelids, and although it has lungs, it also has the remaining tufts of external gills and only the skin is different. The Greater Siren has a long body, but it has no back legs and the front legs are very short and weak, with four thin claws. It lives in water and rises to the surface to breathe, because it mostly uses its lungs. The Greater Siren lives in fairly shallow streams, stagnant waters and swamps, hiding itself by day and coming out at night to get food. It has no teeth, but its jaws have horny plates which it uses to catch worms, water snails, crustaceans and plants. In times of drought, it hides itself in mud and survives within a sort of cocoon for about two months. During this time, its skin dries up and the gills become numb. But when the rain returns, it regains its normal size and the body becomes moist once more.

through its skin and it is very susceptible to dehydration. It can die within a few minutes if exposed to the Sun.

The **Texas Blind Salamander** lives mostly in water below the surface of the ground. It is in danger of extinction because so many have been hunted down and captured.

The **Mudpuppy** is a North American salamander which keeps its larva form when it is adult, with colourful tufts at the sides of its neck, corresponding to external gills. It is nocturnal and lives in the waters of ponds, lakes and rivers.

The tiny **Common Red Spotted Newt** lives in the mountainous

zones of United States. It looks rather like a primitive amphibian.

The **Siberian Salamander** lives within the Arctic Circle. Before hibernating in icy mud, the water in its body is reduced. This is so that its tissues become less dense to avoid the danger of the animal becoming stiff.

CAVE SALAMANDER

The Cave Salamander belongs to the order of Caudata. It is one of the strangest vertebrate animals in Europe. It lives all the time in caves and never goes out in daylight. Its body has no pigment at all and so the blood inside makes it pale pink in colour – only the external gills are a vivid red. The Cave Salamander is a neotenic – becoming adult without undergoing a complete metamorphosis – and so it does not lose its gills before getting lungs.

The eyes are fixed and hidden under the skin. It is not very active, mostly staying hidden underneath stones or in the cold waters inside grottos. But every so often it gets the urge to swim up to the surface, to take a mouthful of air. On these occasions, its skin can dehydrate, but this soon becomes damp and rich in mucus once again, the moment the Cava Salamander gets back into the water.

It feeds mainly on small crustaceans and cave-dwelling creatures and tiny fish. It is very sensitive to the vibrations of water and these help it to find its prey more easily. The female, after having laid her eggs, strongly defends them against any intruders.

Habitat: caves

Breathing: gills and lungs

Reproduction: internal

Length of larvae at birth: 2 cm

Length of adult: 25-30 cm

FIRE SALAMANDER

Habitat: damp, dark places

Breathing: lungs

Reproduction: ovoviviparous

Length of adult: 12-28 cm

The Fire Salamander is the best-known salamander in Europe, especially for its bright colouring, with yellow spots on a black background. Its skin is impregnated with a highly poisonous substance produced by glands directly behind its eyes and nothing can attack it without feeling the effects of the irritant milky liquid which it produces in times of danger.

Slow and lazy, this salamander looks for dark, damp places where it can live in peace. It prefers to hide among layers of moss or rotten wood, underneath stones or in caves. It is very sensitive to heat and dies as soon as the temperature goes above 20°C. In the autumn hundreds of salamanders arrive to settle in particular places to lie underground and spend the winter in hibernation.

Mating takes place on land. The female goes to the water only to give birth to the larvae, which develop inside her body.

Díd you know...

The **Crested Newt** gets its name because of the crest which the male gets on his back during mating time. It is found in western Europe and central Asia.

The **Smooth Newt** lives in almost every part of Europe, especially on the plains. It likes the water of puddles, lakes and reservoirs.

The bright colours of the **Alpine Newt** are only present at mating-time.

During the courting stage, the male of the **Marbled Newt** shows the female its high dorsal crest and vibrates his tail, with which he can hit his own head.

The **Corsican Brook Salamander** is very rare. It is completely nocturnal, never coming out during the day.

The **Italian Cave Salamander** is a small meat-eating salamander. It is not poisonous, but defends itself by changing colour.

TRITURUS CRISTATUS
CRESTED NEWT

TRITURUS VULGARIS
SMOOTH NEWT

PROTEUS ANGUINUS
CAVE SALAMANDER

TRITURUS ALPESTRIS
ALPINE NEWT

TRITURUS MARMORATUS
MARBLED NEWT

EUPROCTUS MONTANUS
CORSICAN BROOK
SALAMANDER

*HYDROMANTES
ITALICUS*
ITALIAN CAVE
SALAMANDER

SALAMANDRINA TERDIGITATA
SPECTACLED SALAMANDER

SALAMANDRA SALAMANDRA
FIRE SALAMANDER

TREE FROG

Habitat: tree-dwelling

Breathing: lungs and through skin

Length of tadpole: about 4 cm

Length of adult: 7-12 cm

The Tree Frog is one of the most popular amphibians in Europe, characterized by its brilliant, shiny green skin and friendly appearance.

With the claws on its legs working like suckers, the Tree Frog can climb trees and bushes easily, staying attached to the leaves, where it finds insects to eat. It skin secretes a mucus and this gives good protection against the danger of dehydration.

It lives near swamps and marshes only until the age of two years. Afterwards it returns to these places only at mating-time, from April to June. Then, after sunset, it is easy to hear the high cry coming from the courting males. The females ready for reproduction are attracted by the croaking and they lay their eggs in late evening. These are attached in small masses to the plants near water and after they become fertilized by the male, the eggs fall into the pond, ready for larvae to develop.

COMMON TOAD

Habitat: land

Breathing: lungs and through the skin

Length of adult: 7-18 cm

The Common Toad has a squat, solid body, large, bulging eyes and a dry skin covered with warts.

It is a very useful animal, because it eats snails, insects and other agricultural pests. Its skin is non-irritant, but in times of danger it can secrete poison from two glands, one at each side of its head.

The toad is land-dwelling and nocturnal. In March, after its winter hibernation, it leaves the woods where it has slept and returns to the ponds to reproduce.

When the male meets a female, it grabs hold of her and takes her to the nearest stretch of water. After some days, the female lays a long chain of eggs which the male then fertilizes in the course of five to ten hours. After reproduction, the male and female separate and return to the woods, fields and gardens.

In autumn, the Common Toad goes back to the place where it spends its winter hibernation.

Did you know...

The male **Common Green Frog** gives out a loud series of sounds to attract a female. Vocal sacs emerge from a split at either side of the mouth and these swell in proportion to the pitch and the duration of the song.

The **Green Toad** has customs which are more aquatic than the Common Toad, and it is more agile. In mountain areas they can reach altitudes of about 1500 m.

The **Yellow Bellied Toad** is found throughout Europe. It has a bright yellow speckled abdomen which it shows the moment it feels threatened, turning over and arching its back to scare away an enemy and sending out a shower of poisonous foam at the same time.

The **Midwife Toad** can be found all over central and southern Europe. It is the male which takes particular care of the eggs. After having fertilized the chain of eggs, it then attaches them around its hind legs, carrying them around with him until they hatch.

The **Common Spadefoot Toad** lives in Europe and western Asia. It has adapted to life on dry, sandy ground. It comes out mainly at night and at dawn buries itself, digging a shelter with the horny growth on its hind claws. At evening, it comes to the surface to catch insects and worms.

The **Common Frog** is the brown frog most widespread throughout Europe. It is found at altitudes up to 2000 m. It lives in woodland during Spring and Summer, returning to the water only to reproduce or to spend the winter.

RANA ESCULENTA
COMMON GREEN FROG

HYLA ARBOREA
EUROPEAN TREE FROG

BUFO VIRIDIS
GREEN TOAD

BUFO BUFO
COMMON EUROPEAN TOAD

PELOBATES FUSCUS
COMMON SPADEFOOT TOAD

ALYTES OBSTETRICANS
MIDWIFE TOAD

BOMBINA VARIEGATA
YELLOW BELLIED TOAD

RANA TEMPORARIA
COMMON FROG

REPTILES

COMMON CHARACTERISTICS

Reptiles are cold-blooded vertebrates, with a skin covered with scales or horny plates, or – as in the case of turtles, tortoises and crocodiles – a bony shell which protects the animal against dehydration. Reptiles do not go through a larva stage, because the egg is enclosed in a shell which is full of liquid containing all that the embryo needs to develop.

EVOLUTION, DISTRIBUTION AND HABITAT

The first reptiles appeared on Earth over 260 million years ago. These were the first vertebrates to live completely free of the water. Reptiles are found all over the world, except for the Antarctic, in places where the temperature is either hot or temperate. Some live in water, others on land.

The Tuatara is a small reptile, about 60 cm long. It belongs to the order of Rhynchocephalia, a group which began 200 million years ago and which were believed to have been extinct. Then at the beginning of the 18th century, some Tuatara were discovered on islands of New Zealand. The remote geographical position of these islands made access difficult and this protected the Tuatara and their home and helped them to survive. It is a species which is still at the risk of extinction and so it is strongly protected.

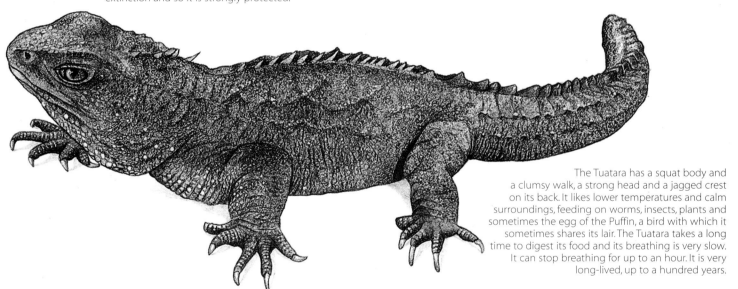

The Tuatara has a squat body and a clumsy walk, a strong head and a jagged crest on its back. It likes lower temperatures and calm surroundings, feeding on worms, insects, plants and sometimes the egg of the Puffin, a bird with which it sometimes shares its lair. The Tuatara takes a long time to digest its food and its breathing is very slow. It can stop breathing for up to an hour. It is very long-lived, up to a hundred years.

BEHAVIOUR

Reptiles have very keen eyesight, which they use to pick out enemies, prey and companions. They can detect smells through the tongue as well as the nose. Some species have skins with bright colours and patterns. The ability to change colour is not only a means of blending in with its background, but also depends on their activity or their mood, such as aggression or fear.

NUTRITION

Most reptiles are carnivores, but there are some herbivore species. The activity of their well-developed saliva glands not only aids ingestion of food but also digestion. In many reptiles, the digestive system is very roomy and 'stretchable', so that many are able to ingest prey considerably larger than them – for example, some snakes can devour a whole deer.

Relatives of dinosaurs

Reptiles were the first animals which were completely land-dwelling. The body is covered with **scales** or horny shields which reduce the evaporation of the skin; this is almost always without glands, so that keeping a constant body temperature depends entirely on the skin taking in heat and not losing it.

Once the scales and the horny plates are completely formed, these do not grow any more, because they are made of dead cells. This means that the skin must be renewed at regular intervals (moulting) especially in the young and during the stages of development. Breathing is by lungs.

Except for snakes, reptiles have two pairs of limbs, each limb having five claws with talons. The jaw is joined to the skull by a bone which enables the mouth to open very wide. The mouth has strong teeth which the reptile uses to grab and to hold its food .

The skull and the skeleton form a rigid bony structure, which gives the reptile the power to attack as well as muscular development.

Reproduction is almost always **oviparous**. The presence of a solid shell indicates internal fertilization, where the egg becomes fertilized inside the female's body and the albumen and shell are formed before it is laid. Some species of reptile are **viviparous** where the fertilized egg develops inside the female body. At birth, the membrane of the egg breaks and the young come out already perfectly formed.

Photographs: top right, a sea turtle, above, the *Furcifer pardalis*, a chameleon from Madagascar. Facing page: an Iguana.

Unlike their dinosaur ancestors, reptiles today are of modest size, except for crocodiles which can grow up to 7 m in length. Present-day species are less numerous than dinosaur species and are divided into four main orders – **Chelonia**, the order to which the tortoise belongs, with its short, squat body, protected with a hard shell; **Rhynchocephalia** an order which today comprises just one special species, the tuatara; **Squamata**. characterized by a body protected by horny-type scales; lizards and snakes also belong to this order; and **Crocodilia**, to which crocodiles belong.

PHYLUM	SUB-PHYLUM	CLASS	ORDER	SUB-ORDER	FAMILY	SPECIESS
CHORDATA	Vertebrates Rhynchocephalia	Reptiles	Chelonia			tortoise
					Tuatara	
				Sauria		lizard
			Squamata	Amphisbaeria		Spiny-Tailed Lizard
				Serpentes		snakes
					Gavialidae	Gavial
			Crocodilia		Alligatoridae	crocodile alligator Caiman

GOPHERUS POLYPHEMUS
GOPHER TORTOISE

CHELODINA LONGICOLLIS
LONG NECKED TURTLE

DERMOCHELYS CORIACEA
LEATHERBACK TURTLE

HYDROMEDUSA
TECTIFERA
SOUTH AMERICAN
TERRAPIN

PELUSIOS NIGER
WEST AFRICAN
BLACK TURTLE

TERRAPENE CAROLINA
COMMON BOX TURTLE

GEOCHELONE PARDALIS
LEOPARD TURTLE

PLATYSTERNON
MEGACEPHALUM
BIG HEADED TURTLE

TRYONIX SPINIFERUS
EASTERN SPINY SOFT
SHELL TURTLE

LEATHERBACK TURTLE

Habitat: the sea

Reproduction: oviparous

Diameter of eggs: 5-6 cm

Length of adult: over 2 m

Weight: up to 600 kg

The Leatherback Turtle is the largest turtle in the world. Its plating consists of hundreds of irregular, bony plates, joined together like a mosaic pattern and covered with a smooth, strong, skin.

Its huge, rounded head, with its hooked jaw cannot withdraw back inside its shell, neither can the limbs, which are like fins.

The Leatherback Turtle is the rarest of sea turtles. It lives by itself in the warmest of seas in Malaysia, Indonesia and Central America – but during the breeding season, the female swims to the land where she digs a nest in the sand, ready to lay her eggs. The Leatherback Turtle is a tireless swimmer, feeding on fish, molluscs, echinoderms and jellyfish, even the poisonous ones. The inside of the mouth and the throat is covered with horny spines which help with the ingestion of slippery prey, like the jellyfish.

COMMON BOX TURTLE

Habitat: land

Reproduction: oviparous

Length of shell at birth: 26-30 mm

Length of shell when adult: 12-16 cm

The Common Box Turtle lives in Mexico and North America. It has a shell with a type of hinge, so that when the turtle withdraws its claws and legs, the front section of the lower shell lifts up. Then the opening of the 'box' closes up, protecting the turtle from its many carnivore enemies.

The Common Box Turtle is an omnivore and so feeds on fruit, berries and other vegetable matter, as well as insects and various tiny animals.

It lives in central areas for most of the year, but in autumn it travels further north, becoming slower and slower and then digging a deep shelter. It likes to stay in one place, and generally spends the whole winter in the same lair. When it wakes, it reproduces; the female can lay fertile eggs up to four years after her last mating.

Did you know...

The **Gopher Tortoise** has a shell about 25 cm long and lives in the central strip of the United States and Mexico. The heat of the deserts and the steppes prevent it from being active during the day, and so it digs an underground tunnel, where it spends the hottest hours. It comes out only in the evening to go in search of grassy plants to eat.

The **Long Necked Turtle** is an Australian species which has highly developed back vertebrae, to which is attached powerful muscles which enable the turtle to bend its neck, like a snake.

Another turtle with a long neck is the **South American Terrapin** which lives in lakes in Argentina. It is mainly active in the evening and the night-time, feeding mainly on water insects.

The **West African Black Turtle** can be found in most parts of Africa. It has a shell about 35 cm long. This species has an extra cover of bony plates which are not visible on the outside.

The **Leopard Tortoise** is a tortoise which lives in the savannah of the African high plains. To go in search of food it will even cross desert zones.

The **Eastern Spiny Soft Shell Turtle** from North America is both agile and aggressive. It has a long neck which it pushes out when it is about to bite.

The **Big Headed Turtle** has an over-sized head which it cannot hide inside its shell. This is, however, covered in hard, bony plates which protect it very well. It lives in the flowing waters of mountains in tropical Asia.

COMMON GECKO

Habitat: land, trees

Reproduction: oviparous

Length of adult: 35-40 cm

The Common Gecko belongs to the family Geckonidae. These reptiles have highly developed eyes, covered with eyelids joined together to form a transparent horny covering. In the Gecko, the eyes have a vertical pupil adapted to night-time vision.
Its legs have five broad claws with adhesive pads and tiny hooks which are able to grasp surfaces. When it climbs, the Gecko moves in the same way as a cat, alternately stretching out and sinking down, then contracting and lifting up each claw. The Common Gecko lives in South-East Asia as far as western Indonesia. It can rapidly darken or lighten the colour of its skin. It lives in large trees and also in houses, where it is always welcome, because it is such an excellent predator of insects and even mice. Perhaps this is why it is considered to be an animal which brings good fortune. Only the male emits the cries which ring out to defend its territory, especially in spring during the mating season.

IGUANA

Habitat: land, trees

Reproduction: oviparous

Lenght at birth: 20-25 cm

Length of adult: 1.5-2 m

The Iguana is the most important member of the family Iguanidae. It has a squat body and a tail which takes up two thirds of its total body length. It has four strong legs with long claws and strong talons. Both sexes have a large sac under the throat. The head has a series of round scales and plates beneath the eardrum and on the back is a crest which is up to 8 cm high in the male. In young Iguanas, this is a deep green colour, in adults it is crossed with wide crossway stripes.
The Iguana is commonly found in Central and Southern America. It lives along the banks of rivers and among the leafy branches of trees. When it senses danger, the Iguana can jump to a height of 5 or 6 m, before diving into water. Its feeding habits vary with age – the young go in search of insects, whilst the adults prefer eating plants. They eat heartily during the rainy season, when vegetation is most plentiful, accumulating reserves of fat at the corners of the jaws which enable an Iguana to survive during periods of drought and shortage of food.

Did you know...

The Australian **Jumping Snake** has a body up to 70 cm long, which is covered in scales. It has a highly-developed tail but no front claws – and its back claws are no more than two tiny, little appendages.

The **Agama** (in the photograph) lives in Africa. Like the chameleon, it can easily change colour if it is disturbed or frightened.

Fischer's Chameleon is also found in Africa. The male uses the horn on its head as a weapon. When it arrives in new surroundings, it settles down by licking the roots of trees.
As well as being able to change colour,

CHAMAELEO MELLERI
MELLERS CHAMELEON

IGUANA IGUANA
IGUANA

CHAMAELEO FISCHERI
FISCHER'S
CHAMELEON

HYDROSAURUS
AMBOIENSIS
ASIAN WATER
DRAGON

PYGOPUS LEPIDOPUS
JUMPING SNAKE

KLAUBERINA
RIVERSIANA
ISLAND NIGHT LIZARD

GEKKO GECKO
COMMON GECKO

GONATODES
ALBOGULARIS
YELLOW HEADED
GECKO

AGAMA AGAMA
COMMON AGAMA

chameleons have a very long and very flexible tongue, which is always moist and sticky. This is an effective weapon when it wants to catch prey.

Common in the Indonesian islands of Moluccas and the Philippines, the **Asian Water Dragon** looks like a dragon, but it is only 1 m long. It spends much of its life in flowing water, where it swims with great

ability, using its flat tail.

The **Yellow Headed Gecko** is from Central America. It has a yellow head and a black body. It is active by day, sometimes even jumping into people's homes.

The **Island Night Lizard** is found only on three islands off the coast of California. It feeds on flowers and on fruit.

Mellers Chameleon is the largest of all those found in Africa. Including its tail, it can reach a length of around 32 cm. Like all other chameleons, it can change colour by increasing or decreasing the concentration of pigment in certain body cells which determine its colouring. It changes colour according to light, temperature, as well as its mood — not because of its surroundings.

ELEPHANT TRUNK SNAKE

Habitat: water

Reproduction: viviparous

Length of adult: 1.10-1.85 cm

The Elephant Trunk Snake is very unusual and easy to identify because of its large body and square-shaped head.

It lives its whole life in the salt water at the mouths of rivers, also going into the sea for short spells. It is a lazy, apathetic creature, which moves extremely slowly and can also remain for a long time on the river bed. When it needs oxygen, it only has to raise its nostrils on the upper part of its nose. The few times it goes on land, it crawls along the river banks with clumsy movements. The body seems to advance independently of its skin, which seems to be too roomy and too pleated – hence the name, the Elephant Trunk Snake.

It eats only fish of various sizes which it catches by remaining perfectly still, trapping them in much the same way as a crocodile. It is always wise to be wary of its poisonous bites, which can cause death, even to humans. Even when it seems to be asleep, it can bite with extreme speed. The female, which gives birth to perfectly-formed young, is more powerful than the male and can reach lengths of over 2 m.

Did you know...

The **Boa Constrictor** lives in Mexico and throughout the whole of South America. It can reach a length of 4.5 m and lives in forests near to swamps. It feeds on small mammals and birds but shows no aggression when confronted by humans.

The **Madagasca Tree Boa** (in photograph) is similar to the Boa Constrictor.

The **Emerald Tree Boa** lives solely in trees in the north of South America and in Brazil. It can grow up to 3 m long and gets its name from its beautiful green colour, crisscrossed with white. Its colouring enables this snake to hide itself perfectly in trees, where it rolls itself up, remaining quite still for days, sometimes for weeks.

The **Sunbeam Snake** is common in southern India and Indo-China. Its body is about 1 m long, covered with brown scales. When these catch the light, they give off the most beautiful shimmering reflections, which is why it is also called 'the rainbow snake'. When excited, it will agitate its tail. It eats small snakes, rodents and birds.

The American **Desert Blind Snake** and the **Worm Snake** which comes from Greece and South-West Asia, are medium-sized snakes. They both like dry places, living hidden in the sub-soil or sheltered by rocks underneath stones. They mostly eat insects, ants and termites.

The **Pipe Snake** is also medium-sized, about 75 - 85 cm in length and scattered throughout South America. It has a vivid red colouring with black rings around the body which makes it look similar to the poisonous **Coral Snake** which has yellow rings either side of black. The Pipe Snake feeds on lizards and smaller snakes.

The **Anaconda** (photograph below) with its 9 m maximum length, is an almost mythical snake. It has amphibian habits, because it spends most of its life in the waters of the basin of the River Amazon and the Orinoco River. It is an excellent swimmer and can remain under water for a long time. Its extremely stretchable muscles enable it to swallow even large mammals. The female gives birth to 30 - 80 young which, when they are born, are about 70 cm long.

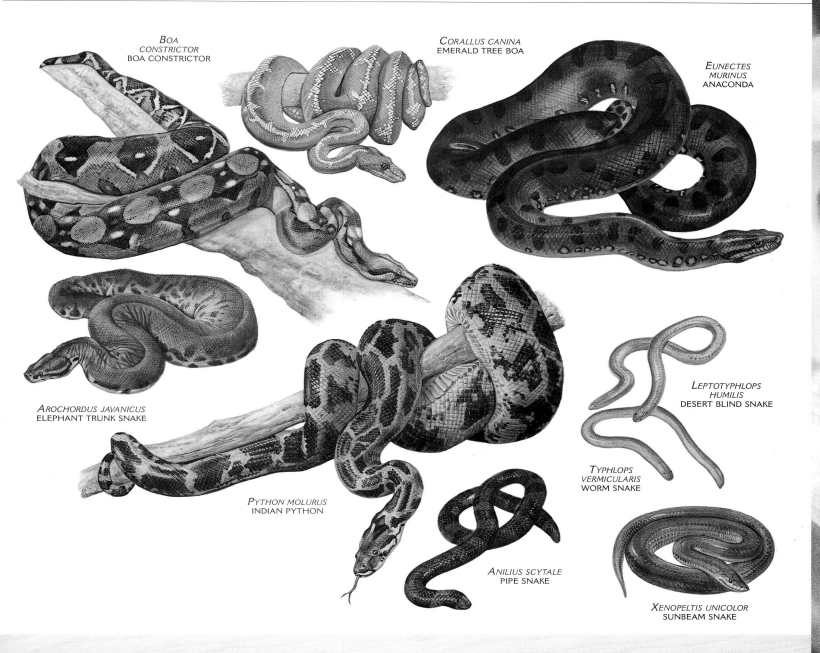

BOA CONSTRICTOR
BOA CONSTRICTOR

CORALLUS CANINA
EMERALD TREE BOA

EUNECTES MURINUS
ANACONDA

AROCHORDUS JAVANICUS
ELEPHANT TRUNK SNAKE

PYTHON MOLURUS
INDIAN PYTHON

LEPTOTYPHLOPS HUMILIS
DESERT BLIND SNAKE

TYPHLOPS VERMICULARIS
WORM SNAKE

ANILIUS SCYTALE
PIPE SNAKE

XENOPELTIS UNICOLOR
SUNBEAM SNAKE

INDIAN PYTHON

Habitat: tropical forests

Reproduction: oviparous

Length of adult: up to 8 m

Weight of adult: up to 110 kg

The Indian Python is one of the longest snakes in the world.
It lives in India, preferring the areas with thick vegetation, such as the jungle. It particularly likes the banks of running water, in which it can sometimes stay immersed for a long time. Although it stays mainly at ground level, the Indian Python can also climb and move among the branches of trees easily.

It has a varied diet which consists of monkeys and different rodents, although it will also attack small deer and birds. Like other members of the python family to which it belongs, the Indian Python has exceptional strength. Its body muscles are so strong that it can wrap its spirals around its prey, strangling it to death. The Indian Python is a nocturnal snake and spends most of its time quite still. It rouses itself and goes into action only when it is hungry. In captivity, it can fast for some months without food and then suddenly decide that it is time to eat. After laying her eggs, the female wraps a spiral of her body around them and does not abandon them until the time that they hatch. When the young are born, they are about 50 cm long.

The Indian Python is a species which is at risk of extinction.

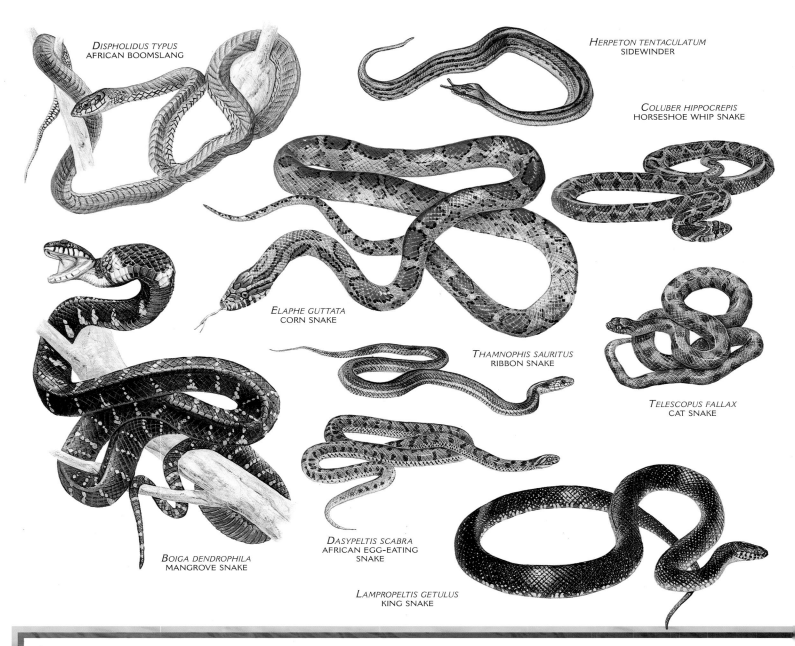

DISPHOLIDUS TYPUS
AFRICAN BOOMSLANG

HERPETON TENTACULATUM
SIDEWINDER

COLUBER HIPPOCREPIS
HORSESHOE WHIP SNAKE

ELAPHE GUTTATA
CORN SNAKE

THAMNOPHIS SAURITUS
RIBBON SNAKE

TELESCOPUS FALLAX
CAT SNAKE

BOIGA DENDROPHILA
MANGROVE SNAKE

DASYPELTIS SCABRA
AFRICAN EGG-EATING
SNAKE

LAMPROPELTIS GETULUS
KING SNAKE

Did you know...

The favourite home of the **African Boomslang** are the branches of trees in tropical Africa.

The **Mangrove Snake** lives in Malaysia and the neighbouring islands. Its diet is comprised of birds, lizards and smaller snakes.

The **Sidewinder** is a water snake from Thailand. It likes salt water with a lot of vegetation.

The **Corn Snake** is a North American species with a most beautiful red-brown pattern.

The **Ribbon Snake** is a thin, medium-size snake, most common in North America.

The **African Egg-Eating Snake** has a diameter equal to the finger of a grown man, yet it can swallow a hen's egg whole.

The **Horseshoe Whip Snake** is very aggressive. At 2 m long, it is the largest snake in Europe.

In Europe we also find the nocturnal **Cat Snake**. This snake is not dangerous to humans.

The **King Snake** is most widespread in the forests of the southern United States and in Mexico, and is often bred in a terrarium.

Like all rattlesnakes, the **Diamond Back Rattlesnake** really does have a tail that makes a rattling sound. It lives in the USA and South America. The female can give birth to up to 60 young.

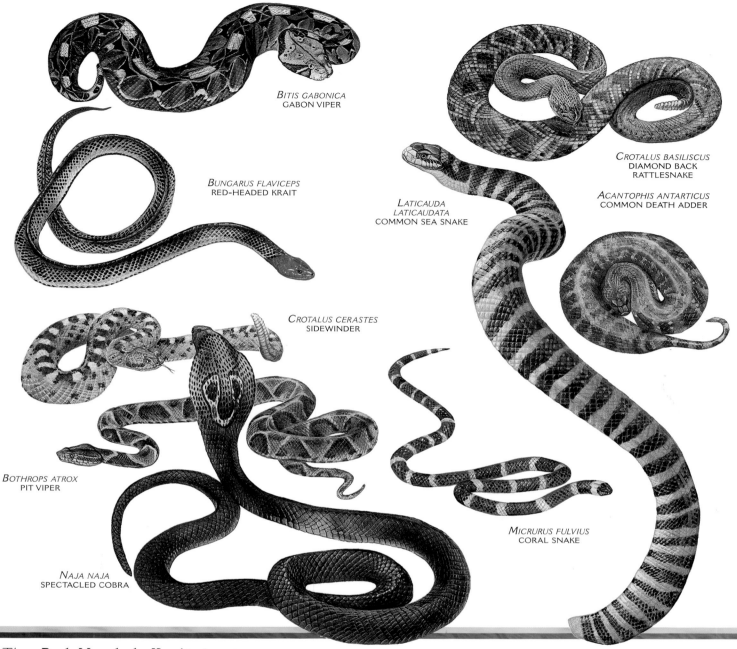

BITIS GABONICA
GABON VIPER

CROTALUS BASILISCUS
DIAMOND BACK
RATTLESNAKE

BUNGARUS FLAVICEPS
RED-HEADED KRAIT

LATICAUDA
LATICAUDATA
COMMON SEA SNAKE

ACANTOPHIS ANTARTICUS
COMMON DEATH ADDER

CROTALUS CERASTES
SIDEWINDER

BOTHROPS ATROX
PIT VIPER

MICRURUS FULVIUS
CORAL SNAKE

NAJA NAJA
SPECTACLED COBRA

The **Red-Headed Krait** is a nocturnal snake. It is poisonous and lives in the forests of South-East Asia.

The **Sidewinder** can grow up to 60-70 cm long. This is also a nocturnal snake, found in the deserts of the USA.

The **Common Sea Snake** lives along the coasts of South-East Asia. Its poison is twice or three times more toxic than land-dwelling poisonous snakes.

The **Common Death Adder** is an Australian snake, so-called because of its highly toxic poison.

The **Spectacled Cobra** lives in Asia. It gets its name from the pattern which appears on its back when it is excited. From a half-open mouth it can spit its highly toxic poison up to a distance of 1 m.

The **Gabon Viper** lives in the rainforests of tropical Africa. The damage it can do with its teeth, up to

38 mm long, adds to the danger of its poison, which is one of the most dangerous of all vipers.

The **Pit Viper** is widespread in the tropical forests of Central America. The female gives birth to up to 70 young at a time.

The **Coral Snake** of North America is a brightly-coloured, beautiful looking snake. It is not aggressive, but its bite is very dangerous, because its poison attacks the nervous system of its victim.

MELANOSUCHUS NIGER
CAIMAN CROCODILE

ALLIGATOR MISSIPPIENSIS
AMERICAN ALLIGATOR

PALEOSUCHUS PALPEBROSUS
DWARF CAIMAN

CAIMAN CROCODYLUS
SPECTACLED CAIMAN

CAIMAN CROCODILE

Reproduction: oviparous

Brood: 35-50 eggs

Length: up to about 5 m

The Caiman Crocodile is the most common crocodile in South America, widespread throughout the Amazon Basin. It resembles its close relative, the alligator, but, unlike the alligator, the skin on its abdomen is reinforced with bony plates. Its favourite habitat is within the calm areas of running water. Often, however, it is also found in the swampy stretches and the forests. These remain flooded for some months in the year and are known by the Brazilians as the 'igapos'.

Very aggressive and hungrier than any other crocodile, the Caiman Crocodile will attack and eat many types of animal. It is a reptile which does not always have a particular liking for certain food, eating anything and everything, and nothing is too big or too small – fish, small mammals, grasshoppers and locusts.

The Caiman Crocodile migrates from the Amazon Basin in the summer to spend the hottest months in lagoons. It will also drink from lagoons at other times, during spells of dry weather.

AMERICAN ALLIGATOR

Reproduction: oviparous

Brood: 20-80 eggs

Length of adult: up to 6 m

More than any other species of Crocodilia, the alligator has been hunted and persecuted for years, because its skin is so much valued in the leather industry. Anti-hunting laws have now been passed to protect crocodiles and the Caiman as well as the alligator.

The geographical distribution of the alligator is at opposite ends of the globe – one species is found in China, another in the United States. They live in rivers and swamps and spend most of their time in water, where they move with surprising rapidity. The alligator has a type of 'radar' on its cheeks. Here is a body zone sensitive enough to sense the least ripple of water and which signals to the alligator the presence of prey.

In winter, the American Alligator hibernates, burying itself in mud.

Did you know...

The **Dwarf Caiman** is one of the smallest crocodiles living, reaching a length of just 145 cm. The shape of its head is very convex (curved), with noticeable bony plates above its eyes and its nose turned up instead of being flat. Despite its fierce appearance, it is not very dangerous. It lives in small groups in the flowing waters of the Amazon Basin, preferring moving water rich with the oxygen of rapids and waterfalls. It eats fish. During the period of drought, it finds a deep well and stays down there, lying for two or three days without eating.

The expression 'crocodile tears' comes from the fact that the **alligator** (in photograph) secretes tears with bubbles of air to protect its highly sensitive eyes.

A close relative of the American Alligator is the **Chinese Alligator** (not illustrated). There are only a few examples of these, in the waters of the Yang-tse Kiang river. It differs from the American Crocodile because it has a shorter nose and its front claws are not webbed.

The **Spectacled Caiman** is the most common caiman in South-Central America. It has quite a short head, its eyes are large with green irises and the bony crest which connects the two sockets gives the Caiman the appearance of wearing spectacles, which is how it gets its name. It lives in slow-flowing water with a muddy bed in the Amazon rainforests. It shares the same water surroundings with the Anaconda, which means that young caiman are often caught by this large snake.

BIRDS

COMMON CHARACTERISTICS

The body is covered with feathers. The mouth is in the form of a beak. Body temperature is constant, as in mammals. The body is built for flight – birds have lungs and very strong pectoral (chest) muscles, a light skeleton with hollow bones. The wings have longer feathers than on the body.

EVOLUTION, DISTRIBUTION AND HABITAT

150 million years ago a group of reptiles similar to the offspring of dinosaurs began to adapt to different surroundings and climates. The front limbs became transformed into wings, so that a bird could maintain flight. After that, birds became creatures of the air – although there are some species which cannot or do not fly. Now, there are birds in all parts of the world, including cities.

Unlike most other birds, the ostrich has a very long neck and long legs covered with tiny feathers. Its legs are very strong, not only to support the weight of the body, but also to sustain the high speed which the bird reaches, with strides up to 4 metres long.

Ostriches mate for life. The female lays her one egg in a depression in the ground, together with the eggs of other female ostriches. Both male and female sit on the egg, but it is the male which takes the most care of the young. An ostrich can live at different temperatures in climate. In winter its body has more feathers which are also thicker. The ostrich is famous for eating strange things! Although it feeds mainly on vegetable matter, it will swallow other objects especially if these are shining.

This male Ostrich can reach a height of 2 metres, the female is smaller. It lives in groups, both small and large, mixing with zebras, antelopes and gazelles.

BEHAVIOUR

Birds react to their surroundings by singing, as well as singing at special times, such as the mating season. Many birds parade and some 'dance' to attract a mate. Birds build nests of different shapes and sizes. Some care for their young, a few leave the rearing to other birds. Only some birds mate for life. Some birds stay in one place, others migrate, using the Sun and stars to find their way.

FEEDING

The type of beak a bird has depends on the food it has. Its diet can include vegetable matter, insects and grubs or food which other creatures, even mammals, cannot get or eat. Many are omnivore and without any particular preference in food. Others have developed a need for a particular diet.

Made to fly

On the Earth there exists at least 8580 species of birds living in all habitats, from the icy wastes of the Antarctic to the torrid climates of the deserts. Some live their lives almost completely at sea. The survival of birds has been mainly due to different foods becoming available and their ability to find and eat them. As well as food being easily found, there is also the dispersal of seeds of different species of plant, as well as some birds being able to eat the remains of dead plants and animals.

The bird's light skeleton has **hollow bones**, a very flexible neck and a wide, smooth breast-bone to support the powerful muscles which are necessary to beat the wings in flight. The wing **feathers** make the flight of a bird the best in the animal kingdom. Each feather is flexible and light, yet very strong. It has a central shaft and from this a series of parallel barbs branch off, each barb slanted down towards the next and with microscopic filaments called **barbules**, closely fitting together to form a surface smooth enough to overcome the resistance of the air. A bird's

feathers, and especially the layer of fine down next to the body, insulate the body. In an adult bird, the top feathers are renewed each year, in the process of moulting during late summer. To slow down the fall of these feathers and also to keep its body waterproof, a bird will then spread itself with a natural grease which it secretes in special glands at the base of the neck.

With birds perching on branches and slowly falling asleep, an automatic reflex of the talons on the claws stops them from falling.

The shape and the strength of the **beak**

Photographs: left, a Buzzard, a bird of the Falciforme order. Facing page: a swan followed by her cygnets.

depends on the diet; strong and hooked in birds of prey, short and cone-shaped in seed-eaters, slender beaks in birds which feed on insects, long and sensitive in those which search for food in mud and slime.

During courtship, many birds dance and carry out particular ritual, showing off the colours of their feathers and how well they can fly and sing. Most birds are particularly dedicated to the care of their eggs, the nest and their young.

PHYLUM	SUB-PHYLUM	CLASS	MAIN ORDERS	SPECIES
CHORDATA	Vertebrates	Birds	Sphenisciformes	penguin
			Procellariiformes	albatross
			Ciconiformes	heron, stork
			Anseriformes	goose, duck
			Falconiformes	falcon
			Galliformes	Pheasant
			Gruiformes	Crane
			Charadriformes	Tern
			Columbiformes	pigeon
			Psittaciformes	parrot
			Cuculiformes	Cuckoo
			Strigiformes	owl
			Caprimulgiformes	Nightjar
			Apodiformes	hummingbird
			Trogoniformes	Trogon
			Coliiformes	Mousebird
			Coraciiformes	Kingfisher
			Piciformes	Woodpecker
			Passeriformes	sparrow, swallow

EUDYPTULA MINOR
LITTLE PENGUIN

MEGADYPTES ANTIPODES
YELLOW EYED PENGUIN

SPHENISCUS DEMERSUS
JACKASS PENGUIN

PYGOCELIS ADELIAE
ADELIE PENGUIN

PYGOSCELIS PAPUA
GENTOO PENGUIN

EUDYPTES CRESTATUS
ROCKHOPPER PENGUIN

APTENODYTES FORSTERI
LITTLE EMPEROR PENGUIN

SPHENISCUS MENDICULUS
GALAPAGOS PENGUIN

Did you know...

The body of a **penguin** is entirely covered with feathers so smooth as to be like a skin. The wings have been transformed into strong flippers – a penguin is a fine swimmer but can no longer fly. The funny walk of the penguin is because the turned-out position of the feet means that the bird cannot keep upright. The short, rigid tail is used as a support.

Penguins belonging to the order of **Spheniciformes**. Other species are the Galapagos Penguin, the Magellan Penguin and the Humbolt Penguin which lives in the freezing waters along the cost of Peru. Numbers of this species have fallen dramatically due to hunting. Deposits of their guano (excrement) is used as fuel.

Although different species of penguin live near the Antarctic, some can be found further north, nesting on a few sub-Antarctic

EMPEROR PENGUIN

Number of eggs: only one, weighing 450 g

Height: 1.35 m

Weight of adult: 45 kg

Home: the Antarctic

The Emperor Penguin is the largest of all living penguins. The only penguin larger than this was a fossilized species discovered in Patagonia at a height of around 1.75 m. All penguins have a body structure which is perfectly adapted to movements under water.

The Emperor Penguin does not swim in the true sense, but 'flies' beneath the water. Athough water is much more dense than air, the bird can reach a remarkable speed by batting its wings like flippers, using its legs as rudders.

To eat, the Emperor Penguin goes hunting for fish and molluscs. It is also an expert diver, reaching depths of up to 250 m as well as being able to stay up to 18 minutes under water.

The Emperor Penguin reproduces in autumn, during the long polar nights. After laying her one egg, the female goes off and the male hatches it. He does not build a nest, but pushes the egg between his feet with his beak. It is wrapped in a pouch-like fold, which is criss-crossed with many blood vessels. These blood vessels keep the egg very warm.

The male fasts for two months, until the egg hatches. The female then returns and begins to provide food for her young. At this point the male, now much, much thinner, goes to the sea to start feeding again.

JACKASS PENGUIN

Number of eggs: 2-3

Height: 60 cm

Speed swimming under water:
20-33 km/h

Home: South Africa

The Jackass Penguin is the only penguin which lives in Africa, on the islands of Dassen and Dyer near to the Cape of Good Hope.

It does not undertake long migrations like other penguins in its family. When it finishes raising its young, the Jackass Penguin is content to gorge itself on the fish in the fresh waters which extend between Africa and the Antarctic Ocean. The Jackass Penguin digs a nest in sandy ground and often builds a proper shelter, which is shielded at the bottom from the rays of the Sun.

The female lays two or three eggs at a time, then she and the male take it in turns to sit on them, and share in the rearing of the young, which lasts for more than eight weeks. On the islands of Dassen and Dyer, the Jackass Penguin form numerous colonies which are always very noisy. Yet, like other large assemblies of penguins, the young penguins and their parents always succeed in finding each other – it seems that it is all a question of the right 'ear' to recognize the 'right' voice. Then they greet each other by stroking each other's neck with their beaks.

islands. One of these is the small **Galapagos Penguin** which lives on the Galapagos Islands, at the same latitude as the Equator.

The smallest penguin, the **Little Penguin**, is only 40 cm long and so is often caught by seals. Snakes, lizards and mice eat its eggs. However, the winter weather and human beings are its enemies too. When it goes out at night to catch fish, it gives a cry rather like a howl.

The male and the female **Adelie Penguin** both stay close to the nest, which is built with flat stones and pebbles placed perfectly together. They return to the same nest each year to hatch their eggs.

The **Rockhopper Penguin** is easily recognized by the tufts of yellow feathers at either side of its head. Its limbs enable it to climb on rocks. This is the reason it got its name.

The **Gentoo Penguin** is about 75 cm tall. It lives on the islands around the Antarctic.

DAPTION CAPENSIS
CAPE PETREL

PUFFINUS GRAVIS
GREAT SHEARWATER

DIOMEDEA NIGRIPES
BLACK FOOTED ALBATROSS

DIOMEDEA EXULARIS
WANDERING ALBATROSS

FULMARUS GLACIALIS
NORTHERN FULMAR

OCEANITES OCEANICUS
WILSONS STORM PETREL

Díd you know...

The **Northern Fulmar**, white as the snow, is found in the seas of the Arctic, whilst the **Cape Petrel** lives in the islands in the Antarctic and also in New Zealand.

The **Black Footed Albatross** lives in the Northern Hemisphere of the world.

The **Wandering Albatross**, a massive and strong flier of the southern oceans. With a length of 140 cm and a wingspan of more than 3 metres, this is the largest sea bird. It builds its nest on the ground and the female lays one egg. From that moment, the hatching lasts 2-3 months and the rearing of the young, in the care of both male and female, lasts between 5-9 months. Albatrosses reproduce only every two years.

Wilsons Storm Petrel is found in the Southern Hemisphere. This bird takes off from the water with its wings open and feet on the surface of the sea, as if it is walking in search of food.

The **Great Shearwater**, recognizable by its characteristic nocturnal calls similar to a lament, nests in the south Atlantic but winters in European seas.

The **Pelican** likes swamps and marshes in summer, and sheltered bays and coastlines in winter. It nests in large colonies and, despite its strange appearance, it is a fine swimmer and flies at speed. The young eat pre-

PHAETON RUBRICAUDA
RED-TAILED TROPIC BIRD

PHALACROCORAX
AURITUS
DOUBLE-BREASTED
CORMORANT

FREGATA ARIEL
LESSER FRIGATE BIRD

SULA LEUCOGASTER
BROWN BOOBY

PELECANUS
CONSPICILLATUS
AUSTRALIAN PELICAN

ANHINGA ANHINGA
AMERICAN DARTER

PHALACROCORAX GAIMARDI
RED-LEGGED CORMORANT

digested food which is collected in a sac under the beak of each parent bird.

The **cormorant** (in the photograph) lives along sea coasts, besides lakes and some rivers in most parts of the world. It swims perfectly, but walks with difficulty. Its talent for catching fish is used by the Chinese who have tamed them to 'fish'.

The **Lesser Frigate Bird** prefers to steal prey from other sea birds. During the mating season the male shows himself off, a vivid red sac swelling out beneath his throat.

The **American Darter**, sometimes called the 'serpent bird', due to the shape of its long neck, lives near lakes and rivers.

The **Brown Booby** catches fish by diving underwater.

The **Double-Crested Cormorant** lines its nest with vegetable matter and algae, held together with mud and remains of food.

The **Red-Tailed Tropic Bird** has an elegant flight. It nests on the most inaccessible rocks in the tropical islands where it lives.

WHITE STORK

The White Stork spends the summer in Europe and the winter in South Africa. It is an expert at soaring and being carried along by currents of air, usually flying above water only if land is in sight. Yet, when it migrates, it has to cross large expanses of open sea without currents of air to help it along. Many storks from Northern Europe cross the Mediterranean then fly over eastern Asia and on to South Africa. It is estimated that a Danish stork undertakes a journey of 13,000 km! Groups from Holland and Spain follow a south-east route towards the Straits of Gibraltar, where they take advantage of the warm rising currents before

Habitat:	swampy areas, farmland rich with water, fields
Wingspan:	170 cm
Length:	100 cm
Food:	reptiles, amphibians, fish, chicks and small mammals, insects, vegetable matter

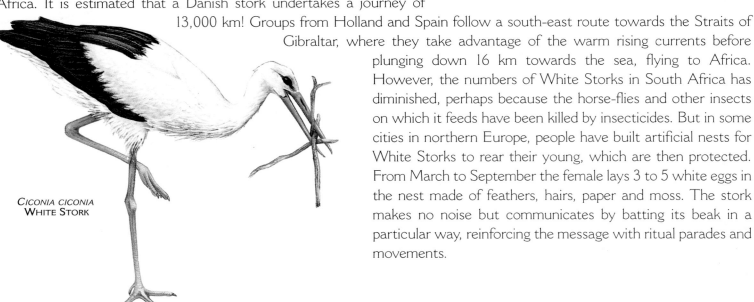

CICONIA CICONIA
WHITE STORK

plunging down 16 km towards the sea, flying to Africa. However, the numbers of White Storks in South Africa has diminished, perhaps because the horse-flies and other insects on which it feeds have been killed by insecticides. But in some cities in northern Europe, people have built artificial nests for White Storks to rear their young, which are then protected. From March to September the female lays 3 to 5 white eggs in the nest made of feathers, hairs, paper and moss. The stork makes no noise but communicates by batting its beak in a particular way, reinforcing the message with ritual parades and movements.

Did you know...

The **Spoonbill** does not have its wide-ended beak from birth. It gets likes this little by little, as the bird grows. The reason for this unusual shape is not yet known.

The **Yellow-Crowned Night Heron** builds large nests with branches woven together in trees, in swamps or on floating vegetation. By day, it remains well-hidden, whilst at night it hunts for fish, reptiles, frogs, crustaceans, insects and vegetables.

The **Marabou Stork** lives in Asia and in the African savannah. Usually it feeds on the rotting meat which is easier to find in dry areas. This bird looks similar to the vulture, with which it often has to compete for the same food.

Probably because of its splendid plumage, the **Scarlet Ibis** (in photograph) with its long, thin, downward curving beak attracts hunters which capture them to sell to zoos. However, in captivity, the Scarlet Ibis pales in colour and becomes a clear pink. For this reason, the owners take care of its diet, enriching it with carotene. It gathers in colonies, together with the White Ibis.

The **Shoebill** or **Whale-Headed Stork** grows up to 120 cm tall. It is lazy, very shy and silent. It flies with great agility keeping its wings firm and taking advantage of the currents of air. It lives in swampy areas of tropical Africa. Special laws protect it from killing because it is at risk of extinction.

There are about 100 species of **bittern**, many living in Europe. It flies very slowly, keeping its neck folded in the form of a letter 'S'. In some species, the head has long feathers, a feature of great importance during the mating season and communication with other bitterns. The thin legs enable the bittern to walk in the water of marshes, swamps, lakes or along sandy coastlines.

TIGRIORNIS LEUCOLOPHUS
WHITE CRESTED BITTERN

EGRETTA GULARIS
WESTERN REEF HERON

NYCTICORAX VIOLACEA
YELLOW-CROWNED
NIGHT HERON

EUDOCINUS RUBER
SCARLET IBIS

AJAIA AJAIA
SPOONBILL

BALAENICEPS REX
SHOEBILL OR
WHALE-HEADED STORK

LEPTOPTILOS
CRUMENIFERUS
MARABOU STORK

BRANTA SANDVICENSIS
HAWAIIAN GOOSE

ANHIMA CORNUTA
HORNED SCREAMER

ANSERANAS
SEMIPALMATA
MAGPIE GOOSE

ANSER ALBIFRONS
WHITE-FRONTED
GOOSE

DENDROCYGNA ARCUATA
WANDERING WHISTLING
DUCK

ANAS CRECCA
TEAL

CYGNUS MELANOCORYPHA
BLACK-NECKED SWAN

MERGUS CUCULLATUS
HOODED MERGANSER

MUTE SWAN

Weight of egg: 350 gr

Weight of adult: 12-18 kg (up to 23)

Wingspan: 2.20-2.50 m

The Mute Swan is the largest bird in Europe. In the wild state, it lives in the area which encircles in the Baltic Sea and in the swampy expanses of northern Germany. It can also be found in northern Asia.

The Mute Swan is recognized by a long neck which is almost serpent-like and a fleshy lump (tubercle) at the base of the beak. Despite its heavy appearance and the comical way in which it walks, there is no bird more elegant in flight. It rises swiftly with majestic batting of wings, keeping its neck straight in front like the stork and the crane. Its wingspan can reach 2.50 m and it is one of the heaviest birds able to fly, reaching speeds of 60-65 km/h. Unlike many other birds which live in pairs only during the mating season, Mute Swans make partners which last all their lives.

This bird builds a large nest with straw and vegetable fibres, slightly raised up above any surrounding water. Once a year, the female lays between 3 to 12 grey-green eggs which she sits on for about 5 weeks. The number of eggs depends on the age of the female – younger females tend to lay more eggs. The chicks are grey, becoming white by about 2 years old. This swan, also called the Royal Swan, makes a cry similar to the sound of a small trumpet. It eats aquatic insects, as well as aquatic vegetable matter. In Europe, they appear in late autumn or in winter and nest in the north of the Alps.

Did you know...

The **Hawaiin Goose** has completely adapted to life on the land, living between the blocks of lava of the Hawaiin volcanoes. As well as being hunted by humans for its meat, it is also in danger from cats, pigs and mice which eat its eggs and its young. This bird was at risk of extinction until the inauguration of a programme of breeding in zoos.

The **White-Fronted Goose** lives in the Arctic tundra in summer, returning to southern Europe in the autumn. Its cry is similar to a laugh. It builds its nest in a simple depression in the ground with twigs and dried grass and lining with feathers.

The small **Teal** is only 35 cm long. It lives in groups near fresh water in summer and coastal waters in winter. It is very common in Europe, and in May the female lays from 8 to 10 white-yellow eggs.

The **Black-Necked Swan** is not very common. Smaller than the Mute Swan, it has shorter legs and a longer body, so that it has to toss itself about with every step. To take off is very tiring for this bird and it needs a long run. It flies rapidly making a characteristic rustling noise. It lives in large groups, in swamps, in ponds and in the marshes of Patagonia.

The **Magpie Goose** lives in Australia, whilst the **Wandering Whistling Duck** is most common in America, Asia and Africa.

Among the tufted ducks is the **Hooded Merganser** with the crest on its head similar to a horse's mane. During summer, this bird can be seen along the coastlines of many Mediterranean countries.

The **Horned Screamer** from Central America has two pointed spurs, about 5 cm long, at the front edges of its wings. Its legs are relatively long and the claws very spread out.

KING VULTURE

Length:	1.10 m
Weight:	3-3.7 kg
Habitat:	tropical forests and savannahs with trees
Home:	from southern Mexico to northern Argentina

This bird 'looks the part' as the king of the vultures. It acquires its distinctive plumage and the vivid colours of the fleshy growth (caruncle) on its head, by the age of 3-4 years. Until then, the young are completely brown.

Although it can kill animals to eat, the King Vulture feeds mostly on the rotting flesh of dead animals, which it can pick out, even when these are covered by vegetation, by a highly-developed sense of smell which is rare in birds. When it makes its appearance at a 'feast' the other vultures give way, scared off by the strength of its beak. It has the habit of flying over the territory.

It does not build a nest. The female lays one egg in the cavity of a stunted tree or a trunk hit by lightning or by old age. Both male and female take it in turns to look after the young.

HAWK

Length of adult:	50-54 cm
Wingspan:	1.15-1.40 m
Weight of adult:	500-1000 g
Lives in:	woodland regions

A hawk is easily recognized by its heavy flight, large wings and short, rounded tail, all of which distinguish it from other daytime birds of prey. There are many species (right, the Bat Hawk of Africa and Asia) and the largest population is found in the hottest regions. At the onset of winter it migrates towards the sunshine of southern countries, where it can continue hunting its prey.

By autumn, many hawks arrive in central and southern Europe. The hawk hunts mostly in open farmland, which it explores from on high with a gliding flight, sometimes staying quite still in the air. Its style of hunting is to trap – it stays at the top of a pole or on a branch where it is easily seen, surveying a wide part of the territory. With its keen eyesight, it can pick out field mice or a vole as soon as the animal puts its nose out of the lair. At the right moment, the hawk throws itself down and grabs the prey in its claws. The hawk nests in forests, among the leaves of trees. The nest is made of twigs lined with leaves and paper.

Did you know...

In **birds of prey** the long fringes of feathers on the wings and the tail act as 'silencers' in flight.

In ancient civilizations, birds of prey were regarded in the same way as gods. One of the most ancient was Garuda, an eagle in Hindu mythology with wings of gold. The Babylonians and the Hittites built temples for the eagle and the most popular Egyptian divinity was Horus, a falcon.

Falcons, eagles, hawks and vultures are **daytime birds of prey** (active from dawn to sunset). These represent two thirds of birds of prey.

The African **Bateleur Eagle** and the **Serpent Eagle** from Asia are both predators of reptiles.

Hawks can see better than humans because the retinas of their eyes are richer in photo-sensitive cells. At the point most dense in photo-sensitive cells, there are a million and a half in the hawk, opposed to the 200,000 in the retina of the human eye.

Like many other falcons, the **Gyrfalcon** is used in the sport of falconry. In this pursuit, a falcon is trained to catch prey and bring it back to a particular spot.

Eagles are very widespread. In Europe, there is the **Royal Eagle** (see photograph), whilst the **Wedge-Tailed Eagle** and the **White-Tailed Eagle** live in Australia, the latter also in Asia.

MACHAERMAMPHUS ALCINOS
BAT HAWK

ROSTHRAMUS SOCIABILIS
EVERGLADE KITE

TERATHOPIUS ECAUDATUS
BATELEUR EAGLE

HALIAËTUS LEUCOGASTER
WHITE-TAILED EAGLE

AQUILA AUDAX
WEDGE-TAILED EAGLE

SARCORAMPHUS PAPA
KING VULTURE

MICROHIERAX CAERULESCENS
RED THIGHED FALCON

FALCO RUSTICOLUS
GYRFALCON

SPILORNIS CHEELA
CRESTED SEA EAGLE

GROUSE

Lives: mountain woodland and clearings up to 3000 m altitude

Length: male 85 cm; female 60 cm

Food: shoots, fir cones and pine needles

There are many types of grouse and they all belong to the Tetraoyndae family in the order of Galliformes. This family also includes the Partridge, the Mountain Pheasant, the Ptarmigan and the Prairie Chicken. The largest member of the grouse family is the Capercaillie (illustrated right). The male Capercaillie is as big as a turkey, with a large head, pale yellow beak, metallic green breast and a large rounded tail. The female is smaller and is sometimes confused with the Mountain Pheasant, from which it is distinguished only by a large reddish patch on the breast and the wider rounded tail. The Capercaillie also has a scarlet caruncle (fleshy growth) above each eye and a bristly 'beard'. It can be found in most mountainous regions of Europe, especially in the east-central chain of the Alps. Because the Capercaillie is still hunted, there are not so many areas in which it lives in the wild. It prefers forests of conifer trees. Here, the Capercaillie moves along the ground in summer and up in the trees in winter. Its nest is a depression in the ground hidden with leaves, feathers and moss, where the female lays her yellow-red eggs spotted with brown in May. These can only be hatched once a year. The chicks are fed with worms and insects, whilst the adults eat vegetable matter.

Did you know...

The order of Galliformes comprises many domesticated birds which have more or less accompanied the development of the human race from ancient times. Birds belonging to this order are not very good fliers. They have a slightly elevated first digit on each claw, a strong, curved beak and very distinctive nostrils to take the position of a bony septum.

A full-grown **Hoatzin** is quite a large bird – about 65 cm long – yet it weighs less than 1 kg. It lives in the swamps of South America.

The **Ocellated Turkey** hides its showy feathers hidden in thick vegetation in small groups of 5-6 individuals. But it seems that the males live alone for some months returning to the females at mating time. It runs quickly and only takes to flight when it is in danger.

The **Congo Peafowl** has sumptuously-coloured feathers.

The **Plumed Quail** is a small member of the pheasant family, very similar to the Common Quail, but with a plume on its head and a brown patch at the throat.

In the United States and the north of Argentina lives the **Great Curassow**, with its backward-sweeping feathers on its crest and a large protruberance (swelling) at the top of its strong beak.

The colourful **Tragopan Satyra** is a species of quail from central Asia. It is in danger of extinction.

The **Mallee Fowl** from Australia lays its eggs in holes in the ground which it then covers with sand or vegetable matter, so that the eggs can be incubated by the warmth of the Sun. The parent birds can attend to the eggs only when the temperature suits them.

The **Spruce Goose** belongs to the same family as the Capercaillie. It has a massive form, sometimes reaching a weight of up to 7 kg. Members of the Tetraoyndae family live in temperate regions and in the Arctic in the Northern Hemisphere.

AGRIOCHARIS OCELLATA
OCELLATED TURKEY

OPISTHOCOMUS HOAZIN
HOATZIN

AFROPAVO CONGENSIS
CONGO PEAFOWL

OREOTYX PICTUS
PLUMED QUAIL

LEIPOA OCELLATA
MALLEE FOWL

CRAX RUBRA
GREAT CURASSOW

SATYRA TRAGOPAN
TRAGOPAN SATYRA

CANACHITES CANADENSIS
SPRUCE GOOSE

RHYNOCHETAS JUBATUS
KAGU

EUPODOTIS
SENEGALENSIS
WHITE-BELLIED
BUSTARD

EURYPYGA HELIAS
SUN BITTERN

CARIAMA CRISTATA
RED-LEGGED SERIEMA

PSOPHIA LEUCOPTERA
PALE-WINGED TRUMPETER

ARAMUS
GUARAUNA
LIMPKIN

PODICA SENEGALENSIS
AFRICAN FINFOOT

TURNIX SUSCITATOR
BARRED-BUTTON QUAIL

NOTORNIS MANTELLI
TAKAHE

Díd you know...

The **Pale-Winged Trumpeter** does not like flying. Even when it has to flee from predators, it prefers to keep its 'feet on the ground' or sometimes to swim in currents of water.

The **Limpkin** is very similar to the heron. It lives in the swamps of the United States and Argentina and feeds on water snails, which it swallows without breaking the shells.

The **Red-Legged Seriema** is found in Brazil, Argentina and Uruguay.

One of the largest examples of dove is the splendid **Victoria Crowned Pigeon** from New Guinea. It is about 65 cm tall and its tuft of feathers of different lengths give it a majestic air.

The **Kagu** exhibits complex parades during which it will use its beak to grasp the feathers on its tail and wings.

The **Takahe** is a species native to New Zealand. It has lost its ability to fly and uses its wings only to swim during the mating season.

The **African Finfoot** can be found throughout almost the whole of Africa. It is an excellent swimmer, with the

PTEROCLES ALCHATA
PIN-TAILED SAND GROUSE

OTODIPHAPS NOBILIS
PHEASANT PIGEON

STREPTOPELIA SENEGALENSIS
LAUGHING DOVE

TRERON CAPELLE
LARGE GREEN PIGEON

LOPHOPHAS PLUMIFERA
PLUMED GUINEAFOWL

PTEROCLES LICHTENSTEINII
LICHENSTEIN SAND GROUSE

GOURA VICTORIAE
VICTORIA CROWNED
PIGEON

COLUMBINA PASSERINA
COMMON GROUND DOVE

habit of carrying its young on its back, even when going under water.

The **Sun Bittern** lives in the rainforests of Central America and Brazil.

The **Lichenstein Sand Grouse** is a bird of the African savannahs, living in groups of up to 400 individuals. Its plumage blends in with its surroundings.

The female **Button Quail** is larger than the male. She is the one who approaches the male at mating time.

The **Pin-Tailed Sand Grouse** nests in Spain, Portugal and parts of northern France.

The **Laughing Dove** also belongs to the dove family, as well as the beautifully-coloured **Pheasant**

Pigeon, the **Plumed Guineafowl** with the plume on its head and the **Common Ground Dove** which has a more rounded shape than the others.

The **Large Green Pigeon** can be found in the tropical zones of Africa and Asia. It lives in groups and is guided along by one adult bird. They travel in search of fruits and berries, which is the only food they can eat.

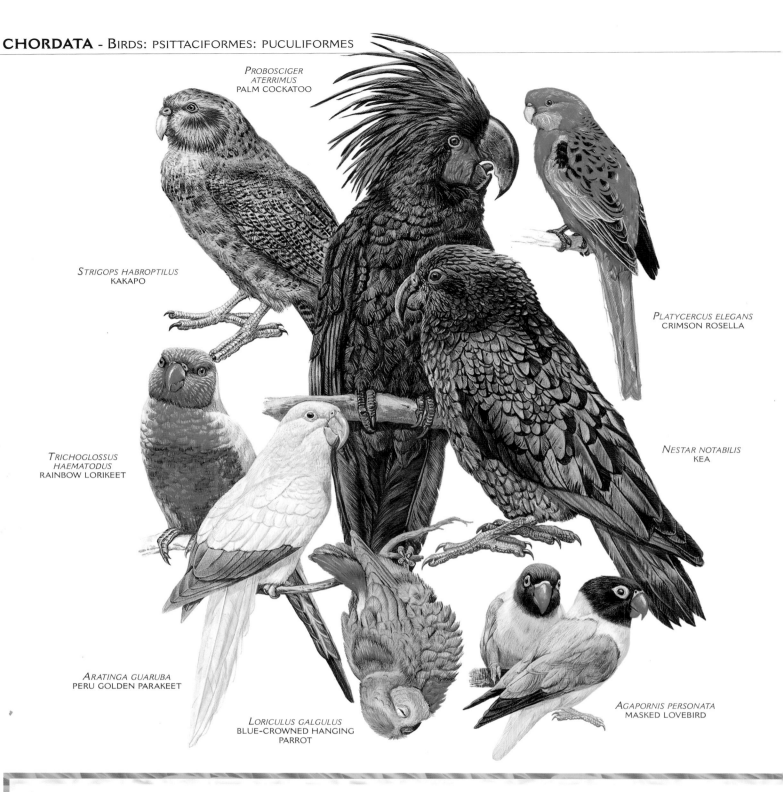

PROBOSCIGER
ATERRIMUS
PALM COCKATOO

STRIGOPS HABROPTILUS
KAKAPO

PLATYCERCUS ELEGANS
CRIMSON ROSELLA

TRICHOGLOSSUS
HAEMATODUS
RAINBOW LORIKEET

NESTAR NOTABILIS
KEA

ARATINGA GUARUBA
PERU GOLDEN PARAKEET

LORICULUS GALGULUS
BLUE-CROWNED HANGING
PARROT

AGAPORNIS PERSONATA
MASKED LOVEBIRD

Did you know...

The **Kea** is a parrot from New Zealand which feeds on fruit and the larvae of insects.

Other members of the parrot family are the **Crimson Rosella**, a very able flier, and the 'hanging parrots' with short, blunt tails, such as the **Blue-Crowned Hanging Parrot** which lives on the ground.

The **Palm Cockatoo** has dark feathers and a strong beak which is large compared to the size of its head.

The **Rainbow Lorikeet** lives in Australia, New Zealand and the islands of Oceania. It eats only nectar, which means that it has to move around according to the flowering of plants.

The **Kakapo** also lives in New Zealand. It spends the day among the roots of trees

and goes hunting at night, sometimes throwing itself down from trees.

In the wild, the little **Golden Parakeet** is found in India, Sri Lanka, South-East Asia and tropical America.

Among the lovebirds of Africa and Madagascar is the **Masked Lovebird**, so-called because of its black 'mask' of feathers which extends from below its nose to the middle of its head.

CENTROPUS MELANOPUS
BLCK-FACED COUCAL

CRYTOPHAGA ANI
SMOOTH-BILLED ANI

CARPOCOCCYX
RADICEUS
GROUND CUCKOO

TURACO PERSA LIVINGSTONII
LIVINGSTONE TAURACO

MUSOPHAGA VIOLACEA
VIOLET TAURACO

CLAMATOR COROMANDOS
RED WING CRESTED CUCKOO

EUDYNAMIS SCOLOPACEA
KOEL (male)

CHRYSOCOCCYX CUPREUS
AFRICAN EMERALD CUCKOO

EUDYNAMIS SCOLOPACEA
KOEL (female)

The Indian **Red Wing Crested Cuckoo** and the **African Emerald Cuckoo** belong to the cuckoo family. These are typical of birds living in tropical zones throughout the world.

The **Violet Tauraco** lives in Africa, in Gambia and Nigeria.

The **Black-Faced Coucal** lives in the Philippines. It is a poor flier and flees from danger by running along the ground.

In China, India and New Guinea the **Koel** is found. Like many other members of the cuckoo family, the female lays her eggs in the nests of other birds, which then incubate the young.

Another parasitic cuckoo is the **African Emerald Cuckoo** with its head coloured in a way which seems

'hooded' and a large beak. It lives in Indo-China and Sumatra.

The **Smooth-Billed Ani** lives in the region of Euro-Asia. It likes to be with other birds of its kind. At hatching time, up to six females may share the same nest.

The **Livingstone Tauraco**, with a straight crest on its head, is also from Africa.

BUFO LACTEUS
EAGLE OWL

PULSATRIX PERSPILLIATA
SPECTACLED OWL

AEGOLUS FUNEREUS
TAWNY OWL

GLAUCIDIUM PASSERINUM
PYGMY OWL

TYPO ALBA
BARN OWL

SPEOTYO CURICULARIA
LITTLE OWL

BARN OWL

Face shape: heart

Length: 30-40 cm

Wingspan: 90-95 cm

Habitat: old buildings, trees

The Barn Owl is a nocturnal bird of prey which can be found almost everywhere, although not in great numbers. Thanks to its special eyesight, it can find its way and capture prey in complete darkness.

Its ears are long clefts hidden at either side of its face, behind the feathers arranged in the shape of a heart. The Barn Owl can detect the slightest sound of a mouse or a vole.

Like many other owls, the exceptional hearing of the Barn Owl is made even better by its facial disc reflecting sound back to its ears. This also enables the owl to detect more easily the direction from which the sound comes.

The Barn Owl eats rodents and other birds such as doves, and also small mammals.

The Barn Owl does not build a nest, but in April and May and sometimes in November or December, the female lays her white eggs in clefts of buildings and trees, or in nests abandoned by other birds.

Thanks to the particular softness of its feathers, the flight of the Barn Owl is silent.

TENGMALM'S OWL

Face shape: roundish

Length: 25 cm

Habitat: conifer forests

Although the Tengmalm's Owl (also called the Boreal Owl) is quite rare in Europe, it can still be found in woodland in the region of the Alps. It is often confused with the Common Barn Owl, but it is smaller.

Tengmalm's Owl comes from the region of the Arctic Circle and likes conifer forests. Here it captures mammals, birds and insects which constitute its diet. It hunts by day as well as by night.

For nesting, it uses natural cavities in trees or nests left free by woodpeckers. The female lays her eggs from April to June, like the Common Barn Owl and the Tawny Owl.

The number of individuals sometimes increases following migration to the north, especially in winter – and this is also true of the Common Barn Owl, especially in central-southern zones of Europe.

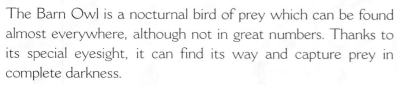

Did you know...

*Nocturnal **birds of prey** have eyes which are more rounded than in other birds and more 'plate-like'. The range of sight in these birds is less, but they can see for long distances.*

*As in all Strigiformes, the eyes of the **Eagle Owl** are forward-looking and at the front of the head – whereas in all other birds the eyes are at the sides. The Eagle Owl cannot see out of the angle of its eye, to look to the side or over its 'shoulder'. So it has to move its head by continual and rapid movements of the neck. It can turn its head 180° from one side to the other.*

***Barn Owls** and **Eagle Owls** are able to see a dead mouse in light from 10 to 100 times weaker than that needed by the normal human eye, and a living mouse in almost complete darkness.*

*In ancient China, the **owl** was considered fierce and a bringer of death. For the North American Indians, however, the Eagle Owl had the power to help and to protect people during the night-time hours.*

*The **Eagle Owl** can find its way by hearing as well as by sight, and by tactile bristles at either side of its beak.*

*The **Pygmy Owl** is only found in a few Alpine areas in Europe. The **Little Owl** and the **Spectacled Owl** are both found in North and South America.*

*In Greek myths, the **owl** was the bird of Athene, the goddess of wisdom, and symbolized the powers of darkness. For Aztecs, the owl was a symbol of the god of the after-life, guardians of the Earth and the forces of nature.*

MARVELLOUS SPATULETAIL

Habitat:	forests
Length:	16 cm
Flight:	rapid taking off, or almost quite still in the air
Food:	nectar

The Marvellous Spatuletail belongs to the Trochilidae family, commonly called hummingbirds, and much admired because of their splendid colouring.

These skilled fliers are generally small, with a roundish head, large eyes and a straight or curved beak, which is sometimes longer than its body.

The hummingbird, like the Marvellous Spatuletail, can be found in the high plains of northern Peru. The unusual appearance of the male makes its dance of love even more charming when he flies around the female showing off the rainbow shafts of light at the ends of his tail feathers. As with other birds in the same group, the male tends to have the more colourful plumage. One exception to this is a hummingbird with violet ears, in which the plumage of the two sexes is not all that different to each other.

ALPINE SWIFT

Habitat: rocks

Length: 20 cm

Speed of flight: up to 200 km/h

Food: insects

In mainland Europe, the Alpine Swift is not too rare, especially in the mountain zones of the Alps and on small and large islands, where it can often be seen flying around steep rocks, before diving into the sea.

The Alpine Swift likes to be with other birds. It feeds mainly on the insects which it catches as it flies, streaking down like lightning.

At nesting-time, Alpine Swift colonies use the clefts in rocks or holes in ruined buildings to lay white-coloured eggs at the end of May. The nest is in the shape of a crown roughly made of straw, feathers and different vegetable matter cemented together with the bird's secretions of saliva.

Did you know...

The order of **Apodiformes** comprises 61 species, scattered around almost every part of the world. Among them are swifts and hummingbirds. Although these birds may seem to be very different, there are many common characteristics, such as very short legs and the way in which the feathers are arranged.

The flight of the **hummingbird** is so perfect that it can fly in any direction, within any space, or stay quite still in the air. With the structure of their shoulder joints together with the highly-developed pectoral (breast) muscles, hummingbirds can flap their wings up to a frequency of 70 flaps per second. In general, hummingbirds are very distinctive, especially during the mating season.

They lead a solitary life and once they have established a hunting territory, they strongly defend it.

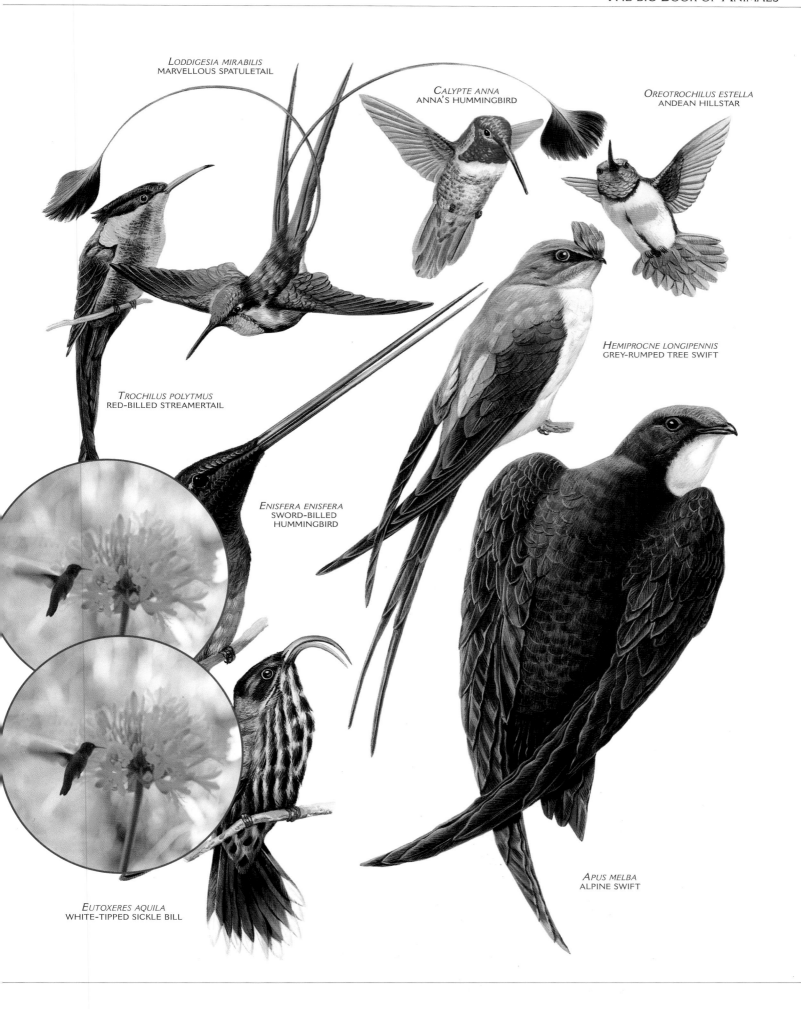

LODDIGESIA MIRABILIS
MARVELLOUS SPATULETAIL

CALYPTE ANNA
ANNA'S HUMMINGBIRD

OREOTROCHILUS ESTELLA
ANDEAN HILLSTAR

TROCHILUS POLYTMUS
RED-BILLED STREAMERTAIL

HEMIPROCNE LONGIPENNIS
GREY-RUMPED TREE SWIFT

ENISFERA ENISFERA
SWORD-BILLED
HUMMINGBIRD

EUTOXERES AQUILA
WHITE-TIPPED SICKLE BILL

APUS MELBA
ALPINE SWIFT

RAMPHASTOS TOCO
TOCO TOUCAN

ANDIGENA
LAMINI ROSTRIS
PLATE-BILLED
MOUNTAIN TOUCAN

PTEROGLOSSUS
BITORQUATUS
RED-NECKED
ARACARI

BUCCO CAPENSIS
COLLARED PUFF BIRD

GALBULA DEA
PARADISE JACAMAR

JYNX TORQUILLA
WRYNECK

INDICATOR INDICATOR
BLACK-THROATED
HONEY GUIDE

Did you know...

All **toucans** have an over-large beak, jaws which are jagged at the edges and a long tongue. The **Toco Toucan** (in photograph), which measures 60 cm long, is among the largest.

The family of Indicatoridae is made up of small birds with short beaks and legs and pointed wings. **The Black-Throated Honey Guide** is found in tropical and southern Africa.

The **Collared Puff Bird** with its huge orange beak is fairly squat and emits low, weak sounds.

The **Red-Necked Aracari** cries in a sharp, awkward way, but it is very colourful, like the **Plate-Billed Mountain Toucan**.

The **Paradise Jacamar**, with its melodious song, has colouring rather like that of the hummingbird.

The **Northern Flicker** is most common in North America. It is particularly colourful and a glutton for

CAMPEPHILUS
PRINCIPALIS
LESSER SPOTTED
WOODPECKER

DENDROCOPUS MAJOR
GREATER SPOTTED
WOODPECKER

MELANERPES
ERYTHROCEPHALUS
RED-HEADED
WOODPECKER

COLAPTES AURATUS
NORTHERN FLICKER

PICUMNUS
MINUTISSIMUS
GUIAMAN PICULET

DRYCOPUS MARTIUS
BLACK WOODPECKER

PICUS PUNICEUS
GREEN WOODPECKER

ants, which it catches by extending its long, moist tongue into the ants' nest.

With its beautiful plumage, the **Green Woodpecker** looks particularly splendid as it rises up in flight.

The **Lesser Spotted Woodpecker** from North America is about 50 cm long and catches insects under the bark of old trees. The killing of these birds has led to their near extinction.

The **Guiaman Piculet** belongs to the family of small woodpeckers and lives in Asia.

The **Red-Headed Woodpecker** is easily recognized by its bright red hood. It lives in Central America.

The **Black Woodpecker** lays its eggs in the cavities of conifer trees.

The **Greater Spotted Woodpecker** lives in woodland, forests and sometimes parks. Its repeated pecking in the bark of tree trunks stuns the insects and the grubs on which it feeds, but it is believed that this is also a way of communication between the sexes.

BLACKCAP

The Blackcap belongs to the order of Passeriformes and the family of Muscicapidae which has over 1500 species with particular similarities. They all have a rather dull brown or grey plumage, sometimes with black, green or red. But, although the plumage of these birds may not be very attractive, their melodious song puts

Number of eggs: 4-6, each about 1.5 g	
Weight of adult: 15-25 g	
Length: 14 cm	
Wingspan: 23 cm	

them among the best songbirds in all the world. The variation of tone and the unending modulation of their song repertoire are extraordinary; each species has an exclusive song and many species are able to recognize the song of their own kind.

The Blackcap is found mostly in Europe. The male has the top of its head clearly defined in black. As with all

SYLVIA ATRICAPILLA
BLACKCAP

Muscicapidae, the Blackcap carries out a very private life in dense woodland or among thick hedges. It does not like to be seen and prefers the quiet, hiding itself among the greenery. At mating time, it builds its nest among honeysuckle or tufts of evergreen trees. Some species of blackcap stay in one place, others prefer to migrate at the first signs of cold weather, when the insects on which it feeds become scarce, returning in spring time.

Did you know...

The **Wryneck** (see page 118) belongs to a family which is mostly non-migratory. However, this bird migrates from the Arctic to spend winter in Africa and southern Asia.

The **Brown Thrasher**, together with the other thirty species of Mimidae (mimics), lives in America. It has a remarkable ability to imitate the songs of other birds.

The **Lyrebird** gets its name from its spectacular tail in the form of a lyre. It lives in Australia. It is quite large and is an excellent mimic of other birds. However, its own song includes phrases which belong only to its species.

The **Cactus Wren** is the symbol of Arizona. It is a very small bird which

lives in desert regions. When it becomes too hot, it opens the beak to lower its internal temperature, breathing very quickly and keeping its wings away from its body.

The **Blue Shrike** uses its beak to skewer its prey.

The **Asian Fairy Bluebird** is one of the most beautiful birds in tropical Asia. It has a plumage of intense blue which makes it very noticeable in the jungle, where it lives and where it eats ripe fruit.

The **Skylark** is common in Europe. Its sweet song heralds the beginning of spring.

The **Pied Wagtail**, common in Europe, belongs to the family of Motacillidae, birds distinguished by their long tails and which move with an elegance, as if they are on tip-toes.

They eat insects which they find in open ground, sheltered by a stone or a bush, where it makes its nest.

The high number of species belonging to the order of Passeriformes includes the Common Sparrow, shown in the photograph. Each species has preferences regarding habitat and diet – and so, to avoid competition for the same places and the same food, they are scattered throughout almost every part of the world, except for the Antarctic.

CAMPYLORHYNEUS BRUNNEICAPULLUS
CACTUS WREN

TOXOSTOMA RUFUM
BROWN THRASHER

IRENA PUELLA
ASIAN FAIRY BLUEBIRD

MENURA NOVAEHOLLANDIAE
LYREBIRD

LEPTOPERUS MADAGASCARNUS
BLUE SHRIKE

MOTACILLA ALBA
PIED WAGTAIL

ALAUDA ARUENSIS
SKYLARK

MAGPIE

Lenght: 46 cm, of which 23 cm is the tail

Number of eggs: 5-9

Habitat: hills and wood plains, parks and marine areas

Food: insects, seeds and eggs

The Magpie has a slender body with black plumage with green-bronze splashes. Its abdomen and the tops of its wings are white.

Magpies live in small family units, sometimes with jackdaws and ravens.

Always ready for combat, the Magpie never hesitates to face predators. It flies with ease, but on the ground it walks heavily, preferring to stay still. It builds its dome-shaped nest with grass and stalks cemented together with mud and lined with dry grass. In April, the female lays between 5–9 white-blue or greenish eggs, sometimes speckled with brown, and for 18 days the female and the male take turns to sit on them. The Magpie eats insects, grain, nuts and the eggs of other birds. It is widespread throughout Europe, Asia, North America and North Africa. The Magpie is protected in central Europe.

JACKDAW

Length: 65-70 cm

Wingspan: 125-140 cm

Number of eggs: 4-8

Food: carrion and small fish, but also game birds

The Jackdaw (in photograph) is the largest member of the Corvidae family and is also among the most intelligent of birds. It has a massive head with a black beak, as large as 10 cm, strong legs and claws and a tail 25 cm long. The feathers are shiny black, with metallic blue and purple splashes. The legs and eyes are also black. Living in North America, northern Africa and throughout Europe, they are also found in the Alps and the Apennines and in the mountain areas of Sardinia and the islands of Tuscany.

The Jackdaw is distrustful and usually lives in the wild and far away from human beings, going to populated areas only when it is cold or hungry.

Jackdaws live in pairs or small groups, whilst the young prefer to be alone. They argue fiercely with companions at mating time and with most other species of birds. Together, male and female Jackdaws prepare large nests ready for blue-green eggs speckled with brown to be laid.

Did you know...

At daybreak throughout Europe and Asia, flocks of **Jackdaws** abandon their night-time homes to go to the fields in search of insects and larvae, grain, molluscs and birds' eggs. They often live together with ravens, and sometimes join with them in the search for food.

To protect itself against shortage of food, **Clark's Nutcracker** hides seeds, pines and nuts ready for the autumn. When the snow falls and covers its food store, this bird can still pick out the exact place where it is. It lives in the mountainous regions of North America.

The **Turquoise Jay**, 32 cm long, is most common in the mountainous regions of the Pacific coastline of the American continent. In Sri Lanka lives a similar bird, the Blue Magpie.

The **raven** is often regarded as a bird bringing bad luck, mostly because of its forbidding appearance and harsh voice.

Among the jays which spend more time on the ground, is the **Persian Ground Jay** which escapes from pursuers by running. It lives in the desert regions of Central Asia.

The **Jay** is often called the 'woodland guard' because at the arrival of a stranger, it alerts the other birds with its cries, so that they can flee from danger. It feeds on nuts, berries, fruit and the larvae of insects, but when rearing its young, it will also steal eggs from the nests of other birds to feed itself and its chicks.

The Jay is over 30 cm long, with purple-red plumage. It lives in all the temperate regions of Europe and Asia.

NUCIFRAGA COLUMBIANA
CLARK'S NUTCRACKER

CYANOLYCA TURCOSA
TURQUOISE JAY

CISSA ORNATA
CEYLON BLUE MAGPIE

PICA PICA
MAGPIE

CORVUS MONEDULA
JACKDAW

PODOCES PANDERI
PERSIAN GROUND JAY

CORVUS CORAX
RAVEN

GARRULUS GLANDARIUS
JAY

MAMMALS

COMMON CHARACTERISTICS

The main thing which distinguishes mammals from other animals is the ability of the female to carry her unborn young and then to feed them with her own milk from her mammary glands (teats). Another important feature is hair on the skin in most species.

EVOLUTION, DISTRIBUTION AND HABITAT

Mammals developed from reptiles - from therapsids, huge lizards which disappeared more than 200 million years ago. Today, mammals live successfully in many different surroundings – deserts, tropical forests, polar zones, oceans – due more than anything else to their ability to regulate their body temperature. Mammals are found in all continents and at all latitudes.

The long and complex development of mammals has altered their external appearance. The skin of a mammal may be covered by hair, fur, spines (as with the porcupine) bony shields and there are also some species with skins which are bare.

The African Elephant (Loxodonta Africana) is the largest mammal in the world. Its size and its weight (average 7 tonnes) is surpassed only by some species of Cetacea, such as the whale. One of the smallest mammal is the Common Shrew (Sorex Araneus) shown above, which weighs only a few grammes.

Mammals include exceptional runners, jumpers, climbers, swimmers and fliers, each one perfectly suited to various surroundings.

BEHAVIOUR

Mammals have a well-developed brain, with a good memory which can receive and select information and learn from it. This has given them an advantage over the rest of the Animal Kingdom, enabling them to adapt most easily to every type of environment.

FOOD

Mammals can be herbivore, carnivore or omnivore (able to eat almost any type of food). The teeth are modified according to the type of food which each mammal eats – well-developed canine teeth for carnivores, molars for herbivores and incisors for rodents.

So many different kinds

Together with birds, mammals represent the most highly developed class of vertebrates. Although they make up only a very small proportion of the Animal Kingdom (5%) mammals have become the masters of the Earth. The development of a nervous system, and especially the **brain**, has enabled them to increase their intelligence, and, as a result, their ability to survive and to rise above other species.

The first mammals were tiny shrews. These appeared on Earth around 200 million years ago at the start of the Mesozoic Era. Unlike their reptile ancestors, mammals were able to regulate their body temperature and to keep this at between 36° and 41°, whatever the external temperature. This phenomena is called homeothermy, or thermal regulation. The female mammal also has **mammary glands** which secrete milk to feed her young.

All mammals – except for the Monotremata such as the duck-billed platypus and the spiny anteater, which lay eggs – are viviparous, meaning that the young develop inside the body of the mother.

The body of a mammal is almost always covered with **hair** which keeps in the warmth and protects the body from the external elements of heat and the cold, water and wind. Some mammals, such as the Porcupine and the Hedgehog have bodies covered with spines; others, such as the Pangolin have scales; other skins are bare – that is, without hair, such as the whale. The skin of a mammal always has **sweat glands** to get rid of perspiration and dead skin cells and **sebaceous glands** to lubricate and protect the skin. Mammals are also distinguished by their exceptionally well-developed senses, which are modified for the life which a mammal leads. One example of this is the acute hearing of bats, the only mammals which can really fly and which find their way by hearing the echo produced by their own cries. Due to their ability to adapt, mammals can live on the land, in the water or fly in the air. There are mammals of all shapes and all sizes.

PHYLUM	SUB-PHYLUM	CLASS	ORDER	SUB-ORDER	SPECIES
CHORDATA	Vertebrates	Mammals	Monotremata		Duck-Billed Platypus
			Marsupialia		kangaroo
			Insectivora		Mole, Fieldmouse
			Chiroptera		bat
			Edentata		sloth
			Pholidota		Pangolin
			Lagomorpha		rabbit
			Rodentia		squirrel, beaver
			Carnivora	Fissipedia	wolf, bear
				Pinnipedia	seal
			Cetacei	Odontoceti	dolphin
				Mysticetes	whale
			Proboscidata		elephant
			Sirenidia		Dugong, Manatee
			Hyracoidea		Hyrax
			Artiodatyl		pig, camel
			Perissodatyl		horse
			Primates	Proscimii	lemur
				Antropoidea	Baboon, Gorilla

DUCK-BILLED PLATYPUS

Reproduction:	oviparous
Number of eggs:	2
Length at birth:	2.5 cm
Length of adult:	30-45 cm
Length of tail:	10-15 cm

The Duck-Billed Platypus belongs to the order of Monotremata, strange animals with some characteristics of birds, some of mammals. The first example of the Duck-Billed Platypus was brought to Europe by a ship which had crossed the Indian Ocean at the end of the eighteenth century. Before then, it was thought that this extraordinary animal was only a fantasy of sailors becalmed in the seas of Asia. As the years passed, other examples were brought to Europe from Australia and finally, in 1884, a study carried out in Australia established that these animals, although mammals, laid eggs. The body of the Duck-Billed Platypus is 400 cm long, covered with thick fur, bristles and fine down. The tail, from 10–15 cm long, is similar to that of a beaver. The nose ends in a horny-type beak, large and flat like that of a duck, with teeth in the young, substituted by horny plates in adults. The front and back legs have webbed feet which enable the Duck-Billed Platypus to swim in the rivers and lakes of Australia and Tasmania where it lives. Underwater it hides its eyes and ears between folds in the skin, finding its way by using its sense of touch,

which is particularly well-developed in the beak. At night it goes hunting for earthworms, small crustaceans and molluscs which it eats in great quantities; during the day it shelters in its lair which it builds in banks sloping down to the water. The lair is in the form of a tunnel which opens out into a round space. When she is ready to lay her eggs, the female lines this space with wet leaves. Then she lays two eggs and rolls herself up around them, enclosing them completely. Ten days later, the young ones are born. Even though they are only 2.5 cm long, they immediately suck the milk which flows from the skin of their mother,

although she does not have proper mammary glands. The young leave the nest after about four months, when their bodies are completely developed and they can go in search of food on their own. These animals have an average life span of about 15 years. The male Duck-Billed Platypus has a hard spur connected to a poisonous gland near to each foot. It is among the few 'poisonous' mammals; its weapon is deadly for other animals, but 'only' causes severe pain to any human victim, and a swelling at the point where the spur pierced the skin.

ORNITHORHYNCHUS ANATINUS
DUCK-BILLED PLATYPUS

*TACHYGLOSSUS
ACULEATUS*
SPINY ANTEATER

SPINY ANTEATER

The Spiny Anteater, or Echidna also belongs to the order of Monotremata. It has a body similar to a Porcupine, about 50 cm long, and completely covered with thick spines. The long nose forms a sort of hard, tube-like beak, with two nostrils at the very end. The mouth, which has a thin opening, has no teeth but the palate is covered with a hard substance which enables the Spiny Anteater to chew its food.

Reproduction: oviparo	
Number of eggs: 1	
Length at birth: 12 mm	
Length of adult: 35-53 cm	
Length of tail: 9 cm	

Its moist, threadlike tongue can project 20 centimetres outside its mouth and its thick, short legs have sharp claws which are ideal for breaking the nests of termites and ants.

There are two species of anteater but the best-known is the Long-Nosed Echidna (illustrated below) from Australia and New Guinea. This animal lives alone and in a variety of surroundings. It settles down without any problems, and although it only has poor vision, it can feel the slightest vibration of the ground. When it senses danger, it rapidly digs a tunnel and is completely buried within a few minutes. It only needs about nine minutes to disappear completely into its underground shelter. Unlike the Duck-Billed Platypus, it does not use this sort of tunnel as a permanent home, but prefers the lair of another animal. If the ground is too hard, and it does not have time to dig, it rolls itself into a ball, like a Hedgehog, anchoring itself to the ground with its claws.

When it needs to, it can also escape very quickly by lifting itself up on its hind legs and running along, hiding itself among the bushes. The Spiny Anteater mainly eats termites and ants which it catches with its long tongue, but in captivity it will also eat minced meat, milk, pieces of bread and almost anything it can get into its mouth. The female lays her egg in a stomach pouch which forms only during the time she carries her young. After about ten days after the egg is laid, the young Spiny Anteater is born, feeding on the milk which flows along the hairs in the stomach pouch of the mother. Here the baby remains for about eight weeks, by which time the young Spiny Anteater begins to sprout spines and reaches a length of 10 cm. At this point, it is hidden by the mother in a safe place, where she goes regularly to feed it.

At one year old, the Spiny Anteater reaches the size of an adult and is ready to mate.

The Spiny Anteater is very long-lived with an average life span of fifty years.

DASYURUS MACULATUS
SPOTTED-TAIL QUOLL

DIDELPHIS VIRGINIANA
VIRGINIA OPOSSUM

PERAMELES NASUTA
LONG-NOSED
BANDICOOT

THYLACINUS
CYNOCEPHALUS
MARSUPIAL WOLF

SARCOPHILUS HARRISI
TASMANIAN DEVIL

ANTECHINUS FLAVIPES
YELLOW-FOOTED
ANTECHINUS
(marsupial mouse)

MYRMECOBIUS FASCIATUS
NUMBAT

NOTORYCTES
MARSUPIAL MOLE

Díd you know...

The **Long-Nosed Bandicoot** is a marsupial of average size, from 21 to 43 cm in length, which lives in Australia, Tasmania and New Guinea. It is similar to a kangaroo, and as large as a badger. The hind legs are longer than the front legs, the nose is very long, the ears are pointed and it has a bristly skin. It feeds on insects and small animals, as well as bulbs and roots.

The **Spotted-Tail Quoll** is sometimes called the tiger cat. It lives in woodland regions and in the mountains along the southern coasts of Tasmania, Australia and New Guinea. It moves as lightly as a cat, and goes hunting for reptiles, birds and rabbits. Sometimes it will even attack small kangaroos.

When the young **marsupial** is born, the mother guides it into a stomach pouch called a 'marsupium'. Here, the baby completes its development.

The **Marsupial Wolf** is also called the 'Tasmanian Tiger' because of the stripes on its back. It is regarded as the largest predator of all marsupials. It looks very much like a dog, with a

TASMANIAN DEVIL

At birth:	blind, without fur, 12 mm long
Incubation:	in marsupium
Number of young:	2-4
Length of adult:	about 50 cm
Length of tail:	23-30 cm
Weight of adult:	4.5-9 kg

The Tasmanian Devil is one of the largest marsupials, belonging to the family of Dasyuridae – animals which are very active and bad-tempered. In the past it was widespread throughout Australia, but now it survives only in Tasmania. It is a strong carnivore which looks rather like a small bear. Its favourite places are remote, rocky places where it can live a secluded existence. During the day it seeks shelter in caves or cavities in rocks, or in shallow lairs which it digs among the roots of trees. It comes out at night to go hunting for reptiles, small mammals and fish. It dives fearlessly into water and also swims underwater to shelter among the tufts of aquatic plants.

The Tasmanian Devil is a poor climber, but it will still go up the trunks of trees to capture a sleeping bird. But it is very quick at running. The name 'devil' is because it is always ready for a fight. But when a Tasmanian Devil is adopted as a baby and brought up with care, it becomes docile and affectionate towards its owner. It reproduces in April and the young are born towards the end of May. They soon find the marsupium where they stay attached to the mammary glands of the mother, feeding on her milk for about 15 weeks.

OPOSSUM

At birth:	blind, without fur
Incubation:	in marsupium
Number of young:	10-20
Length of adult:	60 cm
Length of tail:	30 cm
Weight:	6-7 kg

The Opossum is a marsupial of the Didelphidae family, all of which live in the south and in part of the north of the American continent. It has a pointed nose, large, bare ears, a thick coat and a tail covered with scales. During the day it stays at the bottom of its lair or in the hole of a tree, coming out only after sunset to go in search of food.

The Opossum is an omnivore, feeding on fruit, roots, birds, small mammals, shrimps and eggs. At the least sound, it will either flee and hide under a tree, or show its teeth and bite. But if the danger is great, it will fall down on its side and pretend to be dead. A female can give birth to up to 20 young at any one time. But, as she only has 13 mammary glands in her marsupium, the number of new-born which survive is limited.

---

body longer than 1 m and a tail 50 cm long. There is only one species which lives in Tasmania and this was once thought to be extinct. But unconfirmed sightings have raised hopes that other examples have survived.

*The **Numbat** comes from Australia. It is easily recognized by its zebra-like coat and sharply-pointed nose. It lives among the eucalyptus trees and in woodland, where it uses its long, thin tongue to catch ants and termites to eat. The Numbat moves its tongue at surprising speed, getting it into every corner of a hole.*

*The **Yellow-Footed Antechinus** (marsupial mouse) lives only in Australia. It is a small mammal, rather like a rat, nocturnal and very active and fierce. It climbs easily on the branches of trees and along rocky walls.*

*The **Marsupial Mole**, about 18 cm long, lives in the sandy regions of Australia, and in its appearance and habits is like European moles. Like them, the Marsupial Mole digs underground tunnels (but only a few centimetres deep) and feeds on insects and worms.*

GIANT KANGAROO

At birth: blind, without fur

Incubation: in marsupium

Number of young: 1 or 2 at the most

Weight of adult: 40-70 kg

Length of body: 110-160 cm

Length of tail: 80-110 cm

There are ten species of kangaroo, all belonging to the Macropodidae family. The Giant Kangaroo is found in Australia, Tasmania and New Guinea. It is practically a two-legged animal. From the moment it can move about, it uses only its well-developed hind legs. Its front legs are much shorter and the kangaroo uses these to grasp and to hold. Its long, muscular tail is used for sitting and to keep the body balanced as the kangaroo runs.

The Giant Kangaroo is sometimes called the Grey Kangaroo and it lives in Australia and Tasmania. It eats grass and can withstand drought, going up to two or three months without drinking. It is the largest species of kangaroo and can continue growing throughout its life. It excels in running on its two legs, with a speed which can reach an average of 45 km/h and up to 80 km/h over short distances. It can also clear a length of up to 10 m in one jump. After carrying her young for 30-40 days, the female gives birth to a young kangaroo only as big as a bean, and which finds the marsupium of the mother immediately. There it remains for about eight months, feeding on her milk.

KOALA

At birth: blind, without fur

Incubation: in marsupium (6 months)

Number of young: 1

Weight at birth: 5-6 g

Weight of adult: 14-15 kg

The Koala lives only in some small Australian forests of eucalyptus trees and is not present in any other part of the world.

At the beginning of the 1900s, millions of koalas populated the whole of Australia, but they were hunted to such an extent that the numbers of these charming, shy animals were drastically reduced within just a few years. The Koala is tree-dwelling and descends to the ground only to lick the ground to get the mineral salts which it needs or to move from one tree to another. It is an expert climber and the sharp claws at the end of its paws enable it to scale the highest, smoothest trunks.

It likes to be nocturnal and spends the day with its arms comfortably around a branch.

The Koala lives in groups of around 20 individuals which communicate with each other by loud cries. Its one source of food is the hardest, toughest leaves of a special type of eucalyptus. The rhythm of reproduction of these animals is very slow and this adds to the problems of safeguarding them. However, for many years, the Koala has been protected by the Australian Government, who have also re-introduced the Koala back into the regions where it once lived.

Did you know...

The **Common Wombat** lives in Australia and Tasmania. It is a herbivore marsupial, which looks rather like a rodent, with a squat body covered by bristly fur. It is peaceful and timid, with nocturnal habits. During the day it stays hidden in its lair which it digs in the ground with tunnels up to 30 m long.

The **Sugar Glider** is a small marsupial similar to a squirrel, which lives in Australia. There are three species similar to a flying squirrel, each with a membrane at either side of the body. This enables the Sugar Glider to glide, rather like using a parachute. It can jump like this from one tree to another, without losing height.

The **Tree Kangaroo** is a small kangaroo which lives among the branches of trees, where it can move about easily. In this animal, the two pair of limbs are almost the same

PHALANGER
MACULATUS
SPOTTED CUSCUS

PHASCOLOMIS URSINUS
COMMON WOMBAT

DENDROLAGUS
BENETTIANUS
BENNETTS TREE
KANGAROO

PETROGALE
XANTHOPUS
YELLOW-FOOTED
ROCK WALLABY

PETAURUS BREVICEPS
SUGAR GLIDER

MACROPUS MAJOR
GIANT KANGAROO

PHASCOLARCTOS
CINEREUS
KOALA

length. There are seven similar known species, living in the green forests of Australia and New Guinea.

The **Yellow-Footed Rock Wallaby** belongs to the same family as the kangaroo. Its tail is almost as long as its body, up to 70 cm, and it acts a counterweight as the wallaby jumps and climbs in the rocky regions of Australia. It is a nocturnal animal, which shelters during the day in caves situated in remote places.

The **Spotted Cuscus** is a marsupial with the joints of the claws well developed and perfect for gripping on trees. It has a thick fur, spotted in the male, and a long tail which it can also use for gripping. The Spotted Cuscus is a fine climber and spends its whole life in the trees of the Australian forests, without ever coming down to the ground. It moves slowly and only to hunt for food. For the rest of the time it stays still, sitting on a branch.

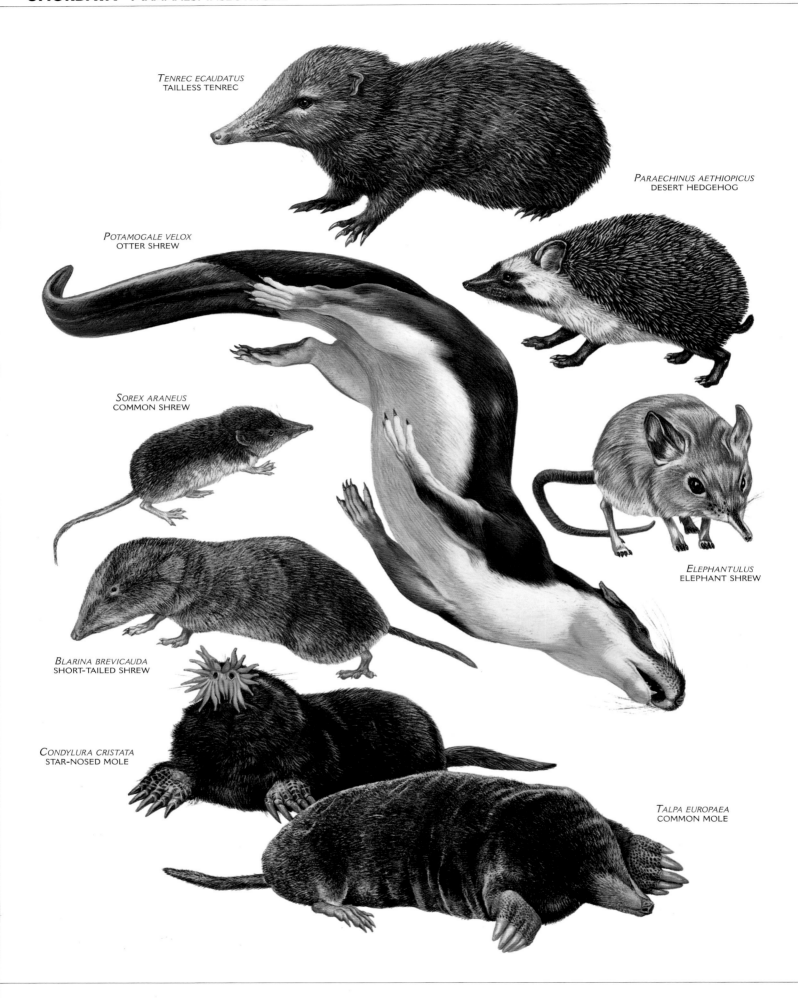

TENREC ECAUDATUS
TAILLESS TENREC

PARAECHINUS AETHIOPICUS
DESERT HEDGEHOG

POTAMOGALE VELOX
OTTER SHREW

SOREX ARANEUS
COMMON SHREW

ELEPHANTULUS
ELEPHANT SHREW

BLARINA BREVICAUDA
SHORT-TAILED SHREW

CONDYLURA CRISTATA
STAR-NOSED MOLE

TALPA EUROPAEA
COMMON MOLE

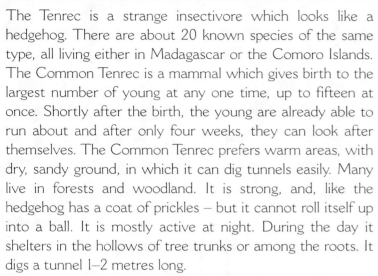

TENREC

Number of young: 12-15

Length of body: 27-39 cm

Length of tail: 1-1.6 cm

The Tenrec is a strange insectivore which looks like a hedgehog. There are about 20 known species of the same type, all living either in Madagascar or the Comoro Islands. The Common Tenrec is a mammal which gives birth to the largest number of young at any one time, up to fifteen at once. Shortly after the birth, the young are already able to run about and after only four weeks, they can look after themselves. The Common Tenrec prefers warm areas, with dry, sandy ground, in which it can dig tunnels easily. Many live in forests and woodland. It is strong, and, like the hedgehog has a coat of prickles – but it cannot roll itself up into a ball. It is mostly active at night. During the day it shelters in the hollows of tree trunks or among the roots. It digs a tunnel 1–2 metres long.

At the beginning of winter, the Tenrec retires into its underground lair and goes into hibernation, its breathing and its heart-rate slowing down. But before hibernation, the Tenrec eats as much as it can and accumulates reserves of fat. During spring and summer, it takes up its nocturnal hunting in search of insects, molluscs, various invertebrates and small reptiles.

COMMON SHREW

Number of young: 5-10

Length of body: 6-8 cm

Length of tail: 3-5 cm

Weight: 6-16 g

The Common Shrew lives mostly in hiding. In Europe there exist many species, all very similar and all belonging to the family of Soricidae. Among these is the Pygmy Shrew, the smallest of all mammals and just 3.5 cm in length.

The Common Shrew is a small animal with a long, sharp nose. It lives mostly in fields and damp areas; generally it hides under stones and bushes, in tunnels which it either digs itself or have already been dug by moles or mice. It is sometimes possible to find them up to about 1900 m in depth.

The main occupation of a Common Shrew is eating all that it can catch and carry in its sharp little teeth. Because it is such a small, warm-blooded animal, it has good reserves of energy. It is the most hungry of all predatory animals. Without food, it can be dying of hunger within just a few hours.

Insects are the most important prey for the Common Shrew, which is why it is so useful to farmers.

Did you know...

Insectivores have a special type of teeth to chew their diet of insects and small animals.

The **Desert Hedgehog** lives in the dry desert regions of Africa. By day it shelters in the warmth of its lair dug in the sandy ground. It can withstand up to ten weeks of total fasting.

The **Elephant Shrew** gets its name from its long nose. It lives in Africa. It has very long hind legs which enable it to move by jumping.

It is nocturnal; in the evening, it goes hunting for locusts and grass-hoppers, which it likes more than anything else.

The **Otter Shrew** likes the water and lives in the slow-flowing currents of the tropical African forests. It is a hungry hunter which searches for crustaceans, insects and fish, digging in the mud with its nose.

The **Mole** is common in Europe, 11–17 cm in length. It uses its broad front feet as tools for digging, living underground in long tunnels dug from soft earth. It has acute senses of hearing, smell and touch to

discover its prey – earthworms, insects, mice, amphibians and reptiles.

The saliva of the **Short-Tailed Shrew**, which lives in North America, contains a poison which acts on the nervous systems of the animals it bites; it can cause severe pain even to humans.

The **Star-Nosed Mole** is an insectivore from the eastern regions of North America. Its nose ends in a crown of 22 hairless appendages, which the animal moves about during its search for food or to move food during a meal.

FLYING FOX

The Flying Fox, or Fruit Bat, is a member of the order Chiroptera, or bats. It is a true giant among bats and native to Indonesia, India and Sri Lanka, where it eats the ripe fruits which abound in forest trees. Unlike other species of bat which live alone, the Flying Fox likes company. Flying Foxes gather in groups of one hundred individuals. By day they look for a place to sleep all together, and this is always a large tree generally without leaves. At twilight, they rise up in ranks to reach the trees which are rich in fruit. They are guided by their own echo-sounding system and by a highly developed sense of smell, which enables them to sense odours, even those present in tiny quantities.

The Flying Fox is also able to withstand strong winds, flying up to the top of trees or above water surfaces.

Number of young: 1

Weight of adult: 650-920 g

Wingspan: 120-170 cm

VAMPIRE BAT

Number of young: 1

Length: 6.5-10 cm

Weight: 25-90 g

Although it feeds only on blood, the Vampire Bat is not really like the popular image of this strange animal. In fact, it is a bat very much like the others. There are three species of Vampire Bat, all living in the tropical regions of South America. One of these is an expert in sucking the blood of chickens and other large birds, whilst the other two prefer the blood of large mammals and will also attack birds and cattle.

Vampire Bats pass the day hidden in the holes of trees or in caves and go in search of their victims when night falls. To find prey, they fly very near the ground, at a height of 1–3 m. When a Vampire Bat has identified a sleeping animal, it lands on the ground and draws near to capture it, moving in a semi-erect position, and jumping over obstacles like a frog. As soon as it nears its victim, it jumps on it and bites it on the neck or on the shoulder. The saliva of the Vampire Bat contains anti-clotting substances, and so the animal bleeds to death, even after the Vampire Bat has gone. Only rarely do Vampire Bats attack humans. It is considered to be a very dangerous animal, not only because it sucks out the blood of its victim, but also because its bite carries disease, including rabies, which is widespread in the areas where the Vampire Bat lives.

Did you know...

Bats are the only mammals really able to fly, because their front limbs have been transformed into wings. Bats have a membrane which extends from the 'finger' of the front claws to either end of its tail. To find its way around, most **bats** have a system based on the perception of sonar or echo. They make high-pitched squeaks at ultrasound – soundwaves not heard by the human ear. These soundwaves rebound off objects which they meet (such as walls, trees or prey) and the echo is then recaptured by the bat. Using this sonar system, it moves about safely and can hunt even in the dark.

The **Greater Bulldog Bat** feeds on the fish which it catches with a particular technique. It flies just above the surface of the water, and using the same sort of echo system as all bats, when it becomes aware of the presence of a fish, it grabs it suddenly with the claws on its foot. It lives in Mexico, northern Argentina and in the Antilles.

The **Small Mouse-Tailed Bat** lives in the dry places of Egypt, in the Middle East and in India. It uses its thin tail as an organ of touch.

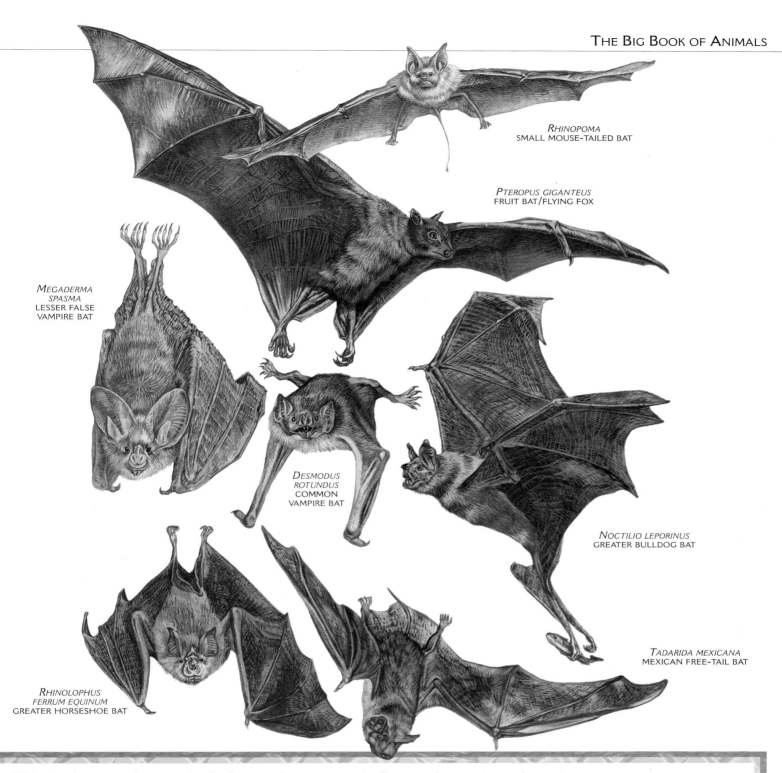

RHINOPOMA
SMALL MOUSE-TAILED BAT

PTEROPUS GIGANTEUS
FRUIT BAT/FLYING FOX

MEGADERMA SPASMA
LESSER FALSE VAMPIRE BAT

DESMODUS ROTUNDUS
COMMON VAMPIRE BAT

NOCTILIO LEPORINUS
GREATER BULLDOG BAT

TADARIDA MEXICANA
MEXICAN FREE-TAIL BAT

RHINOLOPHUS FERRUM EQUINUM
GREATER HORSESHOE BAT

This is almost as long as its body, which makes this bat easily recognized when it takes flight by squeezing into small holes.

The **Lesser False Vampire Bat** lives in South-East Asia. It can be recognized by its large ears and a long sort of bump on its nose. It lives in caves and is a carnivore.

The **Greater Horseshoe Bat** is quite common in Europe. It gets its strange name from its nose which is shaped like a horseshoe. It comes out of its hiding place late at night to go looking for insects, the only food it eats.

At the first sign of winter, the Greater Horseshoe Bat goes into hibernation and falls into a deep sleep. During hibernation, its heartbeat and breathing become slower. It wakes up from its hibernation in the spring.

The **Mexican Free-Tail Bat** belongs to a family of expert fliers which can also move quickly on the ground, thanks to their strong legs and wide feet.

The Mexican Free-Tail Bat lives in flocks of thousands of individuals, inside caves, old buildings and other hiding places, from where they give off a strong musky smell.

135

PANGOLIN

Number of young: 1

Length at birth: 20-30 cm for all species

Length of adult: 75-150 cm according to species

'Pangolin' is the common name for mammals belonging to the order Pholidota. It comes from the Malayan **peng goling** which means 'animal which wraps itself into a ball'. In fact, Pangolins can wrap their bodies completely around themselves. The body is not covered with hair, but with hard scales, one overlapping the other like the tiles on a roof.

There are seven species of Pangolin which are scattered around the hottest and most humid regions of Africa and Asia. Its home is the forest, where it can live on the ground or in the trees. Generally, the largest species live on the ground. The Giant Pangolin prefers to live in the rocky zones of the tropical regions of Africa, where it digs a deep lair under a stone. During the day it rests, going out in search of food at night. This is when it raids nearby savannahs to use the long talons at the end of its claws to tear apart the nests of termites, its favourite food. It can swallow a quantity equal to 2 litres. Once satisfied, it returns to its lair before dawn. The smallest species, such as the Tree Pangolin, prefer to live in trees, which they climb slowly, grasping the branches with their tails.

Pangolins have no teeth and catch termites and ants with their tongues, each one similar to a long sticky tape. In the largest Pangolins, the tongue can be 40 cm long and, when it is not being used, it is rolled up and withdrawn into a chest cavity.

Did you know...

Edentata are mammals which have few or no teeth at all. This order comprises three families to which belong anteaters, sloths and armadillos, all living in South-Central America.

The **Silky Anteater**, with a length of 40 cm and a thick tail, is the smallest in the group of anteaters. It spends its whole life up in the trees.

The **Giant Anteater** can reach 2 m in length, including the tail and 35 kg in weight. Its very long head is filled almost entirely by its long tongue, about 60 m long, which it can extend and retract very rapidly.

The **sloth** is an animal with a thick coat and very long limbs. It moves from one tree to another in tropical forests, with movements which seem to be very slow. It is strictly herbivore.

The **Two-Toed Sloth** spends the whole of its life hanging from branches. Like other species of sloths, it lives in symbiosis with a microscopic algae which settles itself in the skin of the sloth and gives it a greenish colour. This enables it to blend in perfectly with the leafy branches of trees.

The **Giant Armadillo** weighs around 60 kg and is longer than 1.5 m. It is a nocturnal animal and during the day it stays at the bottom of its lair which it digs in the ground.

The **Nine-Banded Armadillo** is the most common and widespread of around 15 species of armadillo.

The **Pink Fairy Armadillo** is the smallest armadillo with a maximum length of only 15 cm. Its back is covered with bony plates but its sides and stomach are covered with a thick coat of white fur. It lives underground, in a network of tunnels.

The **Collared Anteater**, from the same family as anteaters, spends its life in the branches of trees, searching for ants and termites. It has a long tail covered with scales.

CYCLOPES DIDACTYLUS
SILKY ANTEATER

BRADYPUS TRIDACTYLUS
PALE-THROATED THREE-TOED SLOTH

TAMANDUA TETRADACTYLA
COLLARED ANTEATER

CHOLEOPUS DIDACTYLUS
TWO-TOED SLOTH

PRIODONTES GIGANTEUS
GIANT ARMADILLO

DASYPUS NOVEMCINCTUS
NINE-BANDED ARMADILLO

CHLAMYPHORUS TRUNCATUS
PINK FAIRY ARMADILLO

MYRMECOPHAGA TRIDACTYLA
GIANT ANTEATER

Lepus timidus
MOUNTAIN HARE

summer coat

winter coat

Lepus californicus
BLACK-TAILED JACK RABBIT

Sylvilagus
floridanus
EASTERN COTTONTAIL

Ochotona alpina
ALPINE PIKA

Oryctolagus cuiculus
EUROPEAN WILD RABBIT

Lepus europaeus
BROWN HARE

JACK RABBIT

The Jack Rabbit belongs to the order of Lagomorpha. It is distinguished by the length of its ears, the extreme rapidity of its movements and its hind legs which are longer than the front. Also, unlike other rabbits, it gives birth to young which are already covered with fur, have open eyes, and which eat grass from their first day. The Jack Rabbit is common in dry regions covered with undergrowth in the south-east United States to Mexico. It can be most easily recognized by its ears with their large auricles (external part of the ear). As the Jack Rabbit developed, these changed in size and shape to enable the animal to regulate its body temperature in dry climates. The large surface of the auricle disperses excess heat more easily, and so avoids perspiration, which would lose precious water from the body. The Jack Rabbit can live without drinking, getting the water it needs from the fleshy blades of cactus. The Jack Rabbit is active by night, when the temperature is at its lowest. It eats grass, leaves of plants rich in sap and also cultivated plants, causing damage to crops. When the sun rises, it goes back into its lair, which is never very deep.

Teeth: 4 incisors in the jaw; no canine teeth

Rate of reproduction: 4 or more litters per year

Length of adult: 45 cm

Length of ears: 20 cm

ALPINE PIKA

Teeth: 4 incisors in the jaw; no canine teeth

Rate of reproduction: 2-3 litters per year

Length: 20-26 cm

Weight: 100-130 g

The Alpine Pika is a small mammal which, like the Jack Rabbit, belongs to the order of Lagomorpha. It has small ears but no tail. There are 14 species, two of which live in North America and the rest in central and north-east Asia. The Alpine Pika also lives at great heights and can be found in the Himalayas at over 5000 m, the highest altitude at which a mammal can survive. It is also sometimes called the 'whistling hare' because of the long whistles it gives as a signal to its companions. It lives in colonies or in large family groups.

The Alpine Pika builds its lair in woodland beneath roots of trees or digs tunnels in places sheltered by the mountainside. It does not hibernate. Instead, during the summer, it gathers large quantities of grass dried by the Sun and then takes this dried grass to store in its lair, ready to eat during the winter.

The Alpine Pika goes out within a radius of around 200 m from its lair to gather grass, twigs and pieces of bark. It does not fear the cold and goes out into the open even when the temperature descends to below -20°C.

Did you know...

Lagomorphs are distinguished from rodents because they have four incisor teeth instead of two, which grow continually.

The **Mountain Hare** changes the colour of its coat according to the season. In summer it has a red-brown or grey-brownish coat, whilst in winter its coat changes and becomes completely white, to blend in better with the snowy landscape.

The **Eastern Cottontail** is a North American rabbit which lives in humid zones. Unlike other species, it does not fear swampy ground, nor water, where it is a fine swimmer.

The **European Wild Rabbit** is widespread through most of Europe. There are also several species in Asia, Africa and America. It is a sociable animal which lives in small colonies which comprise numerous families. It spends half its life underground, where it digs an intricate series of deep tunnels as its lair. The female gives birth to 5–12 young up to six times a year.

The **Brown Hare** is also widespread in Europe, but it has also settled in America, New Zealand, Australia and the Far East.

GOPHER

Teeth: 2 large incisors, non canine teeth

Number of young: 1-3

length of body: 13-20 cm

Length of tail: 6-10 cm

Weight of adult: 300-400 g

The gopher is a rodent of the family of Geomyidae. There are only a few species, the most common of which is the Eastern Pocket Gopher of North America.

It has two external pouches on its cheeks which are fur-lined and which open instead of lips. These cheek pouches are used to carry both food and the material to line its nest. Thanks to special muscles, a gopher can turn the pouches inside out to empty them of everything inside. Then the cheek pouches go back to normal and the opening is closed by the skin of the face.

A gopher spends its life mostly in its lair, built in an intricate network of tunnels and holes. The male only leaves the lair to go in search of a female. He leaves her directly after mating.

Gophers are burrowing animals with long, strong claws. They are vegetarian and gnaw roots and bulbs.

SQUIRREL

Teeth: 2 large incisors, no canine teeth

Number of young: 3-7

Length of body: 20-28 cm

Length of tail: 14-24 cm

Weight of adult: 230-480 g

The Common Squirrel, or Red Squirrel, lives among the branches of trees in European woodland. It changes its coat in spring and in autumn; during the winter, its tawny coat becomes grey. It is active only during the day, jumping between the branches, where it builds its nest, called a drey. It uses its tail as a counterweight and a rudder when jumping. When it sleeps, the squirrel also uses its tail as a 'cover' and at mating time, as a signal, moving it in a certain way. As it moves, it is guided by hairs at the side of the body which it uses as organs of touch, and with which it can identify obstacles.

The squirrel is a sociable animal, living in small groups made up of different couples, each couple with their own territory. Its food is varied – seeds, berries, buds, mushrooms and toadstools, snails, insects and birds' eggs. It hides its food away in small holes.

Did you know...

The order of **Rodentia** is the largest of mammals and distinguished by their teeth which continue growing throughout their lives. These teeth are kept short by gnawing.

The **Flying Squirrel** from North America is a nocturnal animal. The wide folds in its skin, between its front and back legs at either side of its body, enable it to glide in the air for quite long distances.

The **Black Squirrel** is widespread in Java, Bali and Sumatra. It is a large animal, up to 50 cm long. It can be easily tamed and can live up to 16 years.

The **Desert Kangaroo Rat** is a typical inhabitant of arid surroundings and is nocturnal. It moves by making long jumps with its well-developed hind legs. It uses its tail as a rudder.

The **Marmot** is quite common in the Alps and is active only by day. It is a sociable mammal, which lives in large colonies. In autumn the whole community goes into deep tunnels which they have dug under the rocks. Here the Marmot remains in hibernation for the whole of the winter, its heart-beat and breathing slowing down.

The **Mountain Beaver** is different to the common beaver because of its shorter tail and long, strong claws with which it digs intricate networks of shallow tunnels. It lives in the mountainous regions of the Pacific coasts of North America.

The **Eastern Grey Squirrel** is widespread among oak trees and the woodlands of North America. It is very agile and can reach a speed of 90 km/h over short distances.

RATUFA BICOLOR
BLACK SQUIRREL

GEOMYS BURSARIUS
PLAINS POCKET GOPHER

GLAUCOMYS VOLANS
ASSAPAN
FLYING SQUIRREL

DIPODOMYS DESERTI
DESERT KANGAROO RAT

APLODONTIA RUFA
MOUNTAIN BEAVER

MARMOTA
MARMOTA
ALPINE MARMOT

SCIURUS CAROLINENSIS
EASTERN GREY SQUIRREL

CITELLUS SOUSLICUS
SOUSLIK

SCIURUS VULGARIS
RED SQUIRREL

JACULUS JACULUS
JERBOA

SICISTA BETULINA
NORTHERN BIRCH
MOUSE

MYCROMYS MINUTUS
HARVEST MOUSE

LEMNISCOMYS STRIATUS
STRIPED GRASS MOUSE

SPALAX LEUCODON
MOLE RAT

LEMMUS LEMMUS
LEMMING

GLIS GLIS
FAT DOORMOUSE

*MUSCARDINUS
AVELLANARIUS*
COMMON DOORMOUSE

Did you know...

The **Jerboa** is a small rodent of the African and Asian deserts. It is a nocturnal animal and its strong, well-developed hind legs enable it to jump like a kangaroo.

The **Northern Birch Mouse** is only 5–7 cm long, which makes it the smallest mouse in central Europe. Its hibernation is the longest of all mammals, lasting at least eight months.

The **Mole Rat** lives mainly in the region of the eastern European steppes and in western Asia. Its eyes have become shrunken due to the animal living totally in darkness, deep underground.

The **Lemming** lives in the Tundra of the Artic regions. It is active throughout the year and has many young. It lives in deep lairs which it digs for itself.

The **Fat Dormouse** lives in the woodlands of Europe. Its long hibernation lasts from October to April. Before going into hibernation, it gorges itself on seeds and fruit.

The **Harvest Mouse** is widespread throughout Europe and eastern Asia. It is about 5.5–7.5 cm long.

The **Striped Grass Mouse** from Africa gets its name because its coat is striped with brown and black. It builds a

DOLICHOTIS PATAGONA
MARA

HYSTRIX CRISTATA
AFRICAN PORCUPINE

CTENOMYS
PERUANUS
TUCO TUCO

HYDROCHOERUS
HYDROCHAERIS
CAPYBARA

CHINCHILLA LANIGER
CHINCHILLA

THRYONOMYS
SWINDERIANUS
CANE RAT

CAVIA APEREA
BRAZILIAN GUINEA PIG

CAVIA
GUINEA PIG

ball-shaped nest in the undergrowth.

The **Common Dormouse** is a rodent which can be found in the woodland and countryside areas of Europe. It lives in trees and builds its nest in bushes and among the branches of nut trees, eating the nuts.

The **Capybara** grows to a length of about 1.5 metres. It lives on the banks of the large rivers of South America.

In the **African Porcupine**, a great deal of its fur has been transformed into spines. It can be found in southern Europe, as well as Africa.

The **Tuco Tuco** is a South American rodent. It gets its name from the strange guttural sound that it makes.

In the wild, the **Chinchilla** lives in the highest regions of the Andes mountain chain. It is hunted for its valuable fur, and so it is a protected species.

The **Brazilian Guinea Pig** lives in the grassy expanses of South America.

The **Mara** lives in the pampas and the dry steppes of South America. It can survive without drinking, getting the water it needs from vegetable matter.

The **Guinea Pig** is descended from a wild species reared by the Incas of Peru.

The **Cane Rat** lives in Africa and grows to a length of 60 cm with a weight of 7 kg.

VULPES CORSAC
CORSAC FOX

ALOPEX LAGOPUS
ARCTIC FOX

CANIS LATRANS
COYOTE

VULPES VELOX
SWIFT FOX

VULPES PALLIDA
PALE FOX

VULPES VULPES
RED FOX

CANIS AUREUS
GOLDEN JACKAL

CANIS LUPUS
GREY WOLF

Did you know...

The **Corsac Fox** lives in Mongolia and Mancuria in Asia. It lives in small groups, eating rabbits, marmots and birds.

The **Arctic Fox** lives in Arctic regions, sometimes on ice floes. Its numbers have become drastically reduced, because of its valuable fur. It feeds on rodents, fish, birds and sometimes insects, as well as the remains of the prey of the Polar Bear.

The **coyote** is a distant relative of the wolf. It lives in Alaska, in Canada and throughout North America. Because it is very adaptable, it can often survive on the outskirts of big cities. It is an animal with a great sense of fun and sometimes it can be seen playing with small animals without doing them any harm.

The Swift Fox from North America also belongs to the same family as the Red Fox, as well as the **Pale Fox** which lives in Africa and in parts of

WOLF

Number of young: 4-7

Length: 1-1.50 m

Weight: 25-50 kg

Life span: 16 years

The Common Wolf is a carnivore which is widespread throughout Asia and in North America, but its numbers have been reduced and there are few examples in Europe.

It is one of the most well-known members of the family Canidae, as well as being one of the most intelligent mammals. It is able to adapt to different conditions both in climate and in the land and types of vegetation. All this has enabled the wolf to survive in many regions of the world – in the steppes, scrubland, forests and sometimes in farming areas, where, if it is hungry, it will kill sheep and chickens for food.

The wolf avoids human beings, not because it fears them, but because it prefers to live away from inhabited areas. Only when it is gripped by hunger will it venture towards urban areas in search of food.

The wolf is a sociable animal, which means it likes company. It lives in families or in small packs of two or three pairs with their young. An adult male wolf leads the group as pack leader, and he mates only with the most dominant female. The other members of the group are under the control of the leader.

RED FOX

Number of young: 3-8

Length: 60-70 cm

Weight: 6-10 kg

Life span: about 12 years

The Red Fox belongs to the family Vulpes. It is quite a common animal, living in the woods of Asia, North America and Europe. It is famous for its cunning and its craftiness, and, together with the wolf, is one of the most easily recognizable European carnivores.

The Red Fox can be small to medium size, with a long nose, big ears and bushy tail from 35–40 cm long and it continues to survive despite being the object of so much hunting. It prefers the quiet life, especially in woodland and in the country. It likes to stay in one place, and once it has chosen a home, it stays there and digs a lair in the form of a network of shallow tunnels. But sometimes, the Red Fox does not dig its own lair, but takes possession of a home belonging to another animal, such as a badger or a rabbit, after chasing away the rightful owner.

It lives in small family groups and goes out mostly at night-time. Its diet is made up of small rodents, fish, birds and reptiles. It has earned its dubious fame for theft and plundering because of its liking for poultry and small cattle.

Asia Minor.

Foxes have a 'language' which is very distinctive and communicate to each other by different sounds – loud cries during fights, whimpers, yelps, whines and growls between the mother and her cubs, cries of alarm and howls when they sense danger.

*When two **wolves** fight for the leadership of a pack, the one who loses lays down at the feet of the winner to avoid being torn to pieces. The winner, as a sign of victory, marks his territory with urine, and marks out his hunting territory in the same way.*

*The **Jackal** (in photograph) is a slender, agile canine. The **Golden Jackal** lives in northern Africa and all of southern Asia. It lives in all surroundings, from humid forests to arid zones.*

*MELURSUS
URSINUS*
SLOTH BEAR

*SELENARCTOS
THIBETANUS*
ASIATIC BLACK BEAR

*HELARCTOS
MALAYANUS*
SUN BEAR

TREMARCTOS ORNATUS
SPECTACLED BEAR

URSUS ARCTOS
GRIZZLY BEAR

*THALASSARCTOS
ORNATUS*
POLAR BEAR

*EUARCTOS
AMERICANUS*
AMERICAN BLACK
BEAR

Did you know...

All members of the Ursidae family have massive heads with small ears and a rather clumsy-looking large body with strong, solid legs and strong claws.

The **Spectacled Bear** is the only bear which lives in the Southern Hemisphere in the forests of the Andes, South America.

Here, this bear can reach altitudes of over 3000 m, but it will also descend down to the valleys as well as the moors and pasture areas on the valley bed. It prefers a vegetable diet and often makes a bed among the highest branches of a tree, where it spends the night.

The **Sun Bear** spends most of its time in trees, where it makes a bed of broken branches. It eats fruit, leaves, small

animals and especially ants, which are its favourite food. It destroys young palm trees by eating away the centre.

The **Sloth Bear** is different in many ways to other bears in the Ursidae family. Its coat is long and hairy and its lips are fleshy and extremely mobile. Its bottom lip sticks out, making it look rather like a monkey. It is found on the island of Sri Lanka and in southern

GRIZZLY BEAR

Number of cubs: 1-2

Length of body: 1.50-2.50 m

Weight of adult: 100-350 kg and over

Life span: 30-40 years

The Grizzly Bear is one of the most well-known mammals, found across a vast territory which extends from Europe to northern Asia and from Central to North America. Together with the Polar Bear, it is the largest carnivore in the world, but its size varies according to the region where it lives.

The Grizzly Bear is a solitary animal which lives only with its mate. It is a wanderer, not staying in one place for very long. Its diet is varied and includes vegetables, insects, fish, rodents and sometimes also larger prey such as reindeer and elks. Although it may look good-natured, the Grizzly Bear can change its mood very quickly, but only rarely is it a danger to humans.

When the weather begins to get cold, the Grizzly Bear takes shelter under a large rock or in a cave to spend the winter. It does not go into a proper hibernation, but passes the time mostly sleeping and using up the reserves of fat which it has put on during the summer. The female takes particular care in preparing the winter home ready for her cubs which are born towards the end of December or the beginning of January. She rears them with dedication and does not leave them for almost two years.

POLAR BEAR

Number of cubs: 1 or 2

Length of body: 2 m for the female; 2.5 m for the male

Weight of adult: 320-410 kg; sometimes up to 1 tonne

The habitat of the Polar Bear (in photograph) are the seas of the Arctic Circle covered with layers of floating ice. It has a slender neck and head, small ears and a round body. Its feet have short claws and the 'toes' are joined together with a membrane, which makes it easy for the Polar Bear to swim. The soles of the feet are also covered with fur to prevent it from slipping on the ice. The Polar Bear's coat is creamy-white, enabling it to blend in with its snowy surroundings, as well as being waterproof. The Polar Bear catches fish, sea birds and seals. Despite its massive shape, it can move lightly on the snow and, when it sees prey, it draws near slowly, taking its prey by surprise and killing it with its paw.

Mating takes place only in April. Only at this time the male lives with the female. At all other times it lives alone. In autumn when the female is expecting her cubs, she digs a lair out of the ice and snow ready for her babies when they are born towards the middle of December. The female, and in some cases also the male, pass the winter in one lair in the snow.

India, living in forests and among the trees in the savannahs and the plains. In summer the Sloth Bear goes in search of bee-hives, which it will destroy in order to eat the honey, the larvae and even the bees. It also sucks out termites from their nests.

The **Asian Black Bear** is sometimes called the Collared Bear, because of the long hairs which cover the front and back of its neck and shoulders in a distinctive 'Y' shaped pattern on its black coat. It lives in the forests of the Asiatic mountains at altitudes of between 1400–3300 m. An expert climber, the Asian Black Bear spends most of its time in the trees. During winter it goes lower down into the valleys where it can find food more easily. It eats berries, fruits, buds and leaves.

The **American Black Bear** is one of the most well-known animals of North America. It is a peaceful animal, eating mainly fruit and berries. It is this animal which inspired a toy-maker in New York to make a 'teddy bear' named after the President of the United States at the time, Theodore (or 'Teddy') Roosevelt. From then on, toy bears have always been called 'teddy bears'.

GIANT PANDA

Length of body: up to 1.5 m

Weight of adult: about 100 kg, the female; 120–140 kg, the male

Number of young: 1

The Giant Panda belongs to the family of Ailuridae and lives only in the mountains of western China. It looks rather like a bear, with a massive head, small, round ears and its black and white coat, thick and bristly. For a long time it has been the symbol of the International Association of the Directors of Zoos and from 1961 the emblem of the World Wildlife Fund (WWF).

Although the Giant Panda is regarded as a symbol of animal species in danger, it is at less risk than other animals. Because it lives within such a small, precise area, it can be well-protected by the measures which the Chinese government have put into place to prevent its extinction.

The diet of the Giant Panda consists of vegetable matter, especially bamboo shoots. Sometimes it will also eat rodents and other small animals. It lives mainly on the ground, climbing only rarely – although if it feels threatened, it can climb trees easily. The female rears her one cub in the hole of a tree or an underground lair.

The Giant Panda does not fear the cold and can live at altitudes of up to 3500 m.

COATI

Weight of adult: 3-6 kg and more in the male

Length of body: 75-135 cm (including tail)

Length of tail: 30-70 cm

Number of young: 2-6

The Coati is a small carnivore mammal belonging to the family Procyonidae – raccoons and their close relatives. It can be recognized by its long nose, shaped like the small proboscis of an insect, which it inserts in every hole, every nook and cranny, in its continuous search of something to eat. Its claws have long, strong talons which enable it to climb trees as well as burrowing in the ground. The Coati is an omnivore and eats invertebrates, fruits, birds and small rodents.

The Coati lives in groups of various sizes from 4 to 25 individuals, both male and female. At about two years old, the male leaves its group to lead a solitary life.

In the mating season, each adult male re-joins a group, chasing away all the other males at the time and marking out his territory with its body odours. A short time after the birth of the young, the male leaves the female and takes up his solitary life once again.

As well as being a very active animal, the Coati takes great care over its grooming, combing its coat with its talons and its teeth. It alternates its hunting and grooming for brief moments of rest lying down in the sunshine, whilst the young ones in the group play in the area.

Did you know...

The **Olingo** is a member of the Procyonidae family which lives in Peru and Bolivia as far as the tropical forests of Mexico. It is an animal with a slender body covered with long, soft grey-brown hair. It is nocturnal and lives alone or in pairs, spending most of its time at the top of trees and mainly eating fruit.

The **Red Panda** is an Ailuridae. It is a small raccoon-like mammal which lives in the bamboo forests in the Himalayas at altitudes of between 1800 m and 4000 m. It is a nocturnal animal. It is very elegant and has a thick, soft coat and tail. It lives a solitary life, feeding on the buds of bamboo, roots, pods and fruit.

The **Ringtail**, often called the Ringtail Cat, can be recognized by its long, thick tail with ringed markings in black fur.

It lives both in the rocky plains of North America and in the thick woodland and humid Central America. Strictly nocturnal, it is very quick and agile as it moves, going in search of small mammals, birds and eggs as well as reptiles and fruit.

BASSARICYON
OLINGO

PROCYON CANCRIVORUS
CRAB-EATING RACCOON

AILUROPODA
MELANOLEUCA
GIANT PANDA

POTUS FLAVUS
KINKAJOU

AILURUS FULGENS
RED PANDA

BASSARISCUS ASTUTUS
RINGTAIL

NASUA NASUA
COATI

PROCYON LOTOR
NORTHERN RACCOON

The **Crab-Eating Raccoon** lives in the tropical jungles of South America. It has a larger and thinner body than the Northern Raccoon, its fur is shorter and bristly and its tail is not so bushy. As well as living on the ground, it is also an excellent swimmer.

The **Kinkajou** is a graceful carnivore with a thick and very soft coat of a most beautiful golden colour. It also has a long prehensile tail by which it can hang or settle among the branches of trees in the tropical forests of South America where it lives.

The **Northern Raccoon** lives in the forests of North America and is recognized most of all by its strange habit of washing all its food in water – but not to make sure the food is clean, as many people think. In the wild, the Northern Raccoon does not wash anything and hunts aquatic animals, such as crustaceans, fish, amphibians, which it catches by putting an open claw into water and searching the depths. In captivity, not being able to catch aquatic prey, it gives vent to its instinct by washing whatever objects or food it can get hold of.

Hyaena hyaena
STRIPED HYENA

Proteles cristatus
AARDWOLF

Crocuta crocuta
SPOTTED HYENA

Did you know...

The similarity which the **Aardwolf** has with the Striped Hyena makes it look far more fierce than it actually is, especially when the long, stiff hairs on its back and neck stand on end to make it look even bigger. Generally, it will eat dead animals and birds, but when these are scarce, it may attack cattle. The Aardwolf can be found in South Africa, Tanzania and southern Egypt.

Hyenas are distinguished by having four toes on each foot. They are important animals, because they are scavengers, clearing up the remains of dead animals which other carnivores have left behind. The hyena's strong jaws and sharp teeth can even shatter bone, so they are able to clean carcasses of every last shred of flesh – although a hungry hyena will also attack and kill animals for food.

The **Spotted Hyena** (see photograph, right) is a formidable predator. It hunts by day as well as night, and making its strange-sounding call rather like a peal of

STRIPED HYENA

Weight: from 30 to 45 kg

Length of body: about 1 m

Number of young: 2-4

The Striped Hyena (in photograph) belongs to the family Hyaena, animals which have an appearance similar to the civet and the mongoose. Compared with its two cousins, the Aardwolf and the Spotted Hyena, the Striped Hyena is smaller in size, and it can be found over a wider area. The Spotted Hyena lives in Africa and Asia. Its colouring varies from region to region with shades of yellowish brown to sand. On the back, sides and legs it has black stripes. From its neck to the tail, it has a thick mane of hair which it can stand up straight as it likes. When the Striped Hyena is angry, it becomes a very impressive animal. At twilight and by night, it lives either alone or with a partner, more rarely in small packs. Whilst the Asiatic Striped Hyena feeds on herbivore animals which it captures during the night, the African species faces competition from other predators, such as the Spotted Hyena, and so prefers to eat the remains of carcasses, small prey and sometimes cattle.

Due to its rather timid nature and few bursts of aggression, the Striped Hyena poses no danger to humans. During the day, it lives mostly in a lair which it digs with its sharp claws and which is shaded by the courses of rivers, or in a natural lair such as the network of roots which spread out at the bottom of trees in the Savannah.

AARDWOLF

Weight of adult: 20-32 kg

Length of body: 55-80 cm

Number of young: 2-4

The Aardwolf is the only member of the family of Protelidae and is scattered from the Sudan to South Africa.

Its body structure is typical of hyenas, with a long nose, large, pointed ears and a coat which can vary in colour with black stripes, and a very bushy tail.

It is a mysterious animal, strictly nocturnal and never going out during the day. It spends the daylight hours hidden in the cleft of a rock or inside a lair which has been abandoned by another animal. However, the Aardwolf can also dig a lair for itself, but only in very soft earth.

Despite its appearance it is not a great predator; it does not have many teeth and its diet mainly consists of insects, preferably termites, which the Aardwolf catches in large quantities with its long, sticky tongue. When insects are scarce, the Aardwolf contents itself with small birds or lizards.

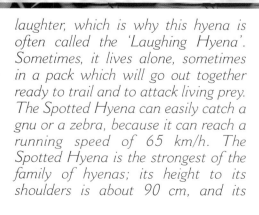

laughter, which is why this hyena is often called the 'Laughing Hyena'. Sometimes, it lives alone, sometimes in a pack which will go out together ready to trail and to attack living prey. The Spotted Hyena can easily catch a gnu or a zebra, because it can reach a running speed of 65 km/h. The Spotted Hyena is the strongest of the family of hyenas; its height to its shoulders is about 90 cm, and its weight averages 85 kg. Unlike the Brown and the Striped Hyena, the Spotted Hyena has a short tail and very small eyes. It lives south of the Tropic of Cancer in the desert zones and the African savannah, often going up into the mountains as well.

The Spotted Hyena is often the object of occult and superstition among many African tribes.

Many people believe that the bile of this animal is both poisonous and able to bring about unexpected death.

LION

The lion is always regarded as king of the African savannah. The male, unlike all members of the cat family, has a thick mane which surrounds his head and protects the neck from the claws of an opponent when it fights.

Of all members of the family Felidae, the lion is the one which likes company the most. It lives in groups of 6–30 individuals made up mostly of female lions and their young, with one or two adult males to protect the group and to ensure reproduction. Each group occupies a definite territory which covers a vast area of around 250 sq km. Its famous roar seems to serve the lion purely as a signal of its presence and to establish territorial limits.

The male lion is very lazy, mostly 'robbing' prey from other carnivores or prey caught by a lioness, who is always more

Weight at birth:	1200-1500 g
Weight of adult:	150-250 kg for males; 120-180 kg, females
Life span:	15-25 years
Number of cubs:	2-4; 5-6 in captivity

active and ready to attack than he is. The female lions are also excellent mothers, forming a very united community together to feed and to rear the young. When the cubs are about six months old, the females take them hunting. At the age of about three years, when they are able to mate, the young male lions leave their families in search of a group where they can be the leader. Whilst the female lions remain in a group for life, the males go away, substituted every two or three years by new arrivals which are stronger and more vigorous.

Did you know...

The **Snow Leopard** can be found among the isolated valleys of the high mountains of central Asia, up to altitudes of 4000 m. It is a medium size, solitary animal, about 1 m long and weighing from 25 to 50 kg and with many features of familiar cat behaviour, purring and eating the remains of food stuck between its claws.

The **Cheetah** is the fastest animal on earth and can reach a speed of 90–98 km/h. It has long legs, a slender body and a long tail. It lives in the African and Asian savannahs and goes hunting by day. With its sharp eyes, the Cheetah can pick out

an antelope at a considerable distance. It chases its prey in a short and extremely fast sprint of 300–400 m.

The **Puma** is a large solitary feline living in North and South America, from Alaska to the extreme end of Patagonia. It fears neither the heat nor the cold and finds itself perfectly at ease either among rocks or among the trees. It mostly eats deer but its diet can be very varied.

The **Clouded Leopard** is one of the most mysterious felines, because it is difficult to observe in its natural surroundings. It is a tree-dwelling animal and lives in the thickest parts of the Asian tropical jungle, leading a very secluded existence. It can be

distinguished from other members of the family by its upper canine teeth which are particularly long and sharp and which remind people of the prehistoric sabre-toothed tiger.

The **Leopard** is a most beautiful predator, elegant and agile. The Black Panther, as well as being wrongly regarded as more fierce, is not truly 'black'. Instead, it is no different to the ordinary male leopard except for the black colour of its coat.

The leopard lives in Africa and the hot regions of Asia, and adapts well to the plains in mountain regions. It is a carnivore which is easily pleased, eating any animal from a mouse to a porcupine, or a gazelle to a zebra.

Uncia uncia
IRBIS

Acinonyx jubatus
CHEETAH

Puma concolor
PUMA

*Neofelis
nebulosa*
CLOUDED
LEOPARD

Panthera pardus
LEOPARD

Panthera leo
LION

TIGER

If the lion is the king of the savannah, then the tiger can be regarded as the ruler of the Asian jungle. It is an extremely agile animal which can clear 5 or 6 m in one jump, leap over obstacles 2 m high and swim with great ability. It is even stronger than its cousin, the lion, and its solitary way of life has made it well-

Weight at birth:	800-1600 g
Weight of adult:	120-280 kg
Life-span:	20 years
Number of young:	usually 2

respected in the Animal Kingdom. The ancient Chinese worshipped the tiger as a creature with supernatural powers. But, despite all this, the tiger has had to overcome continued persecution and now some species are at risk of total extinction. In order to live, the tiger needs three things – an abundance of large wild life (young elephants, goats, wild boar), water and places where it can rest (natural caves or thick vegetation).

The cutting down of forests and expansion of farmland has dramatically reduced the natural home of the tiger. At one time it was present in almost the whole of Asia. Now it survives in some safari parks and in the mangrove forests in the delta of the River Ganges.

Each tiger has its own personal territory where it comes and goes and remains for years. Only the females consider this territory as a place for hunting, moving away solely to find a male to mate with. When they give birth, the female goes in search of shelter. At about eight weeks after the birth, the young begin to follow the mother hunting and they stay with her until they are two or three years old.

*Panthera
tigris*
TIGER

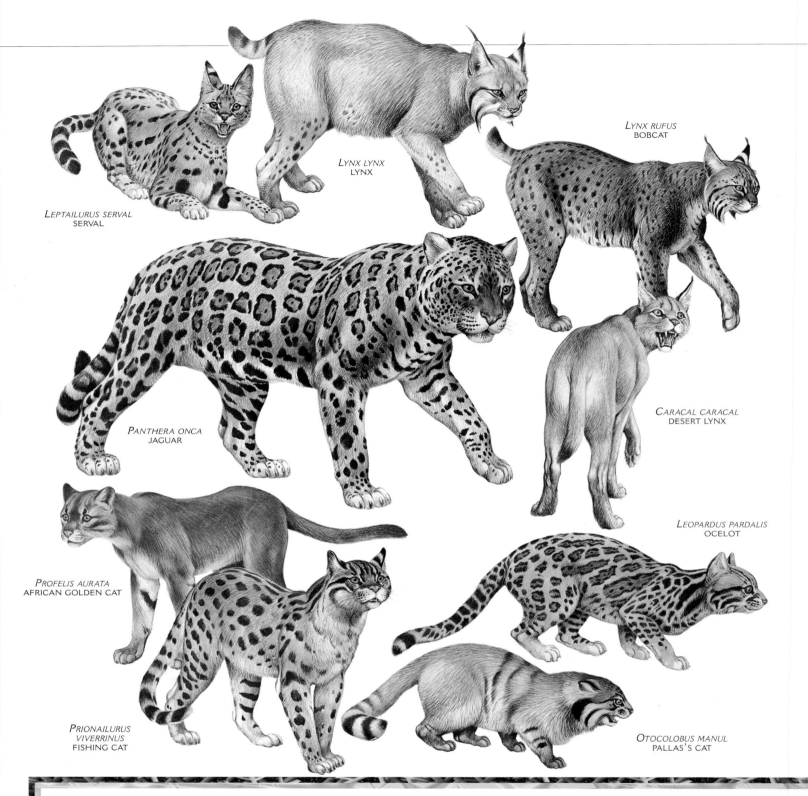

LEPTAILURUS SERVAL
SERVAL

LYNX LYNX
LYNX

LYNX RUFUS
BOBCAT

PANTHERA ONCA
JAGUAR

CARACAL CARACAL
DESERT LYNX

LEOPARDUS PARDALIS
OCELOT

PROFELIS AURATA
AFRICAN GOLDEN CAT

PRIONAILURUS
VIVERRINUS
FISHING CAT

OTOCOLOBUS MANUL
PALLAS'S CAT

Díd you know...

The **Serval** has very strong limbs, ideal for its life in the savannah and among the tall grasses. It has exceptional hearing and can detect the presence of rodents in their network of underground tunnels. Its diet consists of rodents, rabbits, young antelopes and birds.

The **Desert Lynx** likes hot, dry surroundings. It can be found mostly in open areas which have a lot of undergrowth and especially in the open desert regions of India and Pakistan. It is a solitary beast of the night. During the day, it shelters in the lair of a fox or a porcupine.

The **Bobcat** is quite common in the eastern United States. It particularly likes areas dotted with bushes and trees – although it lives in all surroundings, from the forest to the swampy expanses of Florida. It is an excellent hunter, and will kill rabbits and rodents.

The **Ocelot** is a well-known carnivore from South America. It is easily recognized by its beautiful coat, and cat-like ears. The Ocelot has been

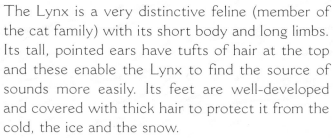

LYNX

Weight at birth: about 200 g

Weight of adult: 11-42 kg

Length of body: 70-110 cm

Number of young: 1-4

The Lynx is a very distinctive feline (member of the cat family) with its short body and long limbs. Its tall, pointed ears have tufts of hair at the top and these enable the Lynx to find the source of sounds more easily. Its feet are well-developed and covered with thick hair to protect it from the cold, the ice and the snow.

The coat of the Lynx can vary in colour, from grey to red, thinly spotted or with no spots at all. The Lynx can be found throughout northern Europe and most of North America, from the flat plains to the sea, and in mountain areas at altitudes of up to 3400 m. But the Lynx is mainly a solitary forest animal and its hunting territory can extend up to 20 sq km in any area – more, if wildlife is scarce. Most of all, the Lynx likes to catch deer, chamois and rabbits. However, it will not ignore smaller prey, which it kills and then swallows in one gulp.

The Lynx is very wary of humans, so it is very difficult for people to observe it for any length of time. It makes its lair in a well-protected place, in small caves or hollow trees. Both male and female leave their territory only to mate and then they return.

JAGUAR

Weight at birth: 700-980 g

Weigh of adult: 45-110 kg

Length of adult: 110-180 cm

Life-span: 22 years

Number of young: 1-4

The Jaguar is the largest feline in America. At one time it was even present in the south-west of the United States. It is still common in the province of Chaco in Argentina and in the Mato Grosso, Brazil. Elsewhere, it is becoming increasingly rare. For many years, the Jaguar has been killed for its precious fur and with the excuse that it attacks cattle, such as horses and sheep.

As well as the savannahs and rainforests, the Jaguar will also live in woodland areas where there is a plentiful supply of water and regions with tall grasses which give it shelter and with running water flowing through it. Its feeding routine is very varied, and it eats a great quantity of small animals – sheep, rodents, monkeys and sloths.

Although it looks rather like the leopard, the Jaguar is less agile and a poor climber, so it prefers to hunt on the ground. But it is an excellent hunter of fish, which it likes very much. It will sit on a rock patting and stroking the water, and, when a fish comes near, the Jaguar will stun it with a vicious blow of its paw at just the right time.

Like all large felines, the Jaguar is mostly nocturnal. It lives alone within its own territory and a male and female remain together only during the mating season.

known from the times of the ancient Aztecs. It has a peaceful nature and rarely attacks humans.

The **African Golden Cat** is a very rare animal which lives in the tropical forests of western Africa. It is larger than the domestic cat and gets its name from the golden colour of its magnificent coat.
It hunts monkeys, squirrels, porcupines and birds.

The **Fishing Cat** is quite widely scattered throughout tropical Asia, where it lives in the humid forests among the mangroves, along the banks of flowing waters and among reeds.
It is a fine climber, but prefers to remain on the ground. It eats molluscs and shrimps, as well as the fish which it catches – hence its name.

Pallas's Cat is a small feline which is broad and squat. It has a long tail which is ringed with black.
It lives in the rocky regions of central Asia and can be found at altitudes of up to 4000 m.
It can withstand the extremely cold climates of Siberia and Mongolia.

WALRUS

Number of young: 1

Length: 3-4.5 m

Length of body: 1.50-2.50 m

Food: invertebrates

Home: Arctic zones of Europe, Asia and North America

Life-span: 12 years in captivity

The Walrus is the giant of the Arctic ice floes, a member of the sub-order of Pinnipeds (aquatic mammals with fins). It is an impressive-looking animal with its long tusks – two long, upper teeth which hang down, and which are present both in the male and female. In the female, however, these tusks are shorter and not as strong. These great teeth are weapons which males sometimes use in fierce battles during the mating season, when two rivals fight for the same female. These tusks also enable the Walrus to search among the mud of the sea bed for the bivalve molluscs which hide there and which the Walrus likes to eat. These are made up mostly of clams which it swallows whole, including the shell. The shell is broken up in its stomach by 'stones' which effectively mince up its food.

Peaceful by nature, the Walrus lives in colonies of various size, sometimes up to a hundred individuals. It spends most of its time dozing lazily on the stony banks. On the ground, the Walrus moves slowly and not without effort, but it can swim at speeds of up to 24 km/h. To find food, the Walrus can go underwater to a depth of 50 m, remaining submerged for about 10 minutes. When the sea is calm, the Walrus can sleep in the water, keeping afloat thanks to two pockets filled with air under its throat, which it inflates like balloons. Strict laws have been put in place to protect the Walrus, because it is hunted for its tusks, its fat and its skin.

CALIFORNIA SEA LION

Weight of male: up to 1 tonne

Length of male: 3.5 m

Feeds on: fish and cephalopod molluscs

Home: Pacific (from Mexico to California)

Life-span: 23 years

The California Sea Lion (in photograph below) is often mistaken for a seal. The main difference is that its rear legs are joined together to make a sort of fin, although it does still have two feet. Its coat is red-brown when dry, black when wet. It can climb rocks and coral reefs, diving from considerable heights. In water, the California Sea Lion is a champion swimmer, achieving speeds of 17–40 km/h and swimming down to depths of up to 75 m. It can also jump up to 2 m high outside the water. On sand, it can run more quickly than a man, although its style is not so elegant as when it is swimming.

At mating-time approaches, the males wait in groups for the arrival of the females, and, after some fierce battles, one conquers a 'harem'. Each female has just one baby, after it develops inside her body for one year. There are many kinds of sea lion, but the California Sea Lion, which lives along the coast of the Pacific Ocean of the United States and Mexico, is the most well-known. Today it is a protected species, but in the nineteenth century it was extensively hunted for its fat. It is the Californian Sea Lion which has astounded spectators by its incredible talent for play. Its remarkable sense of balance makes it unique; it is the only animal that will play naturally with a ball or similar object.

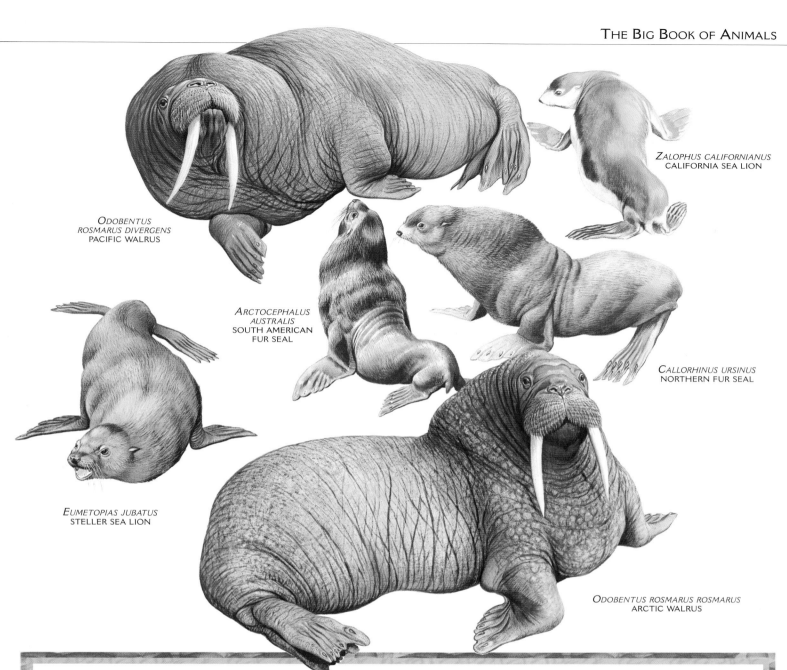

ODOBENTUS
ROSMARUS DIVERGENS
PACIFIC WALRUS

ZALOPHUS CALIFORNIANUS
CALIFORNIA SEA LION

ARCTOCEPHALUS
AUSTRALIS
SOUTH AMERICAN
FUR SEAL

CALLORHINUS URSINUS
NORTHERN FUR SEAL

EUMETOPIAS JUBATUS
STELLER SEA LION

ODOBENTUS ROSMARUS ROSMARUS
ARCTIC WALRUS

Did you know...

Pinnipeds belong to an order of carnivores which have many features in common with other carnivores – in particular, the shape of the skull and their teeth. For example, the long-shaped head of the sea lion is rather like that of a dog. Under the skin, a Pinniped has a considerable layer of fat to insulate the body in very cold waters, and to conserve energy.

Sea lions are members of the family **Otariidae** together with the **Eared Seal** and the **Fur Seal**, indicated by the fact that these animals all have large outer ears. This distinguishes them from other Pinnipeds which, in aquatic animals, are generally provided with some sticking-out structure, like pointed outer ears, which contrasts with the hydrodynamic shape of the body.

The male and female **Steller Sea Lion** live in the Bering Sea on the northern Pacific coast. At the time of reproduction they remain lazily in large groups along the rocky coastline.

In the nineteenth century, the **Northern Fur Seal** was almost completely exterminated by fur-trappers. This reduced numbers considerably; but, fortunately, the American Government have undertaken strict measures to protect the species and numbers have now risen.

The adult **Southern Fur Seal** which lives in the Antarctic, southern Africa and South America is brown-coloured with shades of pale yellow. However, the young seals have a darker back, which is almost black. Like other Pinnipeds, its body length is from 2–2.5 m.

HISTRIOPHOCA FASCIATA
RIBBON SEAL

HYDRURGA LEPTONYX
LEOPARD SEAL

MONACHUS MONACHUS
MEDITERRANEAN MONK SEAL

PHOCA VITULINA
HARBOR SEAL

MIROUNGA
ANGUSTIROSTRIS
ELEPHANT SEAL

PUSA HISPIDA
RINGED SEAL

CYSTOPHORA CRITATA
HOODED SEAL

Did you know...

The family of **Phocidae** is the largest family of Pinnipeds, and comprise animals with a hydrodynamic shape to the body, a very short neck and nostrils which become round during breathing. The short front legs have become flat and plate-like and the rear legs are joined in such a way that the soles of the feet face one another. Many species make a howl similar to that of a dog.

There are at least six million **Ringed Seals** – so many that there has been a census of those which have been studied – but there could be more. Even though they live only in Arctic waters, the Ringed Seal is one of the most common seals. The pups are born from the middle of March to the middle of April.

The **Hooded Seal** gets its name from the nasal cavity in adult males. When it is excited, the male closes its nostrils and this cavity swells with air until it becomes a 'crest' or 'hood' which extends from the point of its nose to

MEDITERRANEAN MONK SEAL

Weight: 250-400 kg

Length: 2 m, sometimes 3 m

Home: Sardinia, Dalmatian Coast (rarely)

The Mediterranean Monk Seal, with its grey-brown, thickish coat, is the only seal which spends its life in warm seas. Because of the development of tourism in the regions where it lives, it is in danger of extinction. It spends long periods of time in the sea, coming on to the beaches of uninhabited zones only at mating time. In the relatively brief time spent on land, its coat becomes covered with green algae which disappears only when the Monk Seal returns to shallow waters or basks in the sun. Today there are quite a few Monk Seals which live in the open seas. Those surviving spend a great deal of time near the coast, and more rarely in places which remain isolated. Also, the places and the surroundings where the Monk Seal reproduces have changed. Many have left the sandy beaches and begun to prefer grottos, and this has certainly helped them to survive. The Monk Seal eats mostly mackerel, but, because of intense fishing and pollution, shoals of these fish are much less numerous today than ten years ago. There is no doubt that the reduction in numbers of these seals is the result of the reduction in their prey.

ELEPHANT SEAL

Weight of male: 3500 kg

Length: 6.5 m

Feeds on: fish

Home: islands in the Southern Hemisphere and along the North American Pacific coast

Life-span: 18 years

The Elephant Seal is the most impressive of Pinnipeds. Only the White Rhinocerous and the elephant weigh more than the male Elephant Seal. Its adaptation to its aquatic life has not only profoundly changed its shape, it has also given it a perfect ease in water, whereas it can only move with incredible effort on land. But, despite the heaviness of its body, the Elephant Seal can move fast enough when it needs to.

The Elephant Seal spends a large part of the year living in groups and finding food. Its teeth, numerous but small, do not enable it to catch large prey, but it can go without food for up to 100 days. In the mating season, Elephant Seals gather together in their favourite places for reproduction – small, secluded islands where, after carrying their young for one year, the females give birth, one seal pup for each couple. Each male will mate with more than one female. So, at mating time, he gathers females around, fighting off rival males to conquer them.

At the end of the summer the Elephant Seals go back to the salty swamps where they moult and the hairs of the previous winter falls off and rots, giving off a horrible smell. There are two different sub-species of Elephant Seal – one lives in the Southern Hemisphere, the other along the eastern coasts of North America, on the eastern side of the Pacific Ocean.

---

behind its eyes for about 20 cm.

*The **Leopard Seal** is the only one in the order of Pinnipeds where the female is larger than the male. This seal is very greedy for penguins, hunting for them as it dives into the sea in an ambush style of attack. The oesophagus (food pipe) of this seal is very elastic, so that it can take in enormous quantities of food.*

*In the past **seals** were very important for some populations – for example, the Inuits or Eskimos, because they provided these people with meat, fat and bone, and so helped them to survive.*

*The **Harbor Seal**, with its shiny, dark coat covered with spots are known to follow fishing boats feeding on the scraps thrown overboard. Occasionally Harbor Seals will haul themselves out of the water on to the dock or even on to a boat. When hauled out, they often lie, with their heads and hind flippers elevated, in what is often referred to as the 'banana-like' position.*

Even though they are wary of humans they have a reputation of being relatively easy to tame.

DUGONG

Weight: 150-200 kg	
Length: up to 3 m	
Feeds on: algae and marine plants	

The Dugong belongs to the family of Sirenidae. It is a close relation of the sea cow, from which the Dugong can be distinguished by the tail fin divided into two parts called lobes.

This gentle animal is a member of a group of mammals which has survived despite a threat to its survival by humans. In the past, the Dugong was much more common and could be found as far south as Japan. Unfortunately, despite the laws made to protect them, secret hunting is still carried out in some countries, because the meat of the Dugong is very delicate, its fat is valuable and its teeth are valuable ivory.

The adult Dugong weighs about 150–200 kg and can grow to a length of up to 3 m. It has a large, round head, connected to the trunk by a very short neck. Its eyes are small and without eyelids, but with a membrane which keeps out dirt. The nostrils are in the shape of a half moon, and they are mobile, able to open and close as the Dugong wants. Its mouth is very large but it has few teeth, with horny plates to chew its food. Its two upper incisors have been transformed into tusks which can reach a length of 20–25 cm, overlapping the lower gums by 5–7 cm.

The Dugong is strictly herbivore, eating marine plants or algae. This is why it always stays near the coast, in water no deeper than 20 m. After a meal, it stays on the sea bed, coming up every so often to the surface to breathe. It breathes every 2–4 minutes, but it can stay immersed up to a quarter of an hour. Its top speed is about 18 km/h.

Mostly silent, this peaceful animal makes whistles and grunts only when it is particularly excited. But at mating time, the males become restless and engage in violent fights. The female Dugong carries her young for 11–12 months. The young are born under water and brought up to the surface immediately to breathe. They take milk from the female for about a year. The oldest Dugongs can live up to 70 years. Dugongs mostly stay in one place, living in pairs or in small family groups, but in the past they also lived in larger groups.

The adult Dugong has practically no enemies except humans, but the young, less than 1.5 m long, can be attacked by sharks and so they never go out alone without an adult. Dugongs live in the tropical waters of Africa, Asia, Australia and in the Indian Ocean. Although it has been known from ancient times, the Dugong has only been studied and described since the nineteenth century.

DUGONG DUGON
DUGONG

BALAENOPTERA PHYSALUS
FIN WHALE

WHALE

Weight:	60 tonnes
Length:	up to 25 m
Feeds on:	plankton

Whales belong to the order of Cetacea, a group of mammals which, at a certain time during their evolution, quite suddenly adapted to enable them to return to the sea. For a long time it was thought that whales might be 'fish which can spurt' but although they do have dorsal and pectoral fins and enormous tails, they are warm-blooded like all other mammals. Also, they breathe with lungs and the female carries her young inside her body. The easiest way to distinguish the whale from fish is to look at the tail. The tail of a mammal in the Cetacea order is horizontal and moves from the top to the bottom – whereas the tail of a fish is upright and moves from side to side. Some species of whale are long and slender, others short and squat; some have enormous dorsal fins, others have no fins at all. Some whales have teeth, others fangs, some with plates arranged like combs attached to the jaw and some which have rigid threads which filter the water and trap food inside. Female whales give birth under water, near to the surface, one baby a time which generally hides at the tail. To begin with, the baby whale is barely able to be pushed to the surface by its mother or an 'assistant whale' to take its first breath.

The Blue Whale is the largest of whales. This well-known whale with its long, hydrodynamic body, dark grey or silver or blue-black can grow up to 26 m. Its head is coloured the same on both sides. The lower lip, the oral cavity and some flanks on the right side are white, whilst those on the left are completely grey. This feature probably dates back to the time when the Blue Whale developed the habit of swimming on its side whilst eating. Another species is the Fin Whale, sometimes called the Finback Whale, so-called because of the ridge on its back and up to 80 or more grooves along its throat and chest to its tummy button.

Communication by whistles, and the intervals between one and another, from 2 to 5, each 10 to 20 seconds, are characteristic of the Fin Whale. Although other whales can remain under water for longer, the Fin Whale can stay immersed only from 5–15 minutes and can reach a depth of 230 m. It can swim rapidly up to 30 km/h and sometimes it will jump completely out of the water.

These jumps and spectacular dives are typical of all whales, but the reason for them is still a mystery; they could be a ritual for courting, a way of signalling something, a strategy to confuse fish or to scare away parasites, a demonstration of strength, or simply for fun.

Whales live in seas throughout the world but they are most common in the temperate waters of the Northern Hemisphere – it is quite common to see whales swimming in the Mediterranean. Some communities migrate south in winter and towards the north in summer, although their moving about is not so predictable as with other Cetacea. At one time they were more numerous, but today many species are still endangered by hunting.

TURSIOPS TRUNCATUS
BOTTLE-NOSED DOLPHIN

DOLPHIN

Weight: 200-370 kg

Length: up to 4 m

Food: fish

With 32 species, the family of dolphins is the largest and most varied of Cetacea. Among these, the examples with prominent beaks (upper jaws) are grouped under the heading of 'dolphins'. Those which can be seen most easily in European seas are the Bottle-Nosed Dolphin and the Stenidae or Long-Snouted Dolphin. The Bottle-Nosed Dolphin, grey-blue with a white stomach, seems always to be smiling and happy, due to the structure of its mouth and the round wrinkles which surround it. Weighing about 200–370 kg and because it is more or less always hungry, it spends a lot of its time hunting in the water and eating from 11–33 kg of fish every day. It is a friendly mammal and lives in groups of 10–20 individuals. These are the creatures we see jumping, swimming in circles, diving and coming to the surface, without, it seems, ever stopping, when we are lucky enough to see them at a distance.

The particular structure of the dolphin's skin gives very little resistance to water, which means that it can swim at incredible speed, by thrusting its nose out in front and propelling itself along by the vertical movements of its tail. It rides the waves on the 'wash' produced by whales as if 'surfing' with its body, just stroking the surface of the water with its tail and jumping out, reaching heights of up to several metres. A dolphin immerses itself for 3 or 4 minutes and it can swim together with sharks and sea turtles or other Cetacea. Members of the group can help each other and even play with fishermen, but only particular male individuals venture out towards any bathers.

Dolphins are found in all 'closed' seas – the Black Sea, the Red Sea, the Mediterranean and the Gulf of California. It seems that some communities migrate, whilst those near the coasts stay in the same zone for years. The dolphin, which is particularly active and curious, is one of the noisiest animals in the ocean; members of the same group 'speak' continually with each other by way of a complex language of cries and whistles.

Thanks to its ability to make sounds and ultrasounds, and to 'read' the sounds of the waves which, as they rebound off objects, echo back to the dolphin and become picked up by the bones of the skull, the dolphin can get a good idea of its surroundings, even in the dark. Many zoologists believe that this animal, with its highly-developed brain, is one of the most intelligent, if not the most intelligent, after humans.

KILLER WHALE

Weight: 2.5-9 tonnes

Length: 7 m

Food: carnivores

Whales belong to the largest species in the family of Delphinidae. The long body, weighing around 2.5–9 tonnes, the enormous dorsal fin of the male – which in individuals can reach up to 1.8 m – and the easily recognized shining black skin, with white splashes above the eyes and its sides and grey behind the dorsal fin, all make whales such as the Killer Whale easy to identify. The main difference between the two sexes is size – the female is about 1 m shorter than the male, which measures on average 7.3 m. The pectoral fins have a typical rounded shape and grow with age.

It is possible to see individual Killer Whales, but a family community, called a 'school', a 'pod' or a 'herd' is more usual, with between 5 to 20 individuals. Two or more schools can unite temporarily to form larger groups, which can comprise up to 150 individuals. The members of a 'school' stay close all their life to a larger 'clan' developing their own means of communication. Whales communicate by high cries and ultrasounds which have the power to scare away all the other marine mammals, except for the largest Cetacea which prefer to keep their distance.

The whale is a carnivore predator with the most varied diet of all Cetacea. It will eat squid, fish, birds, sea turtles, seals and dolphins and even attack animals as large as the Blue Whale. Often a 'school' will work together during a hunt, ignoring all other potential predators. But however hungry they are, whales will not attack humans and aggression within a group is rare. Curious and charming, the whale can travel at a speed of 55 km/h and display all the habits typical of Cetacea – jumping, flapping its fins on the water and slowly emerging until just its head is dry, gradually going back underwater soon after. At times, it is possible to catch sight of a whale rubbing itself on the sand.

It is very difficult to keep a whale in captivity, because it needs to eat a minimum of 50 kg of fresh fish every day, although it can be tamed easily and is as intelligent as other members of its family. The whale lives in most seas but is most commonly seen in cold waters. It prefers deep oceans, but it can also be found within deep bays, in inland seas and in estuaries. It can make its way easily through floating ice packs in search of prey. The whale does not undertake long migrations but stays generally in one area.

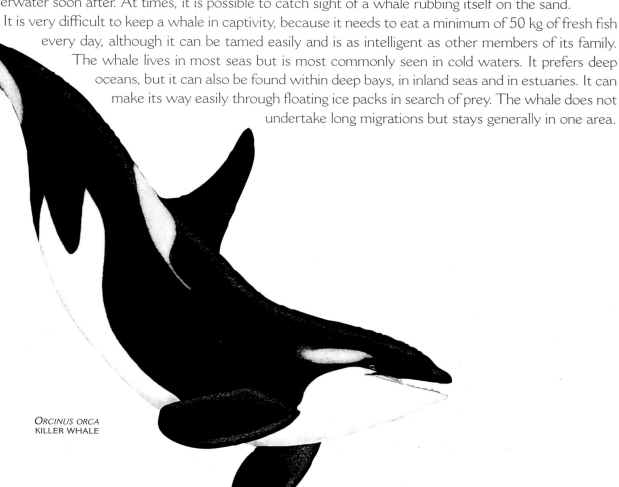

ORCINUS ORCA
KILLER WHALE

ELEPHANT

The land-dwelling mammal which grows to the largest size is the elephant, a member of the order of Proboscidata. In addition to the two famous species, the Indian Elephant and the African Elephant, a third has recently been added, which is the African Forest Elephant. Although they may look similar, the Indian and the African Elephant have quite a few differences. Their common features include a huge head, small eyes and large ears. However, the most noticeable feature is the trunk, which is the result of the elephant's nose fusing with the upper lip. The trunk is very versatile and most useful to the elephant, both as an organ for grasping and for touch, as well as eating, carrying water into its mouth and giving itself a shower. The elephant has a fine sense of hearing and smell, but its eyesight is poor.

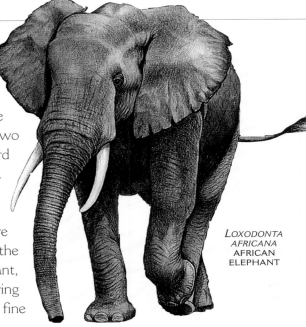

LOXODONTA AFRICANA **AFRICAN ELEPHANT**

Weight:	5 tonnes (Indian Elephant)
	7 tonnes (African Elephant)
Height:	3 m (Indian Elephant)
	3-4 m (African Elephant)
Habitat:	jungle (Indian Elephant)
	Savannah (African Elephant)

The growth of a baby elephant takes about 660 days. At one time, elephants in the wild were nomads, continuously wandering from place to place in order to find the large amounts of food that they need. Now, due to the occupation of vast territories by humans, they have been confined to smaller zones where they have become more stationary animals.

The skeleton of an Indian Elephant has 19 pairs of ribs and 33 caudal (back) vertebrae, whilst the African Elephant has 21 pairs of ribs and 26 caudal vertebrae. In the Indian Elephant the skull is flat at the front, whereas it is very curved in the African Elephant. In the Indian Elephant the legs are shorter than the African Elephant, which can be up to 3.40 m and weigh up to 100 kg. The Indian Elephant is a typical inhabitant of the jungle, avoiding open spaces and the grassy savannah. In mountain areas, it can reach altitudes of up to 3600 m and it lives in herds of 15–30 individuals, always guided by an old female. They prefer to browse juicy grasses and tender plants which grow in the humid undergrowth.

The African Elephant is the largest land-dwelling animal in the world. Only some Cetacea surpass it in weight and size. It weighs at least 7 tonnes, 2 tonnes more than the Indian Elephant, with a body length of about 7 m and a

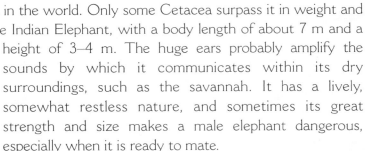

ELEPHAS MAXIMUS **INDIAN ELEPHANT**

height of 3–4 m. The huge ears probably amplify the sounds by which it communicates within its dry surroundings, such as the savannah. It has a lively, somewhat restless nature, and sometimes its great strength and size makes a male elephant dangerous, especially when it is ready to mate.

In the past, there were many examples of the African Elephant. Now, after many years of being hunted and the spread of farmland, resulting in a reduction of its habitat, the population of the African Elephant has diminished. However, many examples survive in reserves in eastern Africa.

HIPPOPOTAMUS AMPHIBIUS

HIPPOPOTAMUS

Weight: 2-3 tonnes

Length: 4.5 m

Habitat: Africa

The Hippopotamus belongs to the order of Artiodactyls and is closely related to pigs and wild boar. Its name means 'river horse' and it is a colossal 2–3 tonnes in weight and 4.5 m in length. It lives only in Africa, south of the Sahara Desert. It is a funny-looking animal, especially when it moves about on land. Its heavy, cylindrical body has short, column-like legs which seem to support it by a miracle.

Although it is not a great swimmer, the Hippopotamus spends most of its time semi-submerged in water, where it seems to be completely at ease. It has colonized the island of Zanzibar, reaching this location by swimming there. It prefers water which is no deeper than 1 metre; it rolls in mud to protect itself from parasites – in fact, rolling itself in mud also enables the Hippopotamus to get rid of them without too much effort.

The Hippopotamus is very important to the environment of a river, because every time it moves, it 'ploughs' the slime and so renews the river bed. Its adaptation to life in the water and on land is mostly due to a valve in its nostrils so that these close completely when it goes underwater. Its tail is almost 50 cm long, whilst the head is enormous, like a horse which could have been drawn by an animal cartoonist. The eyes and the ears are small, but the mouth has an impressive opening, with powerful tusks which can measure up to 60 cm. Its skin is 4 cm thick and without hair. The reddish colouring of the Hippopotamus is due to a red oily substance secreted by glands on its skin and which protects the skin when the Hippopotamus cannot bathe for any length of time.

Towards eight years of age, at the end of the dry season, the Hippopotamus mates in water, and, also in water, the female gives birth after 7–8 months. It feeds on land during the cool hours of sunset, when it separates from its group and goes to graze always in the same place, leaving ridges as a result of its continuous passages. The female stays with her young to defend them from predators – crocodiles, lions and leopards. In case of danger, both the male and female Hippopotamus will gallop towards the water. But when their grazing extends on to cultivated areas, they become a real nuisance to farmers. Uncontrolled hunting and people taking over the territory of the Hippopotamus has resulted in their extinction in some regions,. Today, the Hippopotamus is confined to restricted zones such as national parks, but in time it is hoped that they will be present once again at the delta of the River Nile and in the Middle East.

WILD CAMEL

Weight: 500-600 kg

Food: herbivore

Life-span: 45 years

Habitat: Asiatic deserts

The Wild Camel was identified and distinguished from the domestic camel only at the end of the nineteenth century, in the Gobi Desert, where it still lives today. It has two humps on its back and these are deposits of fat, each hump surmounted by a crest of hair. Some zoos maintain that the Wild Camel is a primitive form of Dromedary, which has just one hump and this continues to be a source of argument. The Wild Camel is also called 'ship of the desert'. At 2 m tall at the shoulder and with a body length of 3 m, it has a tail 50 cm long which ends in a tuft. It can be recognized by a hard area of skin on the knees and some growth on the rear legs. It is a friendly animal and is active by day. Unlike the Dromedary which withstands very hot temperatures, the Wild Camel withstands very well the severe cold and windy climates of the vast Asiatic deserts thanks to its very thick coat which re-grows in winter and insulates the body. During any length of time in which it cannot find water, it can lose up to 30% of its body weight without any ill effect, due to the reserves of liquid which it accumulates in more than 50 water cells in its stomach. This liquid does not depend on the water drunk by the Wild Camel, but is extracted from the vegetable matter which it eats. However, when it comes to an oasis or a rare well in the desert, the Wild Camel can drink up to 140 litres of water.

VICUNA

Height from the withers: 80 cm

Length: 1.5 m

Food: herbivore

Life-span: 20 years

Habitat: Peru, Argentina, Chile

The Vicuna is the smallest South American Camelidae. It is a close relative of the Llama and the Guanaco, but it has adapted even better than them to life in the high mountains. Not only is it never seen below altitudes of about 3500 m, it is not afraid of climbing to over 5000 m. It is one of the few mammals capable of running and jumping in the rarefied atmosphere at such heights. Like all members of the family Camelidae, it lives in groups of 6–12 individuals, among which is one adult male, females with their young and females under one year of age. Although it is careful and rather fussy, it spends a good deal of the day searching for food, browsing among the semi-dry grass of the Puna, the name given to the prairies of the Andes Mountains. It is not afraid of severe cold and so it does migrate away from its territory.

Each group occupies a determined area and they only move around within this.

From the time of the ancient Incas, the Vicuna has been hunted for its fine, silky-soft wool. Despite this type of hunting not being very widespread, it has still brought this animal to the brink of extinction. Fortunately, strict measures have now been taken to protect the Vicuna and to save it.

Did you know...

*Recent studies have put forward a theory that the domestic llama and the Alpaca are descendents of the **Wild Guanaco** which, because it had been tamed and cross-bred by the ancient Incas, became modified so that two new types of animal developed. The Alpaca is often reared because it is a source of abundant precious wool.*

*The **Guanaco** often succeeds in easily out-distancing a rider on horseback who is chasing it. Many times, humans have tried to tame it, but without success and so it is ridden less than the Vicuna. The Guanaco is found more to the south of the Southern Hemisphere and prefers the low hills and the plains of Patagonia. It has long legs and a proud bearing; it lives in groups of various size, from 10 to 30 individuals, but, in the past, before the species became decimated by hunters, it was possible to see herds consisting of some hundreds of individuals in the Argentine pampas.*

*The **Vicuna** and the **Alpaca** can cross-breed, generating fertile individuals.*

LAMA VICUGNA
VICUNA

LAMA GUANICOE
GUANACO

CAMELUS FERUS
WILD CAMEL

YOUNG GUANACO

The **Dromedary** (in photograph) has long eyelashes to protect its eyes from the sand. It can withstand the heat to amazing levels and can go without drinking for up to five days. But, if the temperature is not excessive and it can graze on green grass, it can last 10–15 days without a drink. Now the Dromedary exists only in the domesticated state.

The **Llama** (not illustrated) lives in the Andes mountains. It plays a very important part in the survival of the South American Indians.
They use the Llama as a beast of burden, as well as using its excrement for fuel. They also use its wool to make warm clothes, its hide for footwear and gloves and its fat for making candles.

MOOSE

Height at withers (shoulder): over 2 m

Weight: up to 800 kg

Food: herbivore

Life-span: 20 years

Habitat: humid forests, with lakes and expanses of mud

The Moose is the giant of the Cervidae family. It has an enormous head and an odd-shaped nose which gives it rather a curious appearance. It is a forest animal with a liking for humid areas with lots of lakes and expanses of mud which it can cross safely, thanks to the hooves which it can open wide. It is also a fine swimmer and does not hesitate to cross rivers and expanses of sea. It lives alone, but within small groups – although, in the depths of winter, it is possible to observe numerous Moose working together to dig among the snow to find a source of grass.

During the summer the Moose often grazes in ponds and small lakes, chewing the leaves of water-lilies and other aquatic plants. In winter, the Moose contents itself with worms and young woody shoots which it can reach, thanks to its remarkable height. No other member of the family of Cervidae has such impressive antlers as the male Moose, not only for their length, but also for their span. The female, on the other hand, has no antlers at all. The mating season is from September to the end of October. Mating is temporary and even the mother stays with her baby only until it can eat solid food. The Moose has few natural enemies, among which is the wolf which hunts in packs and so almost always succeeds in catching its prey.

REINDEER

Food: grass and especially lichen

Habitat: tundra

Habitat: Northern territories of Europe, Asia and America

The Reindeer which, in America is better known as the Caribou is a relation of goats and deer and belongs to the same family – but it is the only species in which the female has antlers the same as the male. The Reindeer has very long hooves and its two 'toes' can divide, enabling the animal to step safely, even on snow. As it walks, the Reindeer makes a strange noise which is like a rhythmic crackling. This sound is caused by the rubbing together of the two bones in each leg. The skin of its coat, very thick and warm, covers even the nostrils and the muzzle.

For the people who live in the same regions of the far north, the reindeer is a valuable animal. As well as using it as an animal for pulling sledges, the Lapps and the Inuits cure the skin, eat the meat, use the antlers to make tools and the milk of the female reindeer to make a traditional cheese. These nomad people have tamed reindeer, completing long seasonal migrations across the tundra.

Did you know...

The most recognizable feature of the family of Cervidae is that they have antlers made of bone. These are renewed every year, becoming more and more elaborate as they grow. The budding antlers of young reindeer are covered with a soft, velvety skin.

*The **Wapiti** is a huge American deer, related to the European Red Deer. In the language of the Shawnee Indians its name means 'white deer'. The Wapiti was once very numerous throughout North America, from Canada to the Mexican border, and tens of millions of individuals could be counted, until white settlers began killing them for their skins. As a result, they are still very rare and survive only in some protected areas. However, they can still be found in the Rocky Mountains, in northern Canada and in reserves in the United States.*

ALCES ALCES
MOOSE

CERVUS UNICOLOR
SAMBAR DEER

RANGIFER TARANDUS
WOODLAND REINDEER
OR CARIBOU

CERVUS CANADENSIS
WAPITI

The **Fallow Deer** and **Roe Deer** (not illustrated above) also belong to the family Cervidae. The Fallow Deer has a yellowish-red coat spotted with white in summer. The antlers of the Fallow Deer are flatter than those of other deer and paddle-shaped. The Roe Deer is very small and weighs only 25 kg.

The **Sambar Deer** is considered to be the largest, the most beautiful and the most majestic of all Asiatic deer.
There are many species all varying in size, but all living in forests areas, either alone or in small groups. The most common is the **Indian Sambar** which may be found in

India and throughout South-East Asia, and is recognized by a thick ruff of fur around its neck. It weighs up to 300 kg, whereas the **Malayan Sambar** is the smallest species, weighing only 50 kg. The Malayan Sambar can be found as far south as Japan and on islands nearby.

GIRAFFE

Height at withers (shoulders): 3 m	
Height at head: 6 m	
Weight: 250 kg	

The first giraffes appeared on Earth more than 25 million years ago. The fossilized skulls and bone fragments of giraffes which lived in prehistoric times have enabled experts to be quite certain that these were the ancestors of the giraffes we know today. The prehistoric giraffe did not have such a long neck, and their territory was far more vast, from the south of the Sahara Desert to southern Africa.

Like all mammals with spotted coats, the various species of giraffe display a great variation in colourings and patterns due to cross-breeding. The giraffe is the only mammal which cannot learn to swim, and so any expanses of water are a natural barrier.

Bearing this in mind, it is not surprising to find giraffe communities isolated one from the other, and often with even more different patterns and colourings.

The Chequered Giraffe is the most beautiful among the many species which exist. It is 3 m high at the withers, and, with its very long neck, measures up to 6 m from the top of its head. Add to this, its long legs and the withers so much higher than its pelvis, and this giraffe is unmistakeable. The head, with the long, pointed nose, has two horns rather like those of a camel. The tail is long and terminates in a tuft of hair. Its eyes are at a considerable height, which means that eyesight is the most important sense for the giraffe. A giraffe likes to eat the leaves of the Acacia tree, picking these directly from the branches at 2–6 m high, and by grasping them with its prehensile tongue.

In order to lower its head close enough to the ground to drink, the giraffe can stretch its rear legs very wide apart. Because of its height, the circulation of blood around the giraffe's body is like no other animal, with its heart and network of arteries and veins specially adapted so that the blood can reach its head when this is held high, and yet not rush to the head when this is lowered down.

The habitat of the giraffe is the savannah with high trees, which can be quite sparse. The male lives alone or in small groups. Females live in groups of females and young or groups of young.

GIRAFFA CAMELOPARDALIS GIRAFFE

ANTILOCAPRA AMERICANA
PRONGHORN ANTELOPE

PRONGHORN ANTELOPE

The Pronghorn Antelope is the only surviving species of a family which was scattered across northern America 20 million years ago and comprised many species. Before the arrival of the European settlers, who began to hunt them and to farm the land which had previously been their pastures, the Pronghorn Antelope was still abundant and their population was counted in millions. But by 1923, there were only 30,000. Today, strict measures taken to protect them have brought about an increase and the total population now totals around a half a million.

The male Pronghorn Antelope has a particular type of antler which provides a true link between actual horns and the antlers of Cervidae. Its antlers are divided into two parts and are made of a horny substance, which is renewed each year. Today, the Pronghorn Antelope may be found only in the western United States and, although it can live quite happily up to an altitude of 2000 m, it prefers the borders of the prairies, dry and semi-desert.

Weight: about 50-70 kg	
Length: 1.40 m	
Height at withers (shoulder): about 1 m	
Average speed: 60 km/h	

It is an animal which likes company and which lives in groups of various sizes, although sometimes the older males prefer to live alone.

The Pronghorn Antelope is very timid yet very curious. In the past, settlers attracted their attention by waving handkerchieves tied at the tops of long sticks, and any unwary antelope usually fell into a man-made trap.

The Pronghorn Antelope is the fastest antelope in America. It can gallop even over long distances and reach speeds of up to 80 km/h, as well as covering a length of 6 m in one jump. It eats all vegetable matter which grows on the plain, but needs very little water and can withstand drought for some weeks without drinking.

The Pronghorn Antelope is ready to mate at an age from 15 to 24 months. The female carries her young inside her body from 230–240 days, giving birth to just one baby, rarely two or three,

During the mating season, the males are territorial and the females are isolated afterwards. When the mating season is over, they return to their groups.

YAK

Weight: around 1000 kg

Height at withers (shoulder): more than 2 m

Length of body: 3 m

Number of young: 1

The Wild Yak is a bovine (family of oxen and cows) which has adapted perfectly to life in the high mountains, where the air is thinnest and the most rarefied. It lives in the desert steppes of northern Tibet in groups of 20 to 300 animals, composed mainly of females and their young. The males live alone or grouped together, separated from the rest of the Yaks. Because of the severe climate in which it lives, the Yak has to undertake seasonal migrations, moving to the high plains of up to 5000 m altitude during the summer, when the grass is green, and coming down into the valleys in autumn in search of pastures which are less covered in snow. Thanks to its thick and long-haired coat, which moults at the beginning of June, these animals can withstand temperatures less than -40°C – just like the Musk Ox of the Arctic Tundra. The mating season begins in September and lasts about two months. During this time, the adult males mate with females, after having seen off their rivals. After about nine months, in June, the female gives birth to one baby, which she raises within a year.

The Tibetans and the inhabitants of the western regions of China use the Yak for domestic purposes, by taking the youngest one they can find from the wild. A tamed Yak will then give milk and male and female Yaks become used as working animal for pulling carts and wagons.

AMERICAN BISON

Weight: 450-1350 kg

Height at withers (shoulder): 1.60-1.80 m

Length: 2-3.50 m

Number of young: 1

Life-span: 33 years

The American Bison is a wild bovine, a close relative of the European Bison. It is the most powerful mammal living in the great, grassy plains of North America. Bison are herbivore, eating leaves, shoots and tubers during summer, lichen, moss and dry grass during winter.

During the mating season, males and females gather together in very large groups and the males fight furiously among themselves. The American Bison is a dangerous animal. It will attack at great speed, soon identifying its rival and being led towards its prey by an acute sense of smell and hearing. In the past, the American Bison was much valued by the North American Indians. These people followed the seasonal moves of the herds because they were their means of sustenance, but killing only the number of bison which they needed to survive.

The arrival of European settlers and the progress of the railways towards the west, brought about a massive disappearance. Only a few hundred American Bison survived and these were brought to reserves for reproduction. Today, some ten thousand American Bison live in protected areas.

Did you know...

Bovines constitute a large family in the order of Artiodactyls and include all species of goat, sheep, chamois and oxen. Bovines are herbivore animals with horns and of varying size, from a tiny goat to a giant buffalo. They can be found all over the world, but there are none in their wild state in Australia and southern America.

The **African Buffalo** is truly colossal, without fear of any other animal and considered by hunters the most dangerous prey in the whole of Africa. Despite its mythical strength and its aggression, at heart the African Buffalo likes the quiet life and wants to be left in peace. It lives in herds, each one in the charge of an adult female, in the savannah near to running water, because it needs to drink once or twice every day.

The **Gayal** is a tamed species of wild cattle which is descended from another species, the Gaur. The Gayal can rarely be kept in cattle sheds, because in the wild it lives in groups in the jungle. If it ventures into nearby villages, it will return to the jungle each evening to

SYNCERUS CAFFER
AFRICAN BUFFALO

BOS FRONTALIS
GAYAL

BISON BISON
AMERICAN BISON

POEPHAGUS MUTUS
YAK

BOS JAVANICUS
BANTENG

ANOA
DEPRESSICORNIS
ANOA

renew the supply of natural salt which its body needs.

The **Banteng** is a large-size bovine with a slender body, living in various regions of South-East Asia. It is considered to be the most beautiful of all wild bovines. The male is very different to the female. The male has a dark coat with showy white 'stockings' and pointed horns curving inward.

The female is a beautiful red-brown colour and her antlers are less developed. The Banteng has a shy, timid nature and lives in groups, preferring the thickest parts of the jungle and gathering together in the forest clearings only towards the evening.

The **Anoa** is one of the most primitive of bovines and is found only on the island of Celebes. It is a small size buffalo, only 1.50 m long and with a weight of about 300 kg.

The Anoa leads a very secluded life, hidden in the thickest depths of the forests. Despite its small size, it is a very aggressive, dangerous animal, because of its pointed horns with which it is always ready to fight an enemy. Its diet includes grasses, ferns, saplings, palms, ginger and fallen fruit.

CONNOCHAETES GNU
WHITE -TAILED GNU

HIPPOTRAGUS NIGER
SABLE ANTELOPE

DAMALISCUS DORCAS
BONTEBOK

ADDAX
NASOMACULATUS
ADDAX

ALCELAPHUS
LICHTENSTEINI
LICHENSTEIN'S
HARTBEEST

ORYX LEUCORYX
ARABIAN ORYX

Did you know...

The **Sable Antelope** has a shining black coat which contrasts to the white of its stomach. It lives in the tree-lined savannah of South-East Africa. It needs to drink a lot of water, unlike other antelopes which can withstand thirst very well.

The **Addax** is from the desert regions of North Africa. It is one of the antelopes which are the most wild and difficult to catch, because its large hooves enable it to run at great speed across the sandy ground.

The **Bontebok** is a very elegant African antelope. Only a small number survive in special reserves.

The **Lichenstein's Hartebeest** prefers the forests and the bushy zones of South-East Africa.

The **Gerenuk**, or **Giraffe Antelope**, is one of the most unusual of African bovines, mostly because it can stand erect on its rear legs with its body vertical and its long neck quite straight. It finds this position very useful when it is tearing leaves and twigs from low-growing trees.

The **White-Tailed Gnu** is a rare African animal, with quite a comical appearance. It has a thick beard and tufts of short, erect hair on its nose and between its eyes.

The **Arabian Oryx** is a large antelope recognized mostly by its very pale coat and perfectly suited to the severe conditions of the Arabian and

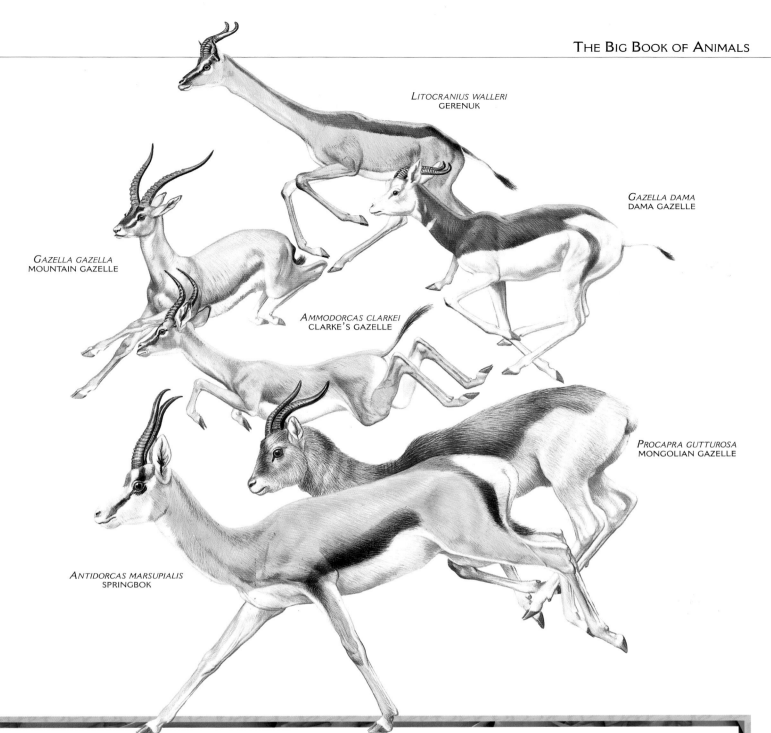

LITOCRANIUS WALLERI
GERENUK

GAZELLA DAMA
DAMA GAZELLE

GAZELLA GAZELLA
MOUNTAIN GAZELLE

AMMODORCAS CLARKEI
CLARKE'S GAZELLE

PROCAPRA GUTTUROSA
MONGOLIAN GAZELLE

ANTIDORCAS MARSUPIALIS
SPRINGBOK

African deserts. It is a wanderer, continuously going in search of food. It lives in small groups in the charge of an old female.

The **Mountain Gazelle** was once common from Arabia to India. Today only a very few examples survive.

The **Dama Gazelle** lives mainly in the dry zones at the far south of the Sahara Desert and is one of the most beautiful gazelles. It trots and runs lifting its front legs high and keeping its head erect, which is why it can

often be mistaken for a little horse from a distance.

The **Dibatag** or **Clarke's Gazelle** lives in the open territories of Somalia. Its legs and long, thin neck makes it similar in appearance to the Gerenuk. But it is smaller in size and its horns curve towards the front in the shape of a scythe.

The **Springbok** (in photograph) is the national emblem of South

Africa. It gets its name because of the many jumps which it makes very quickly and in succession, reaching heights of 3 m.

The **Mongolian Gazelle** belongs to a family which can be found in central Asia. The horns are present only in the males. During the mating season, the males also develop a bulge on the throat, similar to the crop of a cockerel.

ZEBRA

Weight:	300 kg
Height at withers (shoulder):	up to 150 cm
Lives in:	Africa

The Zebra belongs to the order of Perissodatyla, which comprises herbivore medium and large-size animals, distinguished by feet with an odd number of toes which are protected by a strong nail. In equines such as the horse and the zebra, only the third toe on each foot is developed as a hoof. Zebras are elegant animals living in the vast, open spaces, where they run rapidly at the trot and at the gallop, and live in groups. There are three different species of zebra – Grevy's Zebra, the Mountain Zebra and Burchell's Zebra. Grevy's Zebra is the largest, 140–160 cm at the withers. It lives alone in the scrublands of eastern Africa It has a large head, a very long nose, long ears which are large and round and its stripes are more narrow than the other species, except for its abdomen which is white. Its cry is similar to the braying of a donkey. Grevy's Zebras gather together in large mixed groups only at the time of their seasonal migration to find grasses to eat. At other times, the females usually keep apart from the males. Most often, these stay in groups of 6–30 and the males can be very aggressive towards each other, especially at mating time.

The Mountain Zebra lives in Namibia and some parts of South Africa. This is the smallest zebra, only 118–130 cm high

at the withers. It has pointed ears and its stripes are widest on its thighs, more narrow and crosswise on its back. It is a fine climber, most suited to life in mountainous desert regions. Today, both the Mountain Zebra and Grevy's Zebra are endangered species, which means that they are threatened with extinction. Only a very few examples of the Mountain Zebra live in protected zones in South Africa.

There are higher numbers of Burchell's Zebra, which live in the grasslands across eastern and much of southern Africa – hence the reason why this Zebra is sometimes called the 'Zebra of the Steppes'. Burchell's Zebra is recognized by its shorter ears, the long tuft of hair at the end of its tail and the broad stripes across its back which gather into a central dark stripe. It lives in small family groups, with one male at the head and several females with their foals.

EQUUS QUAGGA
BURCHELL'S ZEBRA or ZEBRA OF THE STEPPES

TAPIRUS INDICUS
MALAYAN TAPIR

TAPIR

Weight: up to 300 kg

Height at withers (shoulder): up to 120 cm

Number of young: 1

The Tapir belongs to the family Tapiridae, the least developed family of Perissodatyla. It is considered a 'living fossil' a survivor of a geological age many thousands of years ago, not only because Tapirs today are so much like those of 35–40 million years ago, but also because the areas where they live are very distant one from another. In America, there is Baird's Tapir (also called the Central American Tapir) which may be found from Mexico to Central America. From South America comes the Mountain Tapir which is smaller and lives at altitudes between 2000 m to over 4000 m in the Andes Mountains. Most widespread is the South American Lowland Tapir, from tropical America.

There are three Asian tapirs. The one most similar to the American tapirs is the Malayan Tapir. This is larger than its American relations, and is usually identified by its contrasting coat – black head, shoulders and legs, and white back and abdomen. Like all tapirs, it lives in the tropical and equatorial forest. To look at, it is something of a mixture between a pig, a horse and an elephant. Its strong, squat body moves in a zig-zag fashion when it walks slowly, whilst if it is fleeing, it goes into a fast gallop, hurling itself into thick vegetation.

The tapir has a long nose, mobile and retractable, like an elephant's trunk. But, unlike the elephant, the tapir does not use it for grasping and holding, but for touch and for smelling.

Tapirs prefer to live near flowing water and they are fine swimmers. The Malayan Tapir can also stay for long periods under water, walking on the sea bed. Another feature of tapirs, apart from the Mountain Tapir, is the very strong skin.

The food of the tapir is mainly leaves, shoots, small, tender twigs, but also fruit, grass and water plants. As it moves, the tapir always crosses the same paths and so 'builds' well-marked paths and tunnels through the thick vegetation. Tapirs live alone and they are not very friendly towards one another, except for the mating season. The female gives birth to just one baby at a time. When this is born, it is covered with stripes and little spots.

DICERORHINUS SUMATRENSIS
SUMATRAN RHINO

RHINOCEROS BICORNIS
INDIAN RHINOCEROS

DICEROS BICORNIS
BLACK RHINOCEROS

CERATOTHERIUM SIMUM
WHITE RHINOCEROS

Díd you know...

The family of Rhinocerotidae comprise animals of enormous size which usually have skin without hair and which are most easily recognized by a horn or horns on its muzzle. Its appearance is very heavy. The body is massive, supported by short legs terminating in three toes. The head is huge, with small eyes and wide, paddle-shaped outer ears.

The **Sumatran Rhinoceros** is the only rhinoceros which is partly covered with hair. It is sometimes called the 'hairy rhinoceros' and seems to be descended from an extinct hairy rhinoceros found preserved in the ice of Siberia. It is the smallest species of rhinoceros with a height to the withers which reaches only 1.50 m and an average weight of 600–700 kg. There may be still more examples to be found in Borneo, Myanmar (previously Burma), Thailand, Sumatra and in the Malayan peninsular, but it is difficult to observe them because they hide in the depths of the forests.

The horn of a **rhinoceros** is made

INDIAN RHINOCEROS

Weight: over 2000 kg

Length: 2-4 m

Height at withers (shoulder): 2 m

Life-span: about 47 years

Number of young: 1

The Indian Rhinoceros, also known as the Plated Rhinoceros is a survivor from the prehistoric era and is one of the largest mammals in the world. Its numbers have been reduced to about one thousand, because it was hunted for a long time for its one horn, which was thought to be a valuable tonic. The Indian Rhinoceros has a skin without any hair, covered by a sort of armour plating made of plates of very thick and rigid skin, jointed between each other by areas of thick, softer skin, which enable the plates to move. The Indian Rhinoceros usually lives alone or with one partner at the most and controls a vast territory. This is criss-crossed in all directions by paths battened down by the animal continually coming and going, and these passages sometimes forming types of tunnels through the vegetation. It lives among tall grasses in swampy zones, avoiding the thickest parts of the forest and it also likes to stay immersed in water. The Indian Rhinoceros is a herbivore, eating grass and young shoots which it takes to its mouth using its finger-like appendage on its upper lip. It is active by day and night, but when it senses the presence of a human being, it prefers to move about at night.

WHITE RHINOCEROS

Weight: 3 tonnes

Length of body: 3.50-5 m

Height at withers (shoulder): 1.60-2 m

Life-span: about 40 years

Number of young: 1

The African White Rhinoceros is the largest land-dwelling mammal, after the elephant. It lives in the African savannah. Its muzzle is long and flat and it has two horns, of which the front is the longer and more pointed. It has a highly developed sense of smell, whilst its eyesight and hearing are not so good. It is a sociable animal which likes company and lives in groups of up to 18 individuals, mostly females accompanied by their young. These stay with the mother up to three years old, and then go to find a mate to reproduce.

The day of the White Rhinoceros is influenced very much by weather conditions. If it is very hot, then it rests in shady areas, going out to browse in the evening. In the same way, it rests when there is rain and the temperature lowers. It spends a great deal of its time searching for grass to eat. Like all members of its family, it loves to stay immersed in mud. But, despite their huge size, rhinoceroses can move at a speed of about 45 km/h, even through thick undergrowth.

up keratin, a substance which is also found in its hair. Each horn rests on the hard ridge of the nasal bone. Sometimes the horns wear out, which is when they can often appear to be covered with hair.

The Black Rhinoceros is the only species of rhinoceros which has a reasonable population. It is also the most widespread of the rhinoceros family, living in central-southern Africa and the largest populations are in Tanzania, Mozambique and South Africa.

The habitat of the Black Rhinoceros is partly savannah, partly steppes and it can adapt to altitudes of up to 2000 m.

It has two horns, the first of which can reach a length of more than 50 cm. It is not very tall, about 1.50 m at the withers, whilst its weight can reach 2 tonnes. Its upper lip is particularly long and mobile and the Black Rhinoceros uses this as a sort of grasping finger and to carry leaves and the twigs of bushes and low-growing trees to its mouth.

A rhinoceros has poor sight, but well-developed hearing and a sense of smell as acute as that of a dog.

AYE-AYE

The Aye-Aye is a strange primate. It leads a nocturnal and private life in the remaining strips of forest in Madagascar, living in the holes of tree-trunks which it likes to keep tidy and comfortable for itself. Sometimes it makes a proper nest at the fork of a branch, with twigs and leaves. Since this mammal was first discovered, it has been endlessly discussed and argued about. At first, zoologists believed that the Aye-Aye was a species of squirrel, because its four scalpel-like incisor teeth are similar to those of a rodent. Also, its hands are very strange. The third finger is very thin and very long, compared to the other fingers, and it also has a solid claw which the Aye-Aye uses to extract larvae from the bark of trees. It eats mainly larvae and insects, which it finds simply by putting its head against a tree-trunk. As soon as it knows where its prey is, it quickly chews at the bark with its teeth and digs into the hole it has made with the claw of its third finger.

Length of body: 40 cm; with tail, 100 cm

Food: larvae, insects, dry and fresh fruit

Number of young: 1

Habitat: forest

Home: Madagascar

VERREAUX'S SIFAKA

Length: 95-150 cm including tail

Food: leaves, fruit and shoots

Number of young: 1

Habitat: forest

Home: Madagascar

Verreaux's Sifaka is a Prosimian, a member of a lower order of Primates. It lives only in Madagascar and two species are known – Verreaux's Sifaka and the Diademed Sifaka and each has developed differently according to the surroundings in which it lives - Verreaux's Sifaka lives in hot and humid zones and has a dark coat. The Diademed Sifaka lives in the dry, cold regions of Madagascar, and its coat is pale. It is a friendly animal which lives in groups of 6–10 individuals made up of two families. Like all daytime primates, the Sifaka is very fond of the Sun, and loses no opportunity to bask in the Sun on the branches of trees. It is only at these times that the Sifaka is still, usually chattering to itself. During the times when Sifakas are more active, they talk non-stop among themselves, making a sort of gurgling noise and short sounds. Thanks to a membrane which connects the front limbs to the bottom of its neck and at the trunk, the Sifaka can glide in the air from one branch to another. To gather up ripe fruit, it will also descend to the ground, where it moves by jumping on both feet and extending its long arms to keep its balance. Unlike other Prosimians, it rarely uses its hands to feed itself.

Did you know...

The term 'Primate' was coined by the famous naturalist Carolus Linnaeus as a sign of the Primates' superiority over all other animals. There are two orders of Primates - Prosimians, the lower class, and Anthropoid (man-like), the upper class.

Prosimians are the most ancient group of Primates. The transformation of legs and joints into flat claws have enabled them to perfect their grip and to become the dominant animals of all tree-dwellers. Almost all are nocturnal, with large eyes able to distinguish the minimum variations of intense daylight.

The **Weasel Lemur** is from Madagascar. The big toe of the hind leg has a long, curved nail which enables it to climb. It is covered by a woolly coat which is very thick and it has a short, pointed nose. Its body reaches a length of only 60 cm including the tail. Small and nervous, it is not too well-known because it lives by night.

Other lemurs are active by day. Among these is the **Black Lemur**, black in the male and red-brown in the female, and the **Ring-Tailed Lemur** with its tail ringed with black and white. These also live in Madagascar.

The **Lesser Mouse Lemur** and the **Fork-Marked Lemur** live by night and eat mainly insects. In the driest periods, which are also the most severe for them, they go into hibernation and survive by using up the fat which they have accumulated on their hind legs and in their tail.

PHANER FURCIFER
FORK-MARKED LEMUR

LEPILEMUR MUSTELINUS
WEASEL LEMUR

*PROPITHECUS
VERREAUXI*
VERREAUX'S SIFAKA

LEMUR CATTA
RING-TAILED
LEMUR

*MICROCEBUS
MURINUS*
LESSER MOUSE
LEMUR

LEMUR MACACO
BLACK LEMUR

*DAUBENTONIA
MADAGASCARIENSIS*
AYE-AYE

MACACA IRUS
CRAB-EATING MACAQUE

MACACA NEMESTRINA
PIG-TAILED MACAQUE

*MANDRILLO
LEUCOPHAEUS*
DRILL

*PAPIO
ANUBIS*
OLIVE BABOON

PAPIO HAMADRYAS
SACRED BABOON

CYNOPITHECUS NIGER
CELEBES BLACK APE
(CELEBES CRESTED MACAQUE)

MACACA SILENUS
LONG-TAILED
MACAQUE

*THEROPITHECUS
GELADA*
GELADA

Did you know...

Various species of **macaque** monkeys belong to the family Cercopithecidae, including the **Pig-Tailed Macaque** with its rather forbidding appearance. This monkey is found mostly in south-east Asia and on the islands of Sumatra and Borneo.

The **Crab-Eating Macaque** lives in forests, near rivers and on the coasts of the Sonda Islands, Malaya, Myanmar (formerly Burma) and southern Indo-China.

The **Celebes Crested Macaque** (also known as the **Celebes Black Ape**) is recognized by a vertical tuft of hair on its head. It lives on the island of Celebes.

The **Drill** lives in New Guinea. It spends almost all its life on the ground.

The agile **Long-Tailed Macaque** is regarded as the most handsome of all macaques. It lives in southern India and on the island of Sri Lanka.

Baboons and **Mandrills** are the largest macaques and these are distinguished by their powerful teeth with small tusks in place of normal canine teeth. Both live in the sub-Sahara area of Africa and in southern Arabia. Baboons and mandrills live in small communities — baboons in groups of males, females and young baboons, mandrills in a 'harem' of females

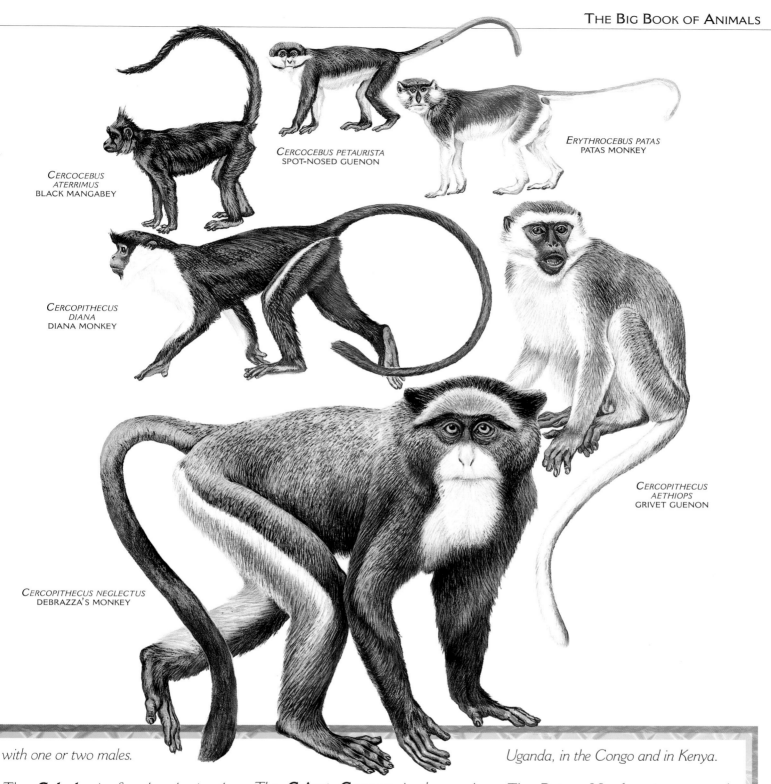

CERCOCEBUS
ATERRIMUS
BLACK MANGABEY

CERCOCEBUS PETAURISTA
SPOT-NOSED GUENON

ERYTHROCEBUS PATAS
PATAS MONKEY

CERCOPITHECUS
DIANA
DIANA MONKEY

CERCOPITHECUS
AETHIOPS
GRIVET GUENON

CERCOPITHECUS NEGLECTUS
DEBRAZZA'S MONKEY

with one or two males.

The **Gelada** is found only in the mountains of Ethiopia and Eritrea.

Monkeys belonging to the Cercopithecidae family are the most multi-coloured of all. They are sometimes called 'Old World Monkeys' because they come from Africa. There are about 100 species and almost all of them live in trees, within tribes of about ten individuals under the control of an elderly male.

The **Grivet Guenon** is the species which is the most widely scattered.

Like the **Spot-Nosed Guenon**, the **Diana Monkey** lives in the rainforests of western Africa. This monkey is known for the bright colours of its coat. The male Diana Monkey has a white 'beard' and whiskers.

The **DeBrazza's Monkey** lives in

Uganda, in the Congo and in Kenya.

The **Patas Monkey** is among the fastest-moving monkeys known. It lives in the dry, arid belt of land south of the Sahara Desert and spends its life mainly on the ground.

Like most other members of the Cercopithecidae family, the **Black Mangabey** has long limbs and a long tail and lives in the forests of equatorial Africa.

CHIMPANZEE

Height: 94-170 cm

Weight of adult: 40-80 kg

Arm span: up to 2 m

Habitat: humid forest, woodland and plains

Home: Equatorial Africa

Of all animals on Earth, the Chimpanzee is the closest relative of human beings. It has an intelligence which is similar to ours. This enables them to use various objects very well and also to display their ability to work out the reason for their actions. For example – to catch ants, a Chimpanzee will dampen a little stick with saliva and poke it into the ant hill, so that the ants will stick to the moist surface. It will throw stones and sticks at enemies to make them go away, clean its skin with the peel of a banana, and collect water to quench its thirst by laying leaves out in the rain.

Although some Chimpanzee communities have adapted to live in the savannah, they generally live in forest areas. According to some zoologists, the species living in the savannah are more developed.

Unlike the gorilla, the Chimpanzee, an anthropoid primate, is tree-dwelling and descends to the ground only when necessary. However, it runs easily on its two feet for long distances. Its social life is very developed – the family comprises an adult male, two or three females and their young. Sometimes, other families join together to make quite a tribe. In general, Chimpanzees are vegetarian, but sometimes the adults catch medium-size mammals. Every evening, chimpanzees prepare on the branches a bed of leaves on which to spend the night.

GORILLA

Height: 1.80 m, male; 1.30 m, female

Weight: 200-270 kg, male; 80-100 kg, female

Food: leaves, seeds, fruit, bamboo shoots and young bunches of bananas

Span of arms: 2-2.75 m

Habitat: forest

Home: Africa

Despite its proverbial strength, and being a true giant among primates, the gorilla is a mainly peaceful animal. It lives in the African jungle and lives quite a secluded life. Three species of gorilla are known – the Western Lowland Gorilla which lives in the coastal zones of the Gulf of Guinea and in the basin of Zaire and in Gabon, the Eastern Lowland Gorilla whose home is the rainforests of the region of the Congo and the Mountain Gorilla which lives among the highest mountains of central Africa up to altitudes of 4000 m, in forests of bamboo. Here, the topmost heights are always wrapped in mist. It may also live in zones bordered by high volcanoes.

Gorillas live in small groups, each one comprising one adult male, two or three females and their young. The male is the undisputed head of the group, who ensures the group's safety and defends their territory. The group does not move about very much, because gorillas can usually get all the food that they need from the jungle all year round. The gorilla is land-dwelling and only the young climb trees and play among the branches. As the male gets old, the hairs on its back become white, rather like older human beings who often become grey-haired.

Did you know...

The **Gibbon** moves only by swinging along and dangling on its long arms, balancing in free flight for up to 15 – 20 m. This type of movement, swinging from one arm to another, is called 'brachiation' and the animal can reach a surprising speed in this way. Sometimes, however, a gibbon acrobat may fall to the ground – the skeleton of a gibbon often shows fractures to its arms. The front legs are shorter and are useful when the animal wants to rest on branches or to pick fruit.

Pan Paniscus – the **Pygmy Chimpanzee** – also lives in Africa.

The name **Orang-Utan** comes from the Malayan **orang-utan** meaning 'man of the woods'. The most surprising feature of this primate is the fact that the different examples all have their own facial features, and, like human beings they can be recognized and distinguished one from the other by the expression on the face of each one. The males also

HYLOBATES LAR
WHITE-HANDED GIBBON

PAN PANISCUS
PYGMY CHIMPANZEE

PONGO PYGMAEUS
ORANG-UTAN

PAN TROGLODYTES
CHIMPANZEE

*SYMPHALANGUS
SYNDACTYLUS*
SIAMANG

GORILLA GORILLA
GORILLA

have beards and whiskers, similar to the anthropoid primates to which they are related.

Unlike the Orang-Utang, which lives alone, the **Siamang** lives in a family group. But, like the Orang-Utang, it has a throat sac which swells up as it cries and works like a sound-box. The cry of the Orang-Utang would be

very soft if it were not for its throat sac to make it louder.

The young female and male **Mountain Gorilla** (in photograph) sleep alone at a certain height from the ground on large branches. The heavy adult males sleep on the ground, on a bed of ferns, grass and twigs.

INDEX

187

GLOSSARY

appendages – an appendage is usually a leg. It can, however, be anything which projects from the central part of the body of an animal, such as a leg, a wing or an antenna.

arachnida – a class of creatures which includes scorpions and spiders. An arachnid has a segmented body divided into two parts. The front part has four pairs of legs, but no antennae.

chelicerae – pincer-like appendages nearest the mouth of arachnids and some crustaceans. The creature uses them to bite its prey and to inject poison into its victim. Spiders also use their chelicerae for spinning silk. Crabs use them to grip their prey.

class – a broad category of animals which have some features in common. Many orders may make up one class.

crustacean – a class of mostly aquatic (water-dwelling) invertebrate animals with a horny or bony outer shell, a pair of appendages on each segment of the body and two pairs of antennae.

evolution – slow process of change, usually over many thousands or millions of years.

family – a group of animals which are closely related. There may be many genuses within a family, and many families within an order.

genus – one or more related species which form part of a family of animals.

habitat – a creature's natural home.

hermaphrodite – an animal with the organs of both sexes, male and female.

invertebrate – without a backbone.

metamorphosis – a complete transformation within the life-cycle of an animal, for example, a larva being transformed into a butterfly.

complete metamorphosis – usually comprises three stages of transformation, e.g. egg, larva, full-grown animal.

incomplete metamorphosis – comprises only two stages, with the egg hatching into an adult animal without going through the larva stage.

mollusc – a creature with a soft, compact body without an internal skeleton and which is sub-divided into a head and a trunk.

nocturnal – living by night and sleeping by day.

order – one section of a class, comprising animals which are quite closely related.

oviparous – egg-laying.

ovoviviparous – where fertilized eggs develop within the female body, but, unlike mammals, these are not nourished by her.

parasite – an animal which lives off another.

pedipalps – second pair of appendages in arachnids. Sometimes these are used for chewing, sometimes as huge, powerful pincers and for gripping, as organs of reproduction and for tasting.

phylum – major group of animals to which many classes may belong.

predator – a hunter of prey.

scavengers – animals which feed on the remains left by others.

sloughing – shedding a dead skin, which has usually become too tight for the animal.

species – a special kind of animal. One or more species can make a genus.

spermatophore – a capsule containing fertile sperm and which some male arachnids deposit on the ground ready for the female to lay her eggs.

symbiosis – where two different species exist together, each one helping the other.

vertebrate – with a backbone.

viviparous – where the young grow inside the body of the female, are nourished by her and born fully developed.